First published in the United Kingdom in 2018
by OMC Investments Limited, 3 Robert Street, Westminster, London WC2N 6RL

Text copyright © OMC Investments Limited

ISBN 978-1-5272-2461-2

Book design and layout by i4 Design Consultants Limited
Printed and bound in Great Britain by Lamport Gilbert Limited, Reading RG2 0TB

Photograph book jacket front cover
Jack Burke, Worthing

Map inside front: Central Europe 1914
Map inside back: Central Europe 1925

Dedicated to all those whose efforts
contributed to the success of Datsun UK

If you can keep your head when all about you
Are losing theirs and blaming it on you,
If you can trust yourself when all men doubt you,
But make allowance for their doubting too;
If you can wait and not be tired by waiting,
Or being lied about, don't deal in lies,
Or being hated, don't give way to hating,
And yet don't look too good, nor talk too wise:

If you can dream — and not make dreams your master;
If you can think — and not make thoughts your aim;
If you can meet with Triumph and Disaster
And treat those two impostors just the same;
If you can bear to hear the truth you've spoken
Twisted by knaves to make a trap for fools,
Or watch the things you gave your life to, broken,
And stoop and build 'em up with worn-out tools:

If you can make one heap of all your winnings
And risk it on one turn of pitch-and-toss,
And lose, and start again at your beginnings
And never breathe a word about your loss;
If you can force your heart and nerve and sinew
To serve your turn long after they are gone,
And so hold on when there is nothing in you
Except the Will which says to them: 'Hold on!'

If you can talk with crowds and keep your virtue,
Or walk with Kings — nor lose the common touch,
If neither foes nor loving friends can hurt you,
If all men count with you, but none too much;
If you can fill the unforgiving minute
With sixty seconds' worth of distance run,
Yours is the Earth and everything that's in it,
And — which is more — you'll be a Man, my son!

RUDYARD KIPLING, "IF —"

THE RT HON LORD TEBBIT CH

Readers of John Laughland's biography of Octav Botnar must prepare themselves not only for a life story but also for a history of Europe's dark 20th Century of conflict, wars and pogroms. They may well, like me, constantly be asking, "What would I have done had I been faced with the alarming choices which the young Oswald Bundorf – as he was originally named – faced in his times?"

I thought that I had known Octav Botnar quite well, but as I read Laughland's book I realised that I had known only one of the three men he had been.

Oswald Bundorf was born in 1913 into a German-speaking Jewish family in the city of Czernowitz. He was but a toddler as the tides of the First World War washed back and forth over his birthplace and as the October Revolution brought Communism first to Imperial Russia in a tide of violence which rose and fell across most of Central Europe and lapped at times even into the West.

At the outbreak of the 1914-1918 war, Czernowitz was situated in Austria. But under the Treaty of Versailles which brought that war to an end, it became part of the kingdom of Romania and the young Bundorf acquired his second nationality.

As Laughland recounts, Bundorf's teenage years brought him into Communist agitation, criminality and jail. Despite the corruption of the state authorities and the brutality of the prison regime, he soon escaped the country and travelled to France, intent on going to Spain to join the Communist side in the Spanish Civil War. By the time he reached Paris, that war was over and Franco victorious, but with the assistance of one his brothers, who bought him false identity papers,

Bundorf joined the French Foreign Legion to fight against Hitler's National Socialist Germany until the surrender of France and the Vichy Pact with Germany. Bundorf was captured by the Germans and interned, but soon escaped to join the Resistance in Paris.

Reading the account of Bundorf's chaotic, violent early life I found it hard to connect that man with the Octav Botnar, businessman and philanthropist, whom I came to know in the late 20th Century.

Perhaps the metamorphosis began in those early post-war years when he returned to Romania and began a new life as Octav Botnar, having changed his name like many others. He remained a Communist but seemed to settle down, marrying Marcela, who in 1952 bore him a daughter, Camelia. He pursued a career in government administration in the Romanian Foreign Trade Service. There, his pride and impulsiveness led to his downfall and expulsion from the Communist Party.

It is hard for anyone born in the United Kingdom to follow the twists and turns of Botnar's persecution by the state and Communist Party through the 1950s and early 1960s, ending in his departure from Romania when his brother, Max, bribed government officials to let him leave with Marcela and Camelia, initially to Israel and thence to Germany.

Max had become well-established in Britain, not least by having worked with our intelligence services during the Second World War and the Cold War. He later acquired the NSU motor car distributorship for the UK and, forgetting numerous slights and quarrels, took Botnar into his firm in Britain. Max was well repaid as Octav ran the firm successfully. Botnar then went on to acquire the Datsun UK distributorship for himself.

As Laughland recounts, Octav Botnar's quick wits and good judgement of people now came into their own with his perception that the richer his dealers became, the more successful his firm would be too. Datsun soon began to outsell its competitors. He began to give money to charities and would eventually become one of the greatest charitable donors in 20th-century Britain.

From here on, the story of Octav Botnar's business career has about it something of the Greek tragedy of Icarus. He persuaded the Nissan top management in Japan that the firm should establish a manufacturing base in Britain to supply the whole European market, just as the Thatcherite reforms in Britain had begun to bite. It fell to me, first as Keith Joseph's deputy at the Department of Industry and later in my own right as Secretary of State for Trade and Industry, to oversee the negotiations which led to the establishment of the Nissan plant at Sunderland.

That led to Botnar's distributorship becoming even more profitable and to eventual quarrels with the management in Japan.

This book explains how that led to the pursuit of Botnar by the British tax authorities, who were never able, despite years of trying, to bring any substantial evidence to court. Botnar left Britain for Switzerland. Tragically, he lost his daughter Camelia in a car accident, but his response was to establish a charitable trust in her name which gave a great deal of money to good causes.

One of those was the Nuffield Orthopaedic Hospital at Oxford where I had become involved in creating one of Europe's leading centres of research into musculo-skeletal disorders.

Whatever others may say, I believe Octav Botnar to have been a good man whom I am proud to claim as a friend.

John Laughland's biography tells its readers why that is so.

CONTENTS

OCTAV BOTNAR – A LIFE

CHAPTER 1

A CHILD OF CZERNOWITZ

If you can dream – and not make dreams your master...

1913, the year of Octav Botnar's birth, was the last year of old Europe. The First World War was to break out the following summer, unleashing unprecedented carnage which would destroy three empires and leave revolution and devastation in its wake. The city of Botnar's birth symbolised, perhaps more than any other, this old order which was soon to pass: Czernowitz was a German-speaking city, the most easterly in the Austrian part of the vast and ramshackle Austro-Hungarian empire, which extended from the shores of Lake Constance deep into what is now Ukraine, and from the wintry Polish city of Krakow to the hot Southern Adriatic city of Dubrovnik. Czernowitz lay on the fringes of the empire, close to the borders of the Russian empire and the Romanian kingdom.

Austria was the immediate cause of the outbreak of the First World War. Her declaration of war on Serbia at the end of July 1914, in reprisal for the assassination of the heir to the imperial throne, Archduke Franz Ferdinand, in Sarajevo, triggered the chain reaction which caused the whole of Europe to be at war within a few days. Austria was also to be the war's main victim. Her empire was completely dismembered after 1918, whereas the German and Russian empires suffered only territorial losses. Austria-Hungary having vanished from the map completely after 1918, the country called "Austria" today is but a tiny rump of the old Austria. The Hungarian kingdom, meanwhile, which was the second constituent part of the empire, lost two thirds of its territory, to Romania and to the new states of Czechoslovakia and Yugoslavia, which were created on its ruins at Versailles.

Czernowitz in 1913 was a peaceful city proud of its sophistication and culture. Its university was famous, as were its theatre and its concert hall. These were the badges of respectability of all major Habsburg cities since the Empress Maria Theresa (1717-1780). Its poets and authors, like Paul Celan and Gregor von Rezzori, were major figures who were to gain international fame in the 20th Century. Rezzori, who was born in Czernowitz in 1914, caricatured the cultural mix and the incipient Balkan corruption of the late Habsburg empire by setting one of his novels in "Czernopol", an evident sarcastic allusion to the city of his birth. Celan's work can only be interpreted in the light of his biography[1], his Central European Jewish origins and probable suicide in Paris symbolising the tortured fate of Europe in the 20th Century. He was three times nominated for the Nobel prize for literature.

Czernowitz's distance from the imperial capital, Vienna, did nothing to dent its sense of importance. It enjoyed calling itself "Little Vienna", rather as the Romanian capital, Bucharest, would call itself "Little Paris" in the inter-war period. Its geographical situation was magnificent: the region, the Bukovina ("Buchenland" in German, the land of the beeches), which was annexed by Romania in 1918 and then by the Soviet Union after the war (it is now in Ukraine) is a lovely part of the world with gently undulating landscapes and beautiful forests in the foothills of the Carpathians.

In contrast to Czernowitz's urbanity and sophistication, in the surrounding villages European peasant life went on as it had for centuries. These villages, which were overwhelmingly given over to small-scale farming[2], contained an immensely rich anthropological heritage composed of Romanians, Ukrainians (then referred to as Ruthenians), Jews, Russian Old Believers (called Lipovans) and others, all living a very traditional, if poor, peasant lifestyle. Czernowitz was thus doubly an outpost, first because it was almost a border town and the last Austrian city before Russia and Romania, and second because it was a foreign entity even with respect to its immediate surroundings.

Just outside the city limits, in the charming but primitive villages, the peasants spoke Romanian or Ukrainian or Yiddish but not the German of the city.

The phenomenon of sophisticated German-speaking towns and cities placed like islands in a sea of non-German peasants was repeated in several other parts of the Austro-Hungarian empire: in Slovakia, for instance, where the Zipser Saxons had lived since the 12th Century, but also in Transylvania, in the great cities of Kronstadt (later Braşov in Romania) and Hermannstadt (later Sibiu). Czernowitz was like these cities – but unlike them in one important respect. Although its urban and German culture differentiated it linguistically and sociologically from its immediate hinterland, Czernowitz was part of its surroundings because of its large Jewish population. The neighbouring regions, especially the Polish parts of the Russian empire to the North and Russian Bessarabia to the East and South, were similarly home to large Jewish populations, as were many of the nearby villages.

In the Bukovina as a whole, Romanian and Ruthenian (Ukrainian) were spoken by 38 per cent and 34 per cent of the population respectively, with 21 per cent of the population being German-speaking. Most of these German speakers were in Czernowitz, where 48.4 per cent of the population had German as its mother tongue. Daily life in the city was therefore conducted in that language. The majority of these German-speakers in Czernowitz were Jews, who comprised 32.8 per cent of the city's population. The assimilated urban Jews of Czernowitz, 95 per cent of whom had German as their mother tongue – and this was the case for Oswald Bundorf, the future Octav Botnar – were therefore separated linguistically by the administrative border in Austrian Galicia. In that region, the majority of whose population was Polish, only 17 per cent of Jews spoke German: instead, they tended to speak Yiddish or Polish. The Jews of Czernowitz were also similarly separated from those in nearby Bessarabia: this originally Romanian-speaking province had been part of the Russian empire since 1812 and

Jews there tended to speak Russian or Yiddish. Yiddish was sometimes looked down on by assimilated German-speaking Jews: the father of Zionism, Theodor Herzl, dismissed it as "a language of the ghetto" and said that Jews in the future Jewish state would have to abandon it.[3]

Religious observance reflected these cultural differences. Whereas in the Bukovina villages, nearly 70 per cent of the population was Orthodox, in Czernowitz Jews formed the largest single group, followed by Catholics (27 per cent, of whom many were Poles, who comprised 17 per cent of the population of the city) and Orthodox (23 per cent, composed of Romanian speakers [15.7 per cent of the population] and Ruthenes or Ukrainians [18 per cent]).[4] Czernowitz was therefore a living symbol of the Habsburg empire, which was about to be submerged in the bloody torrent of 20th-century history. Its genteel reputation and its elegant Habsburg architecture – a sort of Central European Cheltenham – gave it the allure of a haven of peace, inevitably oblivious, like so much of Europe, to the cataclysms which were soon to engulf it and the whole of Europe, and in which Oswald Bundorf was himself to be caught up.

The city was plunged into the vortex of war very early on. Austria declared war on Serbia on 28 July 1914; Austria's ally, Germany, declared war on Russia on 31 July; and Austria declared war on Russia on 6 August. Czernowitz was on the front line. Shortly after the declaration of war, Russian troops quickly overran the Austrian defences and occupied the city by September 1914: by then, there was not even a police force left to protect it. A large part of the population, including many Jews, had fled the Russian advance, in the Jews' case because of the fear of persecution: Russia had a reputation for anti-Semitism, thanks to the repeated pogroms carried out against Jews in the Russian empire, most notoriously in 1905. However, the Russian troops were repulsed in October by an armed resistance group under the leadership of a police colonel, and the city eventually returned to Austrian rule in February 1915. The following year, on 18 June 1916,

Russia took the city again but it was re-taken by Austrian troops on 3 August 1917. The young Emperor Charles visited the city only a few days later to celebrate its liberation, on which occasion he made a point of thanking the Jewish population for its patriotism. The German-speaking Jews of Czernowitz, indeed, were considered as a patriotic bulwark by Vienna in an empire many of whose other ethnic groups were straining for independence.

This back-and-forth between Russian and Austrian rule meant that, in March 1917, Czernowitz was governed by Russia at the time of the first (or "February") Russian revolution. On 15 March 1917 (Gregorian calendar) Emperor Nicholas II abdicated and the events were set in motion which were to lead to the establishment of Communist dictatorship under Lenin by November (the "October" revolution occurred on 7 November 1917, Gregorian calendar: Russia still used the Julian calendar at the time). It took four weeks for the news about the Tsar's abdication to reach Czernowitz, which relied mainly on newspapers from Kiev: these had ceased publication in the second half of March. Even the military and civil authorities in Czernowitz did not know what had happened in Petrograd, the Russian capital.[5]

Once the news did percolate through, Russian rule in Czernowitz collapsed. Russian soldiers started to carry red banners and refused to salute their superiors. Discipline evaporated. The formal proclamation of the new regime took place in the Central Square on 23 April 1917; the military governor of the town, who refused to take down the Tsarist flag, was arrested by his own troops (although released shortly thereafter).[6] The Russian Communists evidently thought that their new political creed would be regarded sympathetically by the Jewish population of Czernowitz: on 1 May 1917, Russian soldiers paraded through the streets of the city to celebrate Labour Day displaying Communist banners, including one with a star of David and the word "Liberty" in Russian *(svoboda)*.[7]

Subsequent to the Austrian recapture of the city in August 1917, however, the Austrian war effort unravelled. Romania rejoined the war on 10 November 1918, having signed a short-lived armistice with Germany in March 1918, and on 12 November Romanian troops entered Czernowitz. Bukovina was to be annexed to the Romanian kingdom. Austria-Hungary, one of the greatest and oldest states in European history – a state whose emperors had called themselves "Roman" until 1806 because they had inherited the title created by Charlemagne in the year 800 – but to whose destruction the Americans were committed as a matter of policy, was erased from the map. A string of successor states took its place, some of which would prove to be unstable or unviable during the course of the 20th Century as well. At the Versailles peace conference in 1919, Romania was to make massive territorial gains and incorporate not only Bukovina but also Transylvania, Bessarabia and Southern Dobrudja. The citizens of the once proud Austrian outpost of Czernowitz became Romanian subjects, incorporated into a state which was utterly foreign to them, and with which they had never had any previous association.

Romania was as new as Austria was old. The two original Romanian principalities, Moldavia and Wallachia, for long under Ottoman suzerainty, had been united since the 1860s and were formally proclaimed an independent kingdom in 1881 with a German dynasty, the Hohenzollern-Sigmaringen. Romania therefore joined Italy and Germany as a newly-united nation-state, just as Greece and Serbia had done earlier in the century as Ottoman rule receded in South-Eastern Europe. The young state was full of promise, a promise which unfortunately was not to be fulfilled: Romania, like so many other states, succumbed to the instability and extremism which racked the whole of Europe in the aftermath of the Great War.

For the Jewish population, the annexation of the Bukovina by Romania was regarded as a *fait accompli* which at least had the advantage, in their eyes, of protecting them from the Russians. This perception persisted even though things were to change in Russia in 1917, when Russia went from being anti-Semitic to pro-Semitic: Communist cosmopolitanism was, for many Jews, the answer to their unresolved national status, and the Russian Communist party contained a disproportionately high number of Jews among its ranks and party cadres. The same was to be true of Romania, where the majority of the tiny Communist party in that country was also composed of Jews: the Romanian state, over the coming two decades, was to respond ever more harshly to what it perceived as a Bolshevik-Jewish threat. Romania was eventually to become a semi-fascist dictatorship allied to Nazi Germany, rather like Italy but with a much more anti-Semitic government. The Jews of Bukovina, in other words, having escaped what they thought would be the frying pan of Russian domination, in fact went into the fire of proto-fascist anti-Semitism when their region was annexed to Romania.

It was into this incipient maelstrom that Oswald Bundorf (who was to change his name to Octav Botnar after the Second World War) was born on 21 October 1913. He was the third son of a family of five children: his eldest brother, Max, born in 1910, was later to Anglicise his surname to Bunford and to make a fortune; his other brother Maurice (Moritz at birth, born in 1912) was to become a doctor in France. There were two younger sisters, Sophia and Henriette.

Like most Jews in the city[8], Bundorf senior had a name in civil life, Adolf, and a religious name, Abraham: he is listed alternatively under the first and then the second in the city registers of 1913 and 1927. The father's full name was Adolf Apsal Tassilo Bundorf and he was originally from the core Austrian lands – what is now the Republic of Austria. Their mother, Amalia, née Berl, by contrast, was from Czernowitz. The children loved her deeply, a devout lady who stayed at home to look after them while their father dealt with his businesses – a restaurant and three properties.[9] They lived in a modest part of the city, near the station, in Bilei Street, although there was some money on Amalia's side of the family.

Religious observance was part of everyday life. Many of those Jewish Communists from Czernowitz who have written memoirs refer to the traditional ceremonies practised at home. Like their future Communist comrades, however, the Bundorf sons – Max, Moritz (Maurice) and Oswald (Octav) – were to grow up with no attachment to Judaism or its practices whatever, Oswald (Octav) becoming an atheist and Max deciding to live as a Christian but also without practising that faith either.

The young Oswald Bundorf had a rudimentary education: primary school until the age of 11 and then evening classes in lieu of secondary school. In 1930 he got a job at a textile company in the town, Klein. It was here that his political activity started. He liaised with the trades unions and became a Communist, joining the Union of Communist Youth (UTC in Romanian, standing for *Uniunea Tineretului Comunist*) in 1931, an organisation founded in 1922 but banned in 1924, like the Romanian Communist Party itself. Bundorf's political activism was a great source of disappointment to his mother. As a believer, she was saddened to see her son becoming a militant atheist. Notwithstanding his mother's reproaches, however, young Oswald followed his political convictions with an intensity approaching recklessness which was to become the hallmark of the rest of his life.

On Monday 21 March 1932, when Bundorf was 18, at around 11 o'clock in the morning, passers-by in the Central Square of Czernowitz (Austriaplatz or Austria Square in German, but renamed Ghica-Voda Square by the Romanian authorities) were surprised by a sudden and rowdy, but evidently pre-planned, demonstration. In a small group of people, a young man pulled out a red flag and started to wave it around. A large crowd of young men and women then ran out from doorways and formed a column, shouting slogans like "Down with war!" and "Long live the Soviet Union". (Bundorf would later say that the demonstration was supposed to celebrate the Paris Commune, although the date of the beginning of that insurrection was 18 March.)

There were only three policemen on the square at the time and so they were outnumbered by the unauthorised demonstrators. One of them grabbed the red flag, at which point the other demonstrators fell upon him. His colleagues came to the rescue and, in the ensuing mêlée, one of the officers was wounded on the head with a knuckle-duster. The policemen's whistles soon attracted reinforcements, and they were able to stop the column which had started to march towards the city hall. The police began to round people up, more or less at random, and about 30 were arrested and taken away. By this time, a police inspector and the head of the police had arrived on the scene.[10]

In staging this otherwise unremarkable unauthorised demonstration, Oswald Bundorf and his comrades – for he was one of the 30 youngsters arrested – had violated, perhaps deliberately, a law passed in Romania in 1924, which bore the name of the Interior Minister who had sponsored it, Gheorghe Mârzescu. It banned extremist political parties, including the Communist Party: Bundorf and his friends had thrown themselves, therefore, into the very centre of the attempt by Romania to hold back the rising tide of Communism which had engulfed neighbouring Russia and which was soon to engulf the whole of Europe. Other countries were to follow Romania's example: Austria, for instance, banned the Communist Party in 1933, the year in which the Communists' arch-enemies, the Nazis, seized power in Germany.

Out of the 30 rounded up in March, 20 were tried later that year, in July, including the young Oswald Bundorf. Following a short trial, Bundorf was sentenced to 15 months in prison, a fine of 10,000 lei, and three years of national disgrace. His was one of the harshest sentences handed down, although six of his co-defendants received 16 months. According to a newspaper report on the trial[11], when the judge read out the sentences, the defendants struck up a lusty rendition of the *Internationale*. The judge angrily demanded who had sung. No hands went up, so Bundorf, who in fact had not sung the anthem but who could not abide the cowardice of those who refused to own up, claimed that he had. He and two others were promptly sentenced to an extra six months in solitary confinement for this act of disrespect to the court.[12] This was to be the first of five times that Botnar was imprisoned throughout his life: he would be detained again, for various reasons, in 1935, 1937, 1940 and 1960. (He was also sentenced in absentia to seven years' imprisonment in 1938, a sentence he would escape by leaving the country.) During his imprisonment, Bundorf's beloved mother visited him regularly; by contrast, his father never did, considering that his son had brought disgrace upon the family.

The fate of the defendants was the subject of a sympathetic and lyrical article by the journalist who reported on it – an attitude which was in stark contrast to the harshness of the state authorities. Helios Hecht, a columnist for the local German-language daily, *Der Tag*, wrote a nice piece after his report of the trial, contrasting the warmth of the summer outside with the coldness and impending winter of the young people's detention. He repeatedly dwelt on their youth, saying that the people sent to the gaol in Czernowitz were hardly out of short trousers. He was touched and delighted by the freshness of their faces and by the almost childish enthusiasm with which they espoused their cause. Of course they were idealists: in corrupt inter-war Romania, the very fact of having ideals, rather than being on the take, was itself an act of rebellion. With great foresight, the journalist predicted that the harsh treatment they had received in pre-trial detention, and would receive while serving their sentences, would harden them. It would turn them into redoubtable fighters, used both to prison life and to practising the art of deception outside prison, whereas if the state had simply allowed them to chant their childish slogans, they might have presented less danger and even been instead a source of useful information. "Now the summer will pass," Hecht wrote, "soon the birds will sing their last songs and the flowers will all sink into death. These young people have been taken away from these beautiful things, and instead they see only the icy faces of the prison guards and the high grey walls of the courtyard and the bitter square of their cells which, day after day, they measure, cross and walk through."[13]

Hecht could not have been more right. The young men sent to prison on that July day were representative of a very small section of Romanian society: the Communist Party was tiny, with only a few hundred members. Once the wheel of fortune had turned, and especially following the entry of Soviet troops into Romanian territory on 23 August 1944, when Romania belatedly switched sides from supporting the Axis to joining the Allies, the Communist Party was to become very important indeed. It would seize power in 1947 and govern the country as a dictatorship until the regime's bloody overthrow at Christmas 1989. One of the factors behind this astonishing reversal of fortune was precisely the experience of future party cadres who were forced to live lives of clandestinity and illegality in the 1930s.

In those early post-war years, therefore, Bundorf's trajectory would be very comparable to that of the future leading lights in the Romanian Communist Party, some of whom, like him, would spend the war years fighting the Germans in the French Resistance. They, too, lived through the Romanian kingdom's prisons, which became veritable academies for future Communists. One police report for Doftana prison, where Romania's future Communist leaders were imprisoned in 1936, shortly after Bundorf, read as follows: "At Doftana, the Communists, though isolated in their cells, carry on political work... hold daily conferences and... discuss subjects of Communist agitation... The prisoners are organised in a collective which includes all Communist prisoners... In addition, there is a Communist group which leads the collective."[14] Boris Holban, né Baruch Bruhman, Oswald Bundorf's future commander in the French Resistance, called Doftana "the Party university" and wrote that, "The majority of party activists left that prison raring to go, prepared to sacrifice their personal lives and to devote themselves entirely to a life of clandestinity."[15]

Holban was one such person; Bundorf was another.

Bundorf's trial and imprisonment were representative of other trends too. Not least because of its geographical proximity to the formerly Russian territory of Bessarabia and Polish Galicia, the Bukovina had a number of Socialist, proto-Communist and Communist organisations, as well as various left-wing Jewish groups, whether Zionist or anti-Zionist. Neighbouring Russia had been home to the *Allgemeine Jüdische Arbeiterbund* (General Jewish Labour Federation), known as the "Bund", a left-wing organisation, many of whose members fled Russia into Bukovina and elsewhere after the anti-Jewish pogroms of 1905.[16] In the same year, the Jewish Socialist Party of Galicia was founded in the Austrian Polish province of that name. By 1917, Russia had become Communist and, for a few months in 1919, a Soviet republic was declared in neighbouring Hungary too.

The Bukovina was therefore typical of the new territories which Romania annexed after the First World War: they changed the nature of the Romanian state from within. Socialist and Communist movements had grown up, and they would continue to grow as the region industrialised: whereas the traditional Romanian economy had been based on small-scale agriculture, trade and retail, Czernowitz in the inter-war period became something of an industrial centre with textile and other factories springing up. This meant that the sociological makeup of the population of Czernowitz was different from the rest of the country, where 80 per cent of the population lived off the land. Naturally, this had an effect on the city's politics: Czernowitz had its own social-democratic newspaper, *Vorwärts* (Forward), and even elected a Social Democrat to the town council as deputy mayor.

Bundorf's trial also throws the ethnic aspect of the early Romanian Communist Party into relief. It is well-known that the Romanian party was overwhelmingly made up of people who were not ethnic Romanians but instead members of Romania's numerous national minorities. In the 1930s, Hungarians made up less than eight per cent of the population of Romania but they accounted for 26 per cent of the membership of the RCP; Jews were four per cent of the population but 18 per cent of the party membership; Russians and Ukrainians three per cent of the population but 10 per cent of the Party; Bulgarians two per cent and 10 per cent. By contrast, ethnic Romanians, who accounted for 72 per cent of the population of Romania, accounted for only 23 per cent of Communist Party members.[17] Even taking into account the very particular ethnic makeup of the city of Czernowitz, it is worth noting that not a single one of Bundorf's 19 co-defendants in July 1932 had a Romanian name: their names were all Ukrainian, Polish, German or Jewish.[18]

Some Jews, in Romania as in neighbouring states, became Communists for reasons which were closely linked to their special status. In an age of nationalism, the Jews were the odd ones out: they were not universally classed as a nation and the issue of statehood for them, Zionism, divided them just as it divided everyone else. Zionism and Communism were linked to the extent that they were both left-wing ideologies, united by a common belief in the possibility of creating a new society.[19] However, they were at odds over the national question: Communists were anti-Zionist because they believed that the status of the Jews would be solved in a future cosmopolitan order, in which all nations would disappear as Marx predicted. The dispute between Communism and Zionism would frequently animate the dinner tables of Jews in Czernowitz, as in other parts of Romania: Ervin Bodnar, né Blum, who, like Oswald Bundorf, joined the French Resistance before returning to Romania after the war to build socialism – where indeed he became acquainted with Bundorf/Botnar – describes how, as an adolescent, he would read *The History of the Communist Party* in bed at night, and during the day argue with his Zionist father about the right solution to the Jewish question.[20]

For some Jews, support for Communism was an existential choice. Prive Friedjung, who was born in 1902 in a village near Czernowitz, entitles her memoir *Memories of a Jewish Communist* because, as she explained to her amanuensis, to have written "Jew and Communist" would have split her personality whereas she considered that these two sides to her character were indissociable.[21] She initially joined Poale Zion, a left-wing Zionist group in Czernowitz, but later converted to Communism which, for her, more closely reflected Jewishness: she writes, "The most important thing for me about Czernowitz was the symbiosis between yiddishistic and revolutionary thought"[22] and, "The percentage of Jewish revolutionaries in the Soviet movement was enormous."[23] Like Friedjung, Irma Mico – whom Bundorf was to meet in Paris during the war, when they both fought in the Resistance, and who was also a Jewish Communist from Czernowitz – exaggerates the already significant role of Jews in the Romanian Communist Party, claiming that, in 1937, 800 out of the 1,000 members of the Romanian Communist Party were Jews[24], a figure which seems impossible but which no doubt reflects her personal perspective and experience.

The conditions of detention in the prison at Czernowitz were grim. Confessions were extracted by violence.[25] In spite of this, the following January, Bundorf himself appeared as a witness in a trial where he testified that, as a prisoner, he had seen people being beaten. In the trial of a Communist woman, Polja Vascauteanu, dubbed "the black Natasha", and her associate Josef Feldmann, where the courtroom was filled to bursting by students eager to follow the proceedings, Vascauteanu denied the various charges against her, alleging, for instance, that a duplicating machine found in her apartment had been given to her by someone called "Grischa".[26] She claimed that her co-defendant, Feldmann, had been subject to terrible beatings, and that water had been thrown over him whenever he was about to lose consciousness. Bundorf testified at that trial that Feldmann had been so badly injured by the torture when he arrived at the prison that the other inmates had had to carry him into his cell.[27] Bundorf's willingness to testify against the prison authorities while himself their prisoner, at no doubt very great personal risk to himself, is testimony to his deep integrity, to his hatred of cowardice and injustice, and to a visceral attachment to his principles.

Bundorf served 16 months in prison, including at a borstal in the Transylvanian town of Cluj. He was released in November 1934, after his mother had used her family's savings to pay a bribe.[28] His brother Max also delved into his pockets for the same purpose.[29] However, Oswald Bundorf's time in prison had done nothing to dent his determination to pursue political activism. Immediately on his return to Czernowitz, he contacted the Union of Communist Youth, which was actively involved in recruiting youngsters in factories. He was, however, soon conscripted into the Romanian army to do his military service, specifically into the 2nd border guard regiment based at Cernavoda on the Bulgarian border, at the other end of the country, which he joined in April 1935.[30]

Military service in the Romanian army at that time was very tough: "drills, endless marching, exercises, fatigue duty, miserable conditions", according to a contemporary of Bundorf's.[31] Conscripts were forbidden from leaving their barracks during the first six months. The regime was harsh and the reluctant were beaten. However, the conscripts were of course given military training, and this was to prove very useful for Bundorf and other Communists a few years later when war broke out.

The police, meanwhile, continued, and even intensified, their hunt for Communists. In May 1935, the young conscript, Bundorf, was again arrested and escorted back to Czernowitz at the request of the Security Inspectorate, having been denounced by two comrades as a Communist agitator. Bundorf persuaded the soldier escorting him to accompany him to his home, where he managed to run away and hide with some acquaintances. Both he and the soldier were subsequently detained and Bundorf was imprisoned for six months in a military prison in Iași (Jassy), where he was subjected to barbarous treatment, taken outside in the middle of winter, naked, and beaten. He was placed in solitary confinement; he was kicked and humiliated in front of other soldiers.

In November 1935[32], together with others, he was freed pending their court appearance and returned to his regiment, where he again tried to organise a Communist group within the army.[33] He was again arrested for this in 1937 and was detained for six months in a military prison in the Black Sea port town of Constanța.[34] The result of all this was that, when his military service came to an end in November 1937, and Bundorf returned to Czernowitz, he had two trials pending against him, one for Communist agitation and the other for trying to give the authorities the slip.

It was at this stage that young Bundorf decided to leave Romania. There was little point in hanging around to face prosecution and imprisonment by a proto-fascist regime, when the Spanish Civil War was raging and Communists from all over the world were flooding into that country to join the International Brigades. This was a great world historical moment which Bundorf was determined not to miss. So Bundorf's decision to leave Romania for Paris can be seen as a political choice. On the one hand, he was a hot-blooded young Communist who wanted to go to fight in Spain; on the other, he needed to get out of an increasingly intolerable political situation in Romania, at a time when his own personal situation could hardly have been worse.

Many years later, in 1952, Bundorf/Botnar was to explain how he had managed to get out of Romania: "At that time, hundreds of people in a similar situation to mine left the country. It was fairly easy to obtain a passport in view of the corruption and the disorganised way the state apparatus operated."[35] Bundorf got his travel documents from the County Prefecture, where no one knew him (he did not apply to the Police Prefecture because they all knew him there). A friend and party comrade, Simon Mautner, helped him by lending him his birth certificate and other papers, which Bundorf submitted along with photographs of himself. He was also helped by his elder brother Max's first wife, Zina (short for Zenaida) Craciunescu (she was later known as Zoé), who knew people at the prefecture. He bribed an official "1,000 or 2,000 lei"[36] to speed up the process, and soon he was on his way to Spain via France with a false passport but very little else.

In March 1938, once he arrived in France, where his brother Maurice was already living and who, like Oswald, was a Communist and a member of the French Communist Party, Bundorf destroyed this false passport and pretended that he had entered the country illegally without papers: this was because the punishment for using false papers carried a harsher fine. He was granted asylum in France, which meant that he had to report to the police every month. Back home in Czernowitz, a military tribunal sentenced him to seven years in prison on the basis of the charges which had originally been brought in 1935.

So by the age of 24, in 1938, Oswald Bundorf was technically a convict on the run. With no professional qualifications to his name, he had spent two terms in prison and now he faced a third custodial sentence at home. He had learned how to live and travel with false papers, how to fight in an army and handle a gun, how to run a clandestine organisation, and how to survive prison and even torture. His prospects seemed bleak. In reality, there could hardly have been a better preparation for the daunting fate which awaited him.

CHAPTER 2

PARIS AND THE WAR

If you can trust yourself when all men doubt you...

Oswald Bundorf arrived in France in the spring of 1938. The world was to be at war a year later and Jews, especially ones with foreign passports living in France, would be deported from France and sent to labour and death camps. With neither work experience nor any formal qualifications, Bundorf was a political refugee with a criminal record in his home country. His situation was dangerously precarious.

By contrast, Oswald's brother Moritz (Maurice) had managed to get a degree in medicine and was practising as a GP in Lyon. Their eldest brother, Max, had obtained a business degree from the University of Vienna after leaving Romania to study there in 1927. Maurice, who was a member of the French Communist Party[37], would later make friends with the legendary leader of the party from 1934 to 1964, Maurice Thorez[38], while Max was on his way to making a fortune, first in Bucharest and later in Istanbul. Young Oswald stayed with Maurice for several months in Lyon before moving to Paris: this would not be the last time in his life that he would need to rely on his brothers for help at a time of extreme crisis.

From the point of view of a young Communist who had spent his life in Romania, France was a promised land in 1938. Under the erratic rule of King Carol, Romania edged ever closer to dictatorship and stepped over the edge at the end of 1937, when the anti-Semitic poet, Octavian Goga, was appointed prime minister. The king did this in a desperate bid to neutralise the rising influence of the fascistic Iron Guard which threatened his rule. Citizenship was revoked for some categories of Jews, especially those who inhabited those territories which Romania had acquired in 1918, like Bukovina. By February 1938, King Carol had suspended the constitution, banned all political parties, and established a royal dictatorship.

France, by contrast, traditionally "the country of human rights" for those on the left, and the home country of both the French Revolution and the Paris Commune, both key reference points for Communists, had had a left-wing government for two years from 1936 to 1938, the *Front populaire* under Léon Blum, which included the Communist Party. The election of this government had occurred after an attempt by royalists to overthrow the republic in riots on 6 February 1934: it was this event which encouraged Maurice Thorez, the leader of the French Communists, to decide to enter into alliance with the socialists, something which he (and his controllers in Moscow) had hitherto opposed.

For those Communists who had arrived in France from countries in Eastern and Central Europe, where the Communist parties were illegal, it was therefore an exhilarating experience to be able to operate legally and publicly. They could shout their slogans without fear of being beaten up by the police; they could attend the legendary *Fête de l'Humanité* organised by the French Communist Party every summer.[39] Paris became the adopted home of the numerous Communist parties which had been banned across Europe: the German Communist Party (banned in 1933), the Austrian (also banned in 1933), and the Czechoslovak (banned in 1938). The same was true of the Polish, Hungarian and Italian Communist parties which also had important bases in Paris, albeit for different reasons.[40] It is difficult to exaggerate the sense of enthusiasm felt in those days by young Communists, for whom the dream of a new society had not yet been tarnished either by knowledge of the excesses and brutality of Stalinism, nor indeed by direct experience of Communist rule in their own countries. It would take another decade before Bundorf, as Octav Botnar, would start to understand the reality of Communist rule in his native Romania, to which he returned after the war ended.

With his own military training and political sympathies, Bundorf's intention in leaving Romania had been to go to fight in Spain. The Spanish Civil War represented an epic conflict for left-wingers all over the world, a sort of Communist crusade against the forces of reaction. Some Jews even thought of the war as their revenge for the Spanish Inquisition.[41] This war between socialist republicans and conservative monarchists gripped the whole world's attention; volunteers poured in, especially to fight on the Republican side, while Europe's fascist powers, Germany and Italy, supported the army-led nationalist rebellion under General Franco. As one historian of the Spanish Civil War has written, the conflict was a war of religion between Catholic and anti-Catholic Spaniards, but onto which foreign powers projected their own political ideologies, communism and fascism, which did indeed then become part of the conflict.[42] Although these projections did not correspond to the original cause of the conflict, they did cause it to take on a world-historical importance, which it continues to enjoy today through the works of literature and art it generated (Hemingway, George Orwell and Picasso being the most obvious examples).

However, by the time Bundorf got to France in 1938, it was too late. The pro-Republican International Brigades were returning, defeated, and the border was closed, as the new French Government applied strictly the non-interventionist policy which Britain had cajoled France and others into at the beginning of the conflict.[43] Bundorf had therefore missed this rendezvous with destiny. Unfortunately a new, much more serious one was just around the corner: the Second World War.

In 1938, things started to go badly wrong on the international stage, including from the Communist point of view. The Republican cause started to unravel in Spain and, in September, Britain and France agreed at Munich to allow Germany, Poland and Hungary to dismember Czechoslovakia (Poland seized the city of Teschen and its surroundings, while Hungary seized Southern Slovakia and Trans-Carpathian Ruthenia, now part of Ukraine). Czechoslovakia was the very state the Allies had helped to create just 20 years previously at Versailles, and whose creation was supposed to put an end to the national question within the Habsburg empire. They had held up Czechoslovakia as a model of national tolerance and modern statehood, an image it largely merited, but which rebounded on them when Hitler demanded self-determination for the Germans in the Western part of the new country, the Sudetenland. The Munich agreement has entered history as the epitome of infamy, when the world's greatest democracies caved in when faced with a brutal German dictator determined to have his way by force. Communists were convinced, moreover, that this Munich agreement was designed not so much to ensure peace as instead to deflect Hitler towards the East, a way of encouraging him to attack the Soviet Union whose Bolshevik regime the Western powers hated. This was almost certainly Poland's calculation when she joined Germany in seizing Czech territory because she also had her eyes on the even greater prize of Ukraine, a vast territory which her elites were then contemplating trying to conquer with German support.

Oswald Bundorf was far from alone in having emigrated from Central or Eastern Europe to France. The first industrial immigrants of this kind were Jews from Russia who started to arrive in France in the 19th Century. In the early 20th Century, the Milliners' Union in Paris was composed almost entirely of Russian Jews and conducted its meetings in Yiddish.[44] After the First World War, in which France lost one and a half million men, a loss which in turn caused a massive drop in the overall birth rate, France actively sought to attract immigrants from Italy, Poland, Czechoslovakia and Spain to help with her economic and demographic recovery. By the early 1930s, there were three million such immigrants in the country. This made France the country with the highest number of immigrants in the world, as a percentage of population. Most of them were economic migrants but there were also political and religious refugees, especially from Central and Eastern Europe. Oswald Bundorf was one of them.

This major wave of immigration had a direct impact on the organisational structure of the French Communist Party. Originally, Communism's ideology did not recognise nationality. Marxism, like the European Union today, proclaimed the free movement of workers as a basic right because it denounced the principle of nationality as bourgeois: the working man "had no country"[45] and was therefore at home everywhere. According to Marxist dogma, the rise of the proletariat would cause national differences to disappear, as they were already doing thanks to the rise of capitalism.[46] However, this cosmopolitanism was soon abandoned because of the sheer weight of numbers of immigrant Communists, some of whom (the Italians, for instance, who were very numerous in France) organised themselves not only in party structures but even into paramilitary groups on a national basis.[47] The French Communist Party therefore acquiesced in the gradual creation of language-based sub-groups, first called *Main d'Oeuvre Etrangère* (Foreign Work Force) and later *Main d'Oeuvre Immigrée* (Immigrant Work Force) or MOI. This latter acronym became widely used.

The outbreak of the Spanish Civil War in 1936 transformed these national sub-structures within the French Communist Party into recruitment organisations for the International Brigades.[48] Precisely because many MOI members had themselves fled anti-Communist or anti-Jewish repression in their home countries, they were determined to do what they could to prevent the Nationalists from crushing the Republicans in Spain. The MOI's structures had the language skills necessary to orient those who came to Paris in the hope of fighting in Spain: people joked that so many languages were spoken that only the few Scandinavian Communists who turned up had any difficulty making themselves understood. The International Committee for Coordination and Information of Aid to Spain grouped together national subsections which were in reality controlled by the respective language groups of the MOI. Communist parties from all over Europe sent representatives to this committee, and each section took care of its national volunteers – their papers, their families, their return to Paris when sick or wounded. Controlled from the Soviet Union, this MOI activity also had a secret function, which was to recruit fighters and party cadres who could be called on one day, if necessary, to defend the Soviet Union itself.

Having been prevented from going to Spain to fight, Bundorf started to work for an association which collected funds for the Republican fighters, Red Aid, of which there was a network in Paris. His work consisted in maintaining contact with volunteers in Spain, in transmitting messages between them and their families back in Romania but in such a way that the Romanian censors would not discover their whereabouts, and in publishing every few months a propaganda newsletter in order to recruit further sponsors for each volunteer. The volunteers were poor but happy, living in shared digs on very little income but convinced that they were engaged in a righteous and historic process.[49]

Through his work, Bundorf entered into contact with many of the men and women who were to become his future comrades in the French Resistance. There was a Romanian committee in Paris, which collected money specifically for Romanian members of the International Brigades, in which Bundorf's future co-resistants, Boris Holban and Irma Mico, were involved.[50] These structures, like other structures created by the French Communist Party, were to become armed cells once France fell under German occupation: they were the germs of the future Resistance. Their military nature was only nourished even further when the defeated Republican fighters returned from Spain. The International Brigades paraded for one last time in Barcelona on 15 November 1938 and the heroine of the Republican cause, Dolores Ibárruri, known as *La Pasionaria*, gave them a ringing send-off by saying, in her speech, "You are the legend." From there, they crossed into France, where many of them were accommodated in camps in or near the Pyrenees.

By March 1939, after German forces occupied the whole of the Czech lands (Bohemia and Moravia) and installed a puppet government in a supposedly independent Slovakia, London and Paris realised the mistake they had made at Munich. The same governments which had sought to appease Hitler now issued him with an ultimatum: any further expansion would lead to war. When German troops invaded Poland on 1 September 1939, the Second World War began.

With the outbreak of war, immigrants in France, especially Jewish immigrants, flocked to join the French army. They were joined in this by the many thousands of former Republican fighters who had fled Spain after Franco's nationalists acquired control of the whole of Spain in March 1939. France was largely unprepared for a German invasion, both technologically and in terms of military strategy. Moreover, because the Great War had been decided by numbers of men alone, the French were delighted to have so many non-French citizens signing up to boost their ranks.

Oswald Bundorf enrolled into one of three new regiments which were created within the French Foreign Legion in October 1939, a month after war was declared, for the purpose of integrating such immigrant soldiers. These regiments were the 21st, 22nd and 23rd *Régiments de marche de volontaires étrangers* (Regiments of Foreign Volunteers) of which Bundorf joined the 22nd. Most of the recruits had fought in Spain. However, their ranks were quickly swelled by economic immigrants from Central Europe, many of whom were Jews or Communists like Bundorf. Such people were just as motivated as the Spanish Republicans to fight the Nazi threat. In total, 10,000 foreigners signed up for the three new regiments.

The camps in which veterans from Spain were housed therefore became the bases of these new regiments. Bundorf was billeted to the camp at Le Barcarès, on a beach on the Mediterranean in Perpignan, where rudimentary tents and shacks were put up from scratch by Spanish Republican refugees, and where French officers started to recruit. The camp housed 10,000 men by March 1939 and nearly 40,000 by August: they were soon sent to other camps elsewhere. For many of the former fighters from Spain, as well as for the Communists of other nationalities who joined, this was but the continuation of their earlier battle, and they hoped to use it to exact revenge for their defeat, this time with the support of Britain and France who had practised a policy of non-intervention in Spain itself.

The conditions in the camp were very difficult. The men slept in shacks; the latrines were outside; the food was dreadful; there were insects everywhere.[51] The wind whipped sand into their faces, onto their dinner plates and into their beds. There were over 50 nationalities in the camp and almost as many languages: many did not speak French. Their uniforms were second-hand. They were given boots of any size and then told to exchange them with their comrades for ones that fitted. They had no braces or belts and so they had to tie up their trousers with string: somehow, this titbit of information made its way into Germany, where Radio Stuttgart announced sarcastically, in 1940, that "the string regiments" had arrived at the front. The men were to adopt this soubriquet proudly and that is how the regiments are fondly remembered today – *Les régiments ficelles.*

Among Oswald Bundorf's comrades was his friend, Maurice Sisterman – a Romanian Jew who was in the 5th Company of the 22nd Regiment, together with Bundorf, who was to be taken prisoner with him in June, and who after the war became Secretary of the *Union des Engagés Volontaires, Anciens Combattants Juifs 1939-1945* (Union of Volunteer Jewish Veterans 1939-1945). This was an association devoted to keeping alive the memory of Jews, especially foreigners, who fought in the French army. Sisterman recalled life in the camp in a memoir published many decades later:

"Most of the 'heroes' of the Barcarès camp were immigrant workers: tailors, carpenters, cobblers, electricians, factory workers, builders, students, young men and men of fifty.

There were also men born in France, or who had settled in the country when they were very young but who had not become French citizens: writers, poets, journalists, artists, actors etc. There were also activists from various Jewish self-help organisations.

In this Jewish community which was ready to fight the Hitlerite hordes there were Communists, Zionists and people with no political affiliation.

The majority of the non-Jews were Spanish Republicans, volunteers who had been freed from internment camps where they had been since Franco's victory. There were also Bulgarians, Yugoslavs, Greeks, Belgians, Swiss, Portuguese and Turks who had been living in France for years. There were even Brazilians, Cubans and Argentinians.

In a word, there was a great mixture of nationalities from more than fifty countries. However, the great majority, as in the First World War, were Jewish volunteers. About 60 per cent or 70 per cent of the 12,000 or 15,000 soldiers at the Barcarès garrison were Jewish...

Our happiest moments were the friendly meetings and conversations in the alleyways between the shacks during free time or in the evenings. We spoke about everything, commenting on the news and giving each other moral support. We were always cheered up by these daily encounters and then passed on feelings of fraternity and optimism in our respective shacks...

In the shack of my own 5th Company there were housed a certain number of Romanian Jews from Transylvania, Bessarabia and Bukovina.

There were also Spaniards who, in the evenings, feeling so near and yet so far from their homeland, expressed their sentiments in melodious songs."[52]

The men were taught to march, and to mount and dismantle their old First World War machine guns. They were told at the outset that they would not have much ammunition. Indeed, during the fighting in June 1940, the soldiers would take guns from fallen comrades because they were so short of arms themselves. The only thing that was good in the regiment, according to one of its veterans, was morale: "We were there to fight and we wanted to fight," said one.[53] This battle spirit was to be betrayed by a French military staff more interested in negotiating an armistice than in fighting for victory. At the end of April 1940, Bundorf's 22nd RMVE and the 21st Regiment were sent to Alsace to join Allied forces already stationed there. For several months during the phoney war, i.e. before the German invasion, French and British troops had been positioned along the Maginot Line, the fortifications built after the First World War along the German border, waiting for the Germans to invade. The attack came at dawn on 10 May 1940, but the Germans simply drove around the Maginot Line and invaded through the Netherlands and Belgium instead. One hundred and thirty-five German divisions, including 10 armoured divisions, invaded Luxembourg, Belgium and the Netherlands. Within a few hours, French and British troops moved to meet the Germans along the Northern part of the line of defence: they had fallen into Hitler's trap, which was to entice the best troops towards him to open up a gap further South.

At this stage, the volunteer regiments knew nothing about the invasion, being hundreds of miles to the South in Alsace where there was no fighting at all. By 14 May, the Germans had crossed into France at Sedan in the Ardennes. By 16 May, when Churchill visited Paris to ascertain the situation, General Gamelin, the commander of the Allied forces in France, told him that France was beaten. Gamelin was thereupon sacked and replaced by General Weygand; at the same time, Marshal Philippe Pétain, the hero of the First World War and the victor of Verdun, was also brought into the government as Deputy Prime Minister.

The two RMVE regiments were then ordered to move from Alsace, the 21st to the Ardennes and the 22nd, with Bundorf, to the south of the town of Péronne, east of Amiens.[54] It took them several exhausting days of travelling by train and bus and marching to get to their destination. German troops arrived at the English Channel on 20 May and the Germans made their offer of a separate armistice with France. On 24 May, in the evening, Bundorf's regiment arrived in the village of Marchélepot, a few kilometres south of Péronne on the Somme. The men's first contact with the Germans took place in a wheat field: there was a firefight and a number of Bundorf's comrades were wounded and killed. In the fields, unmilked cows cried out in agony; it was extremely hot.

At this exact time in Paris, General Weygand also confided in his staff his desire to end the war. However, his honour forbade him to be the one who called for a capitulation of the army; he wanted the Prime Minister, Paul Reynaud, to sue for a political armistice. Reynaud agreed that the war was lost and he too wanted to end the fighting but he insisted that there be no separate peace without the British. In this, he was opposed by Pétain and by the President of the Republic, Albert Lebrun. Both argued that the British had not helped the French and that they had no right of veto if the French wanted to lay down their arms.

On the front, however, the volunteer regiments, like much of the rest of the French army, were determined to fight on, oblivious to the gangrene of defeatism which had infected the military high command and the political elite. The fighting was intense against the Germans, who took the town of Péronne, their intention being to advance west from there to Abbeville and the Channel coast at Boulogne. Bundorf's 3rd battalion withdrew back to Marchélepot. On 24 and 25 May, the front was stabilised between this village and the nearby villages of Misery and Fresnes. The men were heavily outgunned: one gunner said he had been sent to the front line with only 25 cartridges.[55]

The Germans bombed the French troops with a sort of cluster bomb which exploded at a height of three or four metres and killed anyone within a certain radius below. The bodies had to be collected with a spade because men were blown to pieces. Observers needed to locate the source of the artillery fire but the men had no maps: they had to draw their own on pieces of paper or find maps in people's houses. The Germans, by contrast, had French army maps with the legend written in German: they had entered the war properly prepared. Meanwhile, by 4 June, 350,000 French and British troops had escaped across the Channel from Dunkirk. The Germans continued to advance on Paris. On 5 June, Paul Reynaud appointed Jean Prouvost, Paul Baudouin and Brigadier (*général de brigade* in French) Charles de Gaulle to the government: one man determined to continue the war against two determined to stop fighting. Reynaud was keeping his options open.

Bundorf's 22nd RMVE fought on. Morale remained high even though they were badly outgunned. The Germans had planes, tanks and heavy artillery; the RMVE had only old guns and very little ammunition. Yet the 22nd RMVE fought like lions and held their positions for eight days. Were they being treated as cannon fodder, as the International Brigades had been during the Spanish Civil War? That is what some of them believed in later life. "We were sold out," protested one of Bundorf's comrades, Albert Valny, in a documentary made 60 years later.[56]

After the long resistance offered by Bundorf's regiment, two German officers arrived with a French officer carrying a white flag. The men were told they were surrounded and were ordered to surrender. Out of 3,000 men, only half had survived. They were congratulated for their resistance by both their own commander and by the Germans themselves. In 1941, the regiment was commended to the Army Order, one of only 13 such commendations given to infantry regiments throughout the entire war. General Huntziger, the War Minister, wrote in his formal citation:

"Thrown into battle although poorly equipped and having only just been formed, the 22nd Regiment of Foreign Volunteers distinguished itself under the command of Battalion Chief Hermann on 5, 6 and 7 June 1940.

Completely surrounded by German armoured units, violently bombed from the air and by artillery, the regiment resisted all attacks heroically for 48 hours, managing to protect all the localities which constituted the backbone of its position. The regiment surrendered only because of lack of ammunition and because it was crushed by considerable material superiority. The regiment's resistance inspired the admiration of the enemy."[57]

The regiment was awarded the *Croix de guerre*. The admiration of the enemy at the time, however, was soon replaced by the imperatives of Nazi ideology. As soon as the 22nd Regiment started marching out of the village along the road towards the Stalag where they were to be imprisoned at Cambrai, the Germans shouted, "All Jews, step aside!"[58] Those who did – a large percentage of the regiment was Jewish – were given the menial task of carrying the wounded.

With his comrades, Bundorf was taken to a prisoner of war camp, Frontstalag 101 in Cambrai. By 14 June, the Germans were in Paris. Three days later, in Bordeaux, Paul Reynaud resigned and Marshal Pétain announced France's capitulation. On 22 June, the armistice was signed in the same railway carriage at Rethondes near Compiègne where the French had made the Germans sign their capitulation in November 1918. The short Battle of France had taken 100,000 lives in just over a month. The average death rate in the infantry was seven per cent: the figure was considerably higher for the three RMVE Foreign Volunteer regiments, in which between 50 and 60 per cent of the soldiers were killed. These foreigners had served their adopted country better than many of France's own natives.

To be a Jewish prisoner of war in a German Stalag in France in 1940 was not good. Not only were the Nazis in control, the collaborationist regime based at Vichy was also soon to start taking its own anti-Jewish measures. The only safety was in numbers: there were one and a half million prisoners of war in France at the time. Bundorf was one of them.

It was in these unpropitious circumstances that Bundorf unexpectedly made his first acquaintance with people from the country, Britain, which was to become his home 25 years later. There were British prisoners of war in the camp. One day the latrines got blocked. A Tommy cheerfully rolled up his sleeve and reached into the stinking filth with his bare arm to unblock it. This made a deep impression on Bundorf, who shared the same get-up-and-go mentality, and who later would devote his life to encouraging it in others.

He immediately decided that he wanted to learn English and started to take notes on vocabulary in a little book, which he kept for the rest of his life. (See illustration within the photographic pages.) He would carry this notebook in his pocket and fetch it out whenever he could not remember a word. It was forbidden to write anything down in the Stalag so he had to keep it hidden: even having it at all was a small act of defiance against his German captors.

It was also in this Stalag that Bundorf came across a copy of Rudyard Kipling's poem *"If –"* written on a piece of paper. One of the British soldiers must have written it down or had a copy with him.

The poem's clever message of sturdiness, courage, risk-taking, resilience and optimism struck a deep chord with Bundorf. He took its message to heart, especially in the dangerous situation into which world history and his own courage had plunged him.

Kipling's masculine virtues of determination and equanimity in the face of adversity were to serve Bundorf very well throughout his life, which was to be characterised by very dramatic vicissitudes. He never regarded the ups as evidence of his superiority; and he never let the downs get him down. It was all, he argued, part of life's rich tapestry and the key thing was to keep on trying. He was convinced that one's life depended on one's own decisions and that courage, dedication and willpower were essential. You are what you decide to be.[59] He hated wasting time and, on the contrary, packed every available second with work and activity. He made self-improvement into a personal ideology and would very frequently encourage it in others too, sometimes gruffly, pushing them beyond what they initially thought they could do.

Bundorf the prisoner of war was put to work repairing railway tracks. Within a few months, he had befriended French civilian workers who gave him a jacket and a pair of trousers. These enabled him and two other prisoners to escape captivity by hiding in a Paris-bound train on 28 September 1940.[60] The history of the occupation of France is full of such stories of ordinary civilians spontaneously and unexpectedly helping members of the Resistance. It was undoubtedly a major act of daring by Bundorf to escape, because if he had been caught by a German controller in the train, his fate as a foreigner, an escapee and a Jew would have been sealed. As it was, his gamble paid off and he reached the French capital safely in a matter of hours.

CHAPTER 3

THE FRENCH RESISTANCE

If you can keep your head when all about you are losing theirs...

Back in Paris, Bundorf was in danger. The Northern zone of France was occupied by German forces, including the Gestapo and the SS. Foreign Jews would be the first candidates for deportation to the labour and death camps: the fact that the French authorities did release over 75,000 of them to the Germans, a decision which led directly to their murder in death camps, is considered an indelible stain on that country's wartime record. In such a situation, a Jew in Nazi-occupied Europe had only one choice: to go underground. In later life, Uncle Oswald would tell his niece, Amalie, that every man takes his own decisions and that this is the sole factor in determining how a life is lived. Even he, however, would not deny that such choices are taken within a given context. This time, Bundorf had made his rendezvous with destiny and met the challenge with glee. He wanted nothing more than to continue fighting the Nazis. Luckily, Bundorf was able to contact his old friends in the Communist organisations he had worked for in 1938 and 1939. These groups had by now become secret, the French Communist Party having been banned in September 1939, shortly after the Nazi-Soviet Pact and the outbreak of the war. There were lots of other escapees during this period – there were well over a million prisoners of war – and, with them, the Communist Party was able to piece together the embryonic structure which would later form an important part of the Resistance. Some Party members were instructed to return to their countries of origin, others were tasked to remain in France.

Bundorf took evening classes to learn how to build and repair radios. Radio operator was to become his official profession, as indicated on his papers from that period. This, too, became part of his personal philosophy: he never lost his love of making things with his hands and strongly believed that others should do so too. He presented himself to the Soviet authorities in Paris, on the basis that his home town, Czernowitz, had been formally incorporated into the Soviet Union on 2 August 1940, Soviet troops having occupied the territory, and the much larger territory of Bessarabia (which corresponds approximately to today's Moldova), in late June. He asked to be repatriated and his request was approved. Nevertheless, events overtook him because, on 22 June 1941, Nazi Germany invaded the Soviet Union. This event, more than any other, was the definitive event of the Second World War, as it marked the beginning of the cataclysmic battle on the Eastern front between Nazi Germany and the Soviet Union, a battle in which three million German soldiers were to invade Russia, and in which 27 million Soviet citizens were to lose their lives. In sheer scale, it dwarfed all the other fronts of that terrible war.

One of the first people whom Bundorf contacted on his return to Paris was Fanny Gurvitz, who was to become one of the three leaders of the Romanian language section of the MOI and liaison officer for the Romanian section with the rest of the MOI. She would be arrested in April 1943.[61] Another early contact was Aliona Flom, a close comrade of the future military head of the MOI, Boris Holban, Bundorf's commander: Bundorf would work closely with her in the Resistance.[62] In 1945, Bundorf's membership card of the Association of French Partisans and Irregular Forces (*Association Nationale des Amis des Francs-tireurs et Partisans Français*) gave 4, rue du Plateau in the 19th arrondissement as his address: this was where Aliona Flom lived.[63]

The French Resistance started from very modest beginnings. The first Resistance acts consisted of propaganda – sticking up posters or labels on walls, writing graffiti and distributing flyers which criticised the Vichy Government and encouraged resistance against the Germans. The more courageous elements put stickers on German tanks or vehicles while the soldiers were not looking. The purpose of all this was to undermine morale among the occupation forces and to raise it – and awareness – among the French.

Even this work required considerable daring. On one occasion, two German women, both members of the Resistance, were visiting a church in Avignon. They found hymn books in German on the pews. Evidently the church was being prepared for a service for German soldiers. They secretly removed the books from the church in their capes, scribbled propaganda messages in them at home, and returned them to their places in the church. How they would have loved to be able to attend the service to watch the expressions on the Germans' faces as they stood up to sing their hymns![64]

Communist organisations waited, however, until 22 June 1941, the date of the Nazi invasion of the Soviet Union (which Hitler chose to coincide with the first anniversary of the signature of the armistice with France) before really starting to wage an armed struggle against the German occupier. Prior to that, they had followed Party discipline: the line set down in Moscow ordered them to refrain from attacking the Germans, with whom Moscow had signed a non-aggression pact in August 1939. So great, indeed, was the faith of these people in the new creed of Communism, and in its archpriests in Moscow, that they almost blindly followed orders from them and were happy both to ignore the terror of the 1930s and to justify the Nazi-Soviet pact of August 1939.

The attitude of relative passivity changed as soon as the Germano-Soviet war broke out. These MOI groups became an important part of the FTP, *Francs-tireurs et Partisans,* the armed resistance. Their clandestine work, first as Communists and then as anti-German propagandists, meant that they had the know-how and logistical structures to carry out armed activity too. The secret transport of leaflets quickly morphed into the secret transport of guns.

Indeed, the FTP-MOI were the only groups to carry out armed attacks in 1941, the Free French in London not yet having ordered or even approved such tactics. The first such attack was the assassination of a young German naval cadet at the Barbès-Rochechouart metro station in Paris on 21 August 1941, carried out by the young Pierre Georges ("Colonel Fabien").

The Germans reacted to such attacks in exactly the way the *Résistants* wanted them to – sadistically. They would execute a dozen or so hostages, specifically Communists who had been arrested distributing flyers. In other words, an activity which today may seem relatively harmless, handing out leaflets, was something which could lead to one's execution. These Germans therefore fell into the Resistance trap, because their reprisals caused intense resentment among the general public and increased its hatred for them.

Bundorf's initial work was with a part of the MOI known as the *Travail allemand*, created in the summer of 1941 under the leadership of the future Czechoslovak Communist official and then dissident, Artur London. Closely involved in this were German and Austrian nationals, generally Communists who had fled the Nazis to France, and who had to pretend to be from Alsace or Switzerland, as well as German-speaking *Résistants* from East and Central Europe. The work involved spreading propaganda among the German occupation forces, in the form of posters or newspapers with slogans, and by pretending to fraternise with German soldiers in order to sound them out and then tell them that they would lose the war; transmitting information, which then of course was communicated primarily by means of the printed word; and intelligence, by spying on the German war machine, often by means of agents sent to work for the Germans and to inform on them. Some of the spying was of a very high level indeed, for example when some infiltrators were able to get into a position to know about troop movements across occupied Europe.[65]

One of the leading lights in this part of the Resistance was a compatriot of Bundorf's, a Jewish girl from Czernowitz who, like him, was born into a German-speaking family: Irma Mico née Rosenberg. Still alive in 2016, Irma Mico lived to over 100 years old (she was born in 1914). Her sons made a film about her when she was in her nineties[66] and she has given written accounts of her role in chatting up German soldiers in order to extract information from them, and then to sap their morale by telling them that Hitler was leading them to perdition.[67] On occasions, the *Résistants* would even try to recruit soldiers to encourage anti-Hitler thinking among their own fellow soldiers. In one spectacular case, Hans Heisel, an anti-Nazi German naval officer, gave his revolver to a *Résistant*, via such contacts, which was then used to assassinate Julius Ritter, the SS colonel in charge of transporting forced French labour to Germany (the hated *Service du Travail obligatoire*).[68] Heisel appears in the film about Mico, *Das Kind*, where they share reminiscences, both of course speaking their native German.

The *Travail allemand* produced an underground newspaper, *Der Soldat im Westen* (The Soldier in the West) written by German-speaking Communists from Eastern Europe like Bundorf.[69] At its height, it produced 100,000 copies per issue. Bundorf was involved in distributing this newspaper, as well as other propaganda material in French, including drawings (etchings on linoleum) by Aliona Flom's son[70], and leaving this material in places where the target audience would find it. There were about 100 such people of various nationalities, charged with distributing the newspaper and other pamphlets. For security reasons, they operated in small units of three to five men and they were kept apart from the rest of the organisation.[71] One trick Bundorf and his comrades used was to push a wad of leaflets into the swing doors of the metro: when the door was next pushed open, the leaflets would cascade down and scatter everywhere.

On one occasion, Bundorf negotiated the acquisition of a duplicating machine which was capable of printing off the *Travail allemand's* propaganda material. He met a French printer at the home of a friend from Czernowitz. The man had a shop where Bundorf noticed the duplicator. Knowing that he was an anti-fascist, Bundorf asked the man, Fernandez, to print material for the Resistance. He agreed. At first, Bundorf was pleased with the arrangement, but quickly realised that the hand-operated machine was too slow and cumbersome for their purposes. Through Fernandez' connections, he bought for 50,000 old francs of his own money a mechanically operated duplicating machine which was being sold for scrap. They installed it in a basement in an isolated house in the suburbs. The machine was repaired, and material and parts for it were brought with help from MOI comrades. Bundorf had to transport this material himself, which he did using a child's pram (presumably accompanied by a woman, for this was long before the politically correct days in which a father would be seen looking after his children alone). Had he ever been caught doing this, he would have been immediately arrested and tortured, possibly to death. His gamble paid off and the printer was safely delivered: it carried on working until the Liberation, long after Bundorf had himself been moved out of the *Travail allemand*.[72] Others were not so lucky. When a man who printed an underground Yiddish newspaper, Rudolf Zeiler, was denounced and arrested on 29 October 1941, the police found that he had also published an *Appeal to Jews Around the World* on his press. He was handed over to the Germans and shot on 19 December.[73] Accounts of Resistance work are replete with stories about the horrible torture practised on suspects, many of whom managed to refuse to talk even unto death.

On one occasion, Bundorf escaped precisely this fate by a whisker. He was with a comrade from Transylvania, code-named Roger (Bundorf's own *nom de guerre* was Gérard), who was caught surreptitiously leaving propaganda newspapers in the Paris metro. Several years after the event, in a written statement to the authorities of the Communist Party of Romania, Octav Botnar told the chilling story:

"At the end of 1942 or the beginning of 1943, I cannot now remember exactly, after our group had distributed newspapers in German at the Gare de l'Est and in the metro, from where soldiers were leaving for the Eastern Front, I went there with Roger to inspect how this action had been carried out.

I was walking along the corridor of the metro at a distance of two to three metres from Roger, each of us distributing the material on either side. Walking alongside us were German soldiers and French civilians. As we turned a corner, Roger reached into his pocket to throw a pile of our material. Walking towards us were some other Germans who had evidently seen him make this gesture, but whom we had not noticed. He therefore dropped his newspapers as planned. They stopped him and asked to see his identity card. I carried on walking among the other passengers. Then I returned via another entrance to see what was happening, again passing by. The Germans had his identity card and they were waving their arms around. I passed them without stopping. I wanted to turn back but the French police then arrived. I later learned from a comrade who secretly worked with us, a Polish woman, that Roger died three days after his arrest from the torture inflicted on him by the Gestapo. After this, we continued the same methods of operation. They had proved effective even with all their risks."[74]

It was standard Resistance training for such emergencies not to show any emotion. The slightest flicker of recognition from either man risked putting the other in mortal danger. Each occurrence of such situations must have been terrifying and deeply disturbing psychologically. Gilles Perrault explains why people caught working in Resistance propaganda were so appallingly treated by the Gestapo.

"A German soldier killed by the Resistance is written off by his commanders. But a German soldier shaken by a political conversation represented an unacceptable risk for the Nazis. He became the bearer of the virus of doubt which could infect his comrades, demoralise his section or his company, and propagate defeatism at home while on leave. Against this enterprise, which was political in the highest sense of the word, and which although less spectacular than de-railing a train or individual attacks was nonetheless more insidious and more dangerous in the long term because it attacked the Nazis' power at its very heart – the morale and the ideological loyalty of the troops – the Gestapo and all the associated services deployed unfailing vigilance right until the end, and limitless savagery to root it out."[75]

As time went on, Resistance activities in Paris became more and more dangerous. The Germans tightened the noose around the Jews. On 26 May 1942, Jews in the occupied North of the country were required to sew a large yellow star with "Juif" written on it onto their jackets. To avoid this, and to pursue his Resistance activities, Bundorf had at least two false identities during the Resistance – Charles Gerber, born in Sonceboz in the Bernese Jura in Switzerland, and Charles Just. Pretending to be of Swiss origin was a common way for *Résistants* to cover up their strange accents in French. The Nazis' programme of extermination also started to bite in France: on 16 and 17 June, 14,500 men, women and children were arrested in Paris and deported to Auschwitz: only about 100 survived. A total of 40,000 Jews were deported from France that year.

Bundorf himself was directly affected by this unimaginable barbarism. He had fallen in love with a woman from Czernowitz, "Coca" Semel, born in 1918, five years his junior. (One of his Communist comrades from Czernowitz had been Jacob Semel, perhaps her brother[76].) She had a daughter by another man, named Fuhrmann, and on 25 September 1942, she was deported from Drancy, a collection centre north of Paris, to Auschwitz together with her 16-month-old baby girl, Nadine, who had been born in May 1941. Both mother and daughter were killed the moment they arrived at the death camp, on 30 September 1942.[77]

Such acts only strengthened the resolve of the fighters. Between autumn 1942 and November 1943, the FTP-MOI in Paris carried out 230 acts of armed attack and sabotage. It is for this reason that one historian rightly calls the detachments commanded by Boris Holban "the most courageous and deadly arm of the Communist resistance in the Paris area".[78] This was in spite of the fact that the total number of Resistance fighters in the Paris region then was less than 100[79], for the most part very young men and women who were essentially amateurs being chased by a professional police force.

When the hated programme of obligatory work service in Germany (*Service du Travail obligatoire*) was introduced in 1943, this helped the *maquis* (the Resistance) because people joined it in order to escape the draft. The police stepped up their operations as well, creating the *Brigades spéciales* to track down Resistance cells. Several of these were crushed. Torture was widely practised in order to get people to talk; if possible, they would be turned and released to work as informers. When the so-called Manouchian group was arrested in 1944, its 23 Resistance fighters, comrades of Bundorf, all of them foreigners and most of them Jews, were executed by the Gestapo: Vichy France and its German controllers made much of the fact that none of the partisans was French.[80]

This meant that Resistance operatives lived in mortal danger, not only from the Nazis and the police but also from their own comrades. Boris Holban tells a chilling story of how one of their comrades had been arrested by the Gestapo, turned, and then released to infiltrate their group once more in order to betray them. His wife had been kept hostage as a guarantee. Joseph Davidovitch had been one of Holban's closest and oldest comrades: he and his friends could hardly believe it when they were tipped off by a policeman that he had been recruited while in detention. They decided to agree to meet him in order to find out what he knew and to test their theory.

A team was set up for this purpose and Davidovitch was secretly watched by his former comrades. His movements convinced them that he had become an informer. A safe house was found in a suburb. Cristina Luca, the head of MOI intelligence, whom Bundorf knew well, and who, like him and Holban, returned to Romania after the war, was sent to collect Davidovitch. He was brought to the safe house. The suspect started by trying to pretend that the story of his escape was true, but he was forced, under cross-examination, to admit that he had been lying and that he was in fact working for the Gestapo. The group of four men withdrew to consider the situation and their verdict was unanimous: he had to be executed there and then. They knifed him to death in the kitchen and then had to dispose of the corpse, at night and under curfew, no mean feat in an occupied city.[81] Such events occurred often in the Resistance, and a fictional one, no doubt inspired by reality, is recounted in Jean-Pierre Melville's film *Army of Shadows*, based on Joseph Kessel's novel of the same name, in which, at the end, the character played by Simone Signoret is gunned down in broad daylight by her comrades, because the Gestapo have forced her to speak by torturing her daughter.

Bundorf himself was closely involved in a very similar affair. Having been promoted in 1943, he ended up in charge of a group of

Czechs and Poles within the *Travail allemand*.[82] One Monday morning in January 1944, Irma Mico had one of her regular appointments with "Nicolas" (his real name was Armand) Avramescu, a technical officer within the *Travail allemand* who printed the leaflets and newspapers produced in German. She met him about twice a week to discuss where to plant their publicity material, on the basis of information she and her comrades had gleaned from chatting to German soldiers. The arrangement was that she would travel to one metro station, he to another, and they would then appear to meet by chance in the street between the two stops.

Just as Irma Mico came out of her station, an alarm sounded and everyone rushed for cover. Mico sheltered near a newspaper kiosk. As she ran to hide, she noticed a man who remained on the pavement opposite and whom she immediately guessed was a secret policeman. Once the alarm was over, she decided not to walk towards the other metro station as planned, but instead to abandon the rendezvous and to return to the same place at the same time the next day. This was standard Resistance practice for failed meetings. When she got back to her comrades, one of them unexpectedly embraced her with joy and told her that Avramescu had been caught and he had betrayed all his appointments to the police. Irma Mico realised then that the policeman she had seen had in fact been waiting to grab her. She was later able to confirm her hunch for certain by information gleaned from another comrade who was in police custody at the time.[83]

A few days after the Liberation, in August 1944, this same Avramescu was discovered wearing Free French uniform. He was trying to pass himself off as a member of the Resistance. One of his comrades recognised him. They arrested him and took him to the barracks in the rue de Reuilly in the 12th arrondissement, where hundreds of other FTP-MOI fighters including Bundorf were billeted following their integration into the regular army of liberated France. Boris Holban, for instance, set up the *Bataillon Liberté* there; another group, the *Compagnie Rayman*, had another son of Czernowitz, Sigmund Tumin, as its deputy commander.

In the barracks, Avramescu was taken down to the cellars and executed.[84] The difference, however, from other similar executions was that this one occurred after the Liberation, and after the promulgation of the legal government. It therefore counted as an act of revenge, an illegal settling of accounts, and therefore an act of murder. It is estimated that some 9,000 people were killed in this way, as old scores were settled in the weeks following the Liberation. Such executions were often carried out by former members of the Resistance.[85]

Several years later, Octav Botnar would tell the Romanian security police that he had been the person who had killed Avramescu, and that after the war he had been wanted for questioning by the French police for this reason.[86] He told the Romanian authorities this in response to the claim by his enemies in Romania that it was suspicious that he himself had not been betrayed by the turncoat. Botnar was to inform the Romanian police that Avramescu had indeed tried to betray him to the Gestapo, but that he had known only his old address. Many other comrades had not been so lucky, and his betrayal therefore led to their arrest and death. The interrogation, conducted in August 1960, went like this:

"Question: Why did you maintain contact with your brother through an address with the name PERIANU VICTORIA?

Answer (Botnar): I gave this address with my mother-in-law's name to MAURICE out of prudence for him, because in a certain period – 1950-1954 – a number of persons from Romania who had a 'suspicious' situation were expelled from France. I was wanted in France in the years after the war, because I executed a certain AVRAMESCU ARMAND, who had been in Spain, had then been active in the Resistance and on being detained by the Gestapo, had betrayed a great number of activists.

Maurice knew about me being followed and so did Max, who in 1949 was detained in my place for 48 hours. I was also told about this by VICTOR IONESCU, who was in France at that time.

For this reason, to avoid him being endangered in any way, I gave Maurice this address which he used in writing to me, using for the sender the maiden name of his wife... (Minute signed Botnar Octav)."[87]

Shortly after Avramescu was turned by the Gestapo in January 1944, but long before his execution, Cristina Luca (born Bianca Marcusohn, she is better known by the married name she took after the war, Boico), the FTP-MOI's head of intelligence, with whom Bundorf cooperated on a daily basis, reassigned him from propaganda to actual fighting duties.[88] As the war went on and the Allied pincer tightened on the German armies, Bundorf was given more and more important tasks within the Resistance. It was as a fighter that he was to participate in the liberation of Paris. Luca put him in touch with members of the underground, whom he organised into a fighting group in the southern suburb of Étampes; he then travelled with her to Arpajon, also south of Paris, to set up another group of *maquisards*. Finally, he was the liaison officer for a group of over 30 Soviet former prisoners of war whom he moved from the south to the north of Paris, and alongside whom he himself fought the Germans at Pierrefitte-sur-Seine, a northern suburb which was liberated on 20 August, a week before Paris itself, Free French forces having first engaged the Germans there on 12 August.[89]

For the rest of his life, he felt that Paris was his city, as he had fought for its freedom and shared in the paroxysm of euphoria centred on the Hôtel de Ville.

These actions were to merit Botnar, 50 years later, a eulogistic attestation by Holban, the military commander of the Parisian immigrant *Résistants*. Holban wrote:

"Octav Botnar, alias Gérard, operated under my command between November 1942 and August 1944, during which time he was engaged in most courageous and effective operations, right up to the Liberation of Paris on 25th August 1944. As a member of the FTP-MOI *(Francs Tireurs et partisans – main-d'oeuvre immigrée)*, he took part in numerous actions of sabotage and armed attacks against the occupier, in Paris and in the wider Paris region, and was engaged in the battle for the liberation of Paris itself."[90]

His comrade, Irma Mico, similarly wrote:

"In the years 1941-43, Octav Botnar and I were members of the same Resistance network, namely the TA *(Travail anti-allemand)*. He distributed leaflets in places frequented by the German army, such as railway stations, the Metro and close to their barracks. These leaflets were produced by us with the aim of passing information to and demoralising the soldiers of the Wehrmacht. Later on, he led several groups carrying out the same work (a group of Czechs and another group of Polish, amongst others). Throughout this whole period, Octav Botnar, working under the name of Gérard, displayed sang-froid composure, courage and energy. These qualities were a requisite as this was a particularly dangerous area of activity. Many of our comrades in action were arrested, tortured, deported or shot."[91]

Years later, under interrogation by the Securitate in Bucharest, Octav Botnar would be presented with claims that neither Holban nor Cristina Luca-Boico had liked him. His enemies claimed that he had been conceited, short-tempered, impulsive, unable to accept criticism, and that he had caused problems for the Party and the Resistance hierarchy by being undisciplined. They claimed that he put the organisation in danger, for instance by disobeying rules about how and where to arrange meetings. Naturally such accusations were very damaging in Communist Romania, where loyalty to the Party was everything, and where personal rivalries could easily be settled by a well-placed denunciation. Botnar denied that he was guilty of insubordination but he did admit that his relationships with his superiors were sometimes difficult. "I had disagreements with these colleagues (Cristina Luca, Boris Holban, Alexandru Buican) which degenerated into enmity," he wrote in 1952.[92] "These were caused partly by defects in my own character but also by them, who were presumptuous and full of vanity."

There seems little doubt, therefore, that even during the war Bundorf had a reputation for being anarchic and for questioning his superiors. Fifty years later, another leading figure in the Resistance, Georges Filip-Lefort, born Gheorghe Grünfeld in Transylvania in 1919, who played a major role in the organisation in Lyon, wrote an affidavit for Botnar, in which he described his record in the Resistance as "exceptional" and "particularly courageous".[93] He wrote:

"This activity (the *Travail allemand*) was reserved for especially brave volunteers who had a perfect command of German. They carried out very sensitive and extremely dangerous missions among members of the Wehrmacht."

In a note written on a postcard in Romanian and French – he and Botnar evidently used both languages interchangeably – which he enclosed with the formal affidavit, Filip-Lefort took Botnar to task for pestering two other Resistance comrades, Holban and Mico, into giving him similar affidavits. He had evidently told Botnar to let him take care of it, an instruction Botnar had ignored. He wrote:

"Oh well, you always were stubborn. God made you that way."

CHAPTER 4

BUILDING SOCIALISM

If you can bear to hear the truth you've spoken
Twisted by knaves to make a trap for fools...

It is impossible to exaggerate the sense of euphoria felt by those who had fought for the liberation of Paris. Having adopted the city as a second home, following expulsion or flight from their home countries, and having seen it and the whole of France then languish for four years under Nazi occupation, the immigrants in the Resistance felt that the victory to which they had made such a decisive contribution justified their pre-war engagement in favour of Communism. Even in the Spanish Civil War, anti-fascism had been the guiding principle of Communists. Now, they had pulled off a victory on a world scale after five years of global conflict. History seemed to be on their side, as they had won in the most atrocious war ever fought. What could possibly stop them now?

The Red Army had liberated Europe from the Nazi tyranny and its troops were stationed all over Central and Eastern Europe, including in Berlin and the eastern part of Germany. The Cold War and the division of Europe into two ideologically and geopolitically hostile blocks still lay several years in the future; it did not really break out until 1948 after the Prague coup and the Berlin airlift. Those Communists who had fought fascism, first in Spain and then in the world war, naturally expected to reap political dividends from their victory, including in their home countries. The need for Party cadres to return to their home countries was especially strong in Romania, where the Communist Party had been tiny.[94]

One of the leading lights of the Romanian Communist Party, Ana Pauker, travelled to Paris in May 1945 to encourage those

Romanian Communists who had sought exile in France to return to their home country, where the new regime, of which the Communists were a part, needed men and women with talent. Romania had been an ally of the Axis powers during the war, even joining Nazi Germany in its attack on the Soviet Union in 1941, and her sudden and belated changing of sides – King Michael arrested the pro-German leader, Marshal Antonescu, on 23 August 1944, and joined the Allies – meant that the Communists (and their Soviet backers) had few natural allies within the country. Any expatriate talent needed to be recalled home.

Oswald Bundorf attended the meeting Pauker addressed and answered her call by agreeing to return to Romania. The Communist Party had played a role in the overthrow of Marshal Antonescu, in August 1944 – a role it was grossly to exaggerate once it had seized total power in Romania – and so the Party was now not only legal but even included in the new government. The Soviet forces in Romania naturally encouraged this because they wanted to ensure friendly governments in the countries they now occupied: all the USSR's Central European neighbours had had pro-Nazi governments during the war (the only exceptions being Poland and the Czech lands which had no governments because the Germans administered them directly).

A Liberation Committee was set up in the Romanian embassy in Paris, in the rue Saint-Dominique, manned by Communist Party officials and former Resistance fighters. The job of this committee was to repatriate as many ex-Resistance fighters as possible, as well as liberated prisoners of war. A large number of such people were flown back to Romania in the immediate aftermath of the war, travelling via Italy and Yugoslavia with the help of the French and Yugoslav Communist Parties.[95] Bundorf waited in Paris until 1946. When he did return to Romania in March, his route took him through Italy. He was later to boast that, on the way, he had slept in Mussolini's bed[96], which implies that he stopped at Gargnano on Lake Garda where the Italian dictator had a villa.

Oswald Bundorf had personal reasons for remaining in France for a few extra months after the end of the war. He had married a French woman, Raymonde Anonge, in 1946. Their prospects seemed excellent in his home country: although Bundorf was not a senior Communist Party official, his Resistance record would count strongly in his favour. Few foresaw that Romanian Communism would be as dictatorial as Soviet Communism under Stalin. Few, indeed, even accepted that Stalin's Soviet Union was a dictatorship at all. When Stalin died in 1953, Botnar (as he was known by then) mourned his death.[97]

It was through the return of people like Bundorf that much of the apparatus of the Communist Party, and even some governmental posts, were staffed. Many of its leaders, as we have seen, had cut their teeth in the prisons of pre-war Romania before fighting in the Spanish Civil War and then spending years underground in the French Resistance, where betrayal was a constant danger punished by death. To be sure, Stalinism existed all over Communist Europe but the Romanian regime very quickly acquired a particularly nasty quality: as historians of Romania make clear, the apparatus of a police state was set up immediately the Communist Party seized control of the country in 1948. Once in power, party cadres retained the same habits of deviousness and dissimulation which had been so essential for survival underground before and during the war.[98] Politics for them was struggle and nothing else. Enemies had to be ruthlessly sought out and destroyed, in peacetime as in war. The paranoia continued to reach ever greater heights until the regime came to a spectacular end in the bloody conflagration of Christmas 1989, when Nicolae Ceaușescu, the successor of the original Stalinist dictator, and his wife Elena, were executed after a brief show trial by a kangaroo court.[99]

Like many of his compatriots who returned to Romania after the war, Bundorf was encouraged to change his name. Just as Vichy France had denounced the French Resistance as nothing but a gang of Jews and other foreigners, so the Romanian Communist Party had been denounced in Romania throughout the pre-war and wartime years as a Jewish conspiracy. The new regime needed to shake off this image, and so many of the returnees changed their names to sound less Jewish. Baruch Bruhman became Boris Holban; Ervin Blum became Ervin Bodnar[100]; Gheorghiu Grünfeld became Georges Filip-Lefort; Sigmund Tumin (from Czernowitz) became Ion Marinescu; and Oswald Bundorf became Octav Botnar. It was by this name that he was to be known for the rest of his life.

Initially, Botnar was assigned to work in the Communist Party itself, in the agitprop section of the Bucharest regional section of the Party, producing official Party publications. Evidently the Party cadres thought that his experience distributing anti-fascist propaganda in the French Resistance had given him valuable experience for this. However, within a year, in April 1947, he was transferred to a post within the administration which was to give him valuable experience for his future career as a businessman. He was employed first in economic planning, at the Office of Economic Control, from June 1947 until January 1948, working in the research and documentation office, and then in the Ministry of Foreign Trade.

This second job involved recovering funds which had been placed abroad and which the new regime decided to appropriate for itself. He had to undertake foreign trips for this work, and of course his knowledge of foreign languages, especially French and German, was an asset. In March 1948, he was given a short foreign posting, to Brussels, where for three months he was commercial attaché at the Romanian embassy to Belgium and the Netherlands.

Although Botnar's new career appeared to get off to a promising start, he also very quickly rubbed his colleagues up the wrong way,

Central Square, Czernowitz in 1934. Botnar took part in a pro-Communist demonstration here in 1932 at the age of 18 which led to his arrest and his first period of imprisonment.

Acknowledgement of Botnar's application for a carte d'identité in February 1940 (see handwritten date left centre). France was yet to fall to German occupation, and Botnar was still able to use his real name – at that time Oswald Bundorf.

Marchélepot, France: Memorial to Botnar's 22nd Regiment of Foreign Volunteers who fought valiantly to hold the line against the advancing Germans in May/June 1940. Botnar was captured and made prisoner of war. France fell to the Germans two weeks later.

Two pages of Botnar's hand-made dictionary of translations which he began as a prisoner of war in a German Stalag in 1940. He kept it for the rest of his life.

False identity papers using the alias Charles Gerber, a supposed Swiss, born in Sonceboz in the Bernese Jura. Pretending to be Swiss was a common way for Résistants to "explain" their unusual French accents.

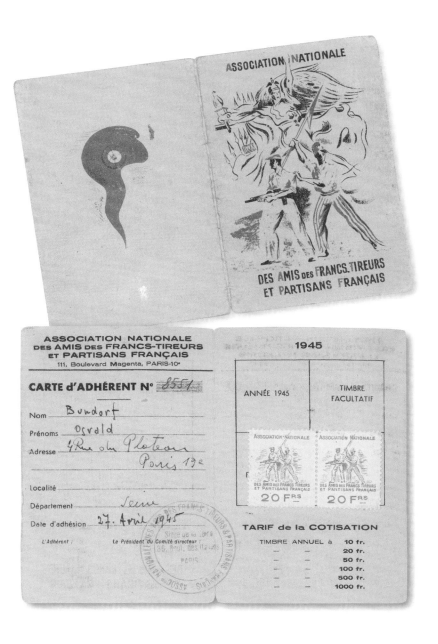

Post-Liberation, and produced shortly before VE Day, Botnar's membership card of the Association Nationale des Amis des Francs-Tireurs et Partisans Français.

Botnar always looked on Paris as his city, having fought for its freedom. These documents are testimony to his allegiance to the French capital, although it was not long before he was persuaded to return to Romania.

Botnar with his baby daughter Camelia (1952/3).

An early photograph of Botnar with his wife Marcela and daughter Camelia.

Botnar pictured shortly after his release from the labour camp in Periprava in the Danube Delta (1964). Emaciated and undernourished, he weighed just six stone (40 kg).

refusing to take orders – just as he had allegedly done in the Resistance – and refusing to submit to the discipline required of a Party member and a civil servant. He quarrelled with the head of the delegation in Brussels and tried to pull rank on him by reminding him that he, Botnar, had been a member of the French Communist Party and not just the Romanian.[101] He complained about the accommodation offered him in the premises of the Legation, saying that the room they proposed to give him was unfit to live in. He refused to let his colleagues inspect his suitcases on the occasion of a business trip to Paris. Such behaviour counted, in the eyes of his colleagues, as acts of insubordination which were considered proof of his vanity. For good measure, his enemies added that he was bringing the country itself into disrepute by his indiscipline.

Whilst in Bucharest in July 1948, having been recalled on a pretext from an overseas business trip, Botnar was dismissed without warning from his job and thenceforth retained in Romania. A few months after his return to Bucharest, he received a letter from his wife, Raymonde, who had remained in Paris in the rooms he had rented on the edge of the 17th arrondissement under one of his Resistance pseudonyms (Charles Just), asking him to join her. He could not, and she did not want to join him in Romania. She decided to stay in France.[102]

It is not clear why the couple separated. Maybe Raymonde sensed the way the regime was evolving. Maybe she had been unhappy in Bucharest, in a country whose language she probably did not speak. It is also possible that Botnar refused to join her in France because of the Avramescu affair. As we saw in the last chapter, Botnar would take precautions to protect his brother Maurice from fall-out for the execution, by asking him to write to him at his mother-in-law's address, for fear that the French authorities would make the connection with him. He may have needed to protect himself from arrest by the French authorities. This was certainly the belief of one of the numerous people who informed on Octav Botnar in later years: while in prison, the Securitate put a "cellmate" in with him who was in reality working for them. When the issue arose of which countries Botnar might try to leave for after his release from prison, the cellmate/informer wrote that Botnar would not be able to go and live in France:

> "because in France the danger of being made responsible for killing Avramescu persisted (which I am sure was the main reason why he had not followed his first wife in 1948, although he admits he had loved her so much that for a couple of years he had not been able to grow close to any other woman!)".[103]

According to this account, then, Botnar was heartbroken. Whatever the truth, Octav Botnar and Raymonde Anonge divorced by 1950. On Raymonde's return to Paris, there was a row between Botnar and his brother, Max. According to Botnar's version of events over a decade later, Max had wanted to take possession of the flat in Paris, even though Botnar was only its tenant.[104] This argument led to a split and the two brothers did not talk or correspond for 10 years. He told his other brother, Maurice, that he held Max responsible for provoking the row, and that he did not want to have anything more to do with him. The brothers were not to meet again until 1957.

In addition to his personal problems, Botnar was cross that he had been tricked into returning to Romania in 1948. He did everything to make his displeasure known. He sent several memos and letters to the Central Committee of the Romanian Workers' Party (as the Communist Party had renamed itself), and even to the head of state himself, Gheorghe Gheorghiu-Dej, protesting at the ruse which had been used to get him back into the country, and initially asking to be allowed to rejoin his wife whom he had left behind in Western Europe. He argued that she had been ill and had had to return to France for this reason.[105] He tried to practise some self-criticism, a common Communist gesture, and said that no doubt he had made some mistakes as anyone could, especially in view of his difficult family situation. It was to no avail: there is no record of the Romanian President having even read the letter, still less sending a reply.

Unfortunately for Botnar, as for many Romanians, the culture of mutual suspicion and denunciation had already started to bite. Any dissidence was treated as evidence of hostility to the state. A few professional rivalries and personal disputes were enough to sabotage anyone's position. Draconian laws were passed to enforce absolute obedience to the Party and the state, such as the introduction of the death penalty for "economic sabotage"[106] – as Botnar was to discover because he was to fall from grace on precisely this charge. Indeed, so crazy was the obsession with security that, as soon as the Securitate had been set up, its officers were instructed to spy and eavesdrop on each other, and even on the most senior party figures. Ana Pauker and Alexandru Bârlădeanu, for whom Botnar was to work, were spied on; so was the future party leader, Nicolae Ceauşescu, and the former head of the Securitate, Gheorghe Pintilie. Even Gheorghiu-Dej himself, the head of the Party and the head of state, had his phone tapped from 1949 onwards.[107] As a result, although Botnar moved quickly into interesting jobs involving foreign trade, and even did a short stint in the foreign intelligence service for a few months in 1948, he was himself spied on and denounced. The informants who were keeping tabs on him noted what they called his insolence, his quick tongue and the way he was happy to criticise his comrades and superiors. This was to count badly against him.

In August 1949, Botnar was demoted and moved to the Customs Office as an inspector. Following complaints that he had tried to sidestep his boss by writing to the Minister himself to air his concerns that imports were being restricted to the detriment of the national economy, Botnar was again accused of insubordination by his colleagues. He refused to submit to various disciplinary procedures; this only aggravated the situation. His boss, meanwhile, absconded from the country while on a trip abroad and was never seen again.

Having divorced his first wife, Botnar met Marcela Perian, whom he was to marry, in 1951. At the time of their marriage she was 23 and he 37. According to Marcela, after knowing each other for a few months, she had married Botnar in her lunch hour, in a dingy Bucharest registry office.[108] Marcela was a carpenter's daughter from the Western Transylvanian town of Alba Iulia. Her father had died when she was a young girl, after years of illness. She had done well at school, where she learned foreign languages. This enabled her to get a job at the National Tourist Office. Only people who were regarded as totally reliable by the regime were given such jobs because they involved regular contact with foreigners, something of which the Romanian regime was to have a pathological fear for over four decades: the social status and political background of potential employees' parents were vetted for this purpose. The children of non-Communists or, worse, anti-Communists, needed not apply. Marcela passed the test. The fact that her elder brother, Eugen Perian, had been a Securitate officer since 1948 undoubtedly helped[109]: he was to be sent to London from 1952 to 1957 as Third Secretary at the Embassy, where he set up the Securitate espionage unit. Indeed, he was to write reports for his controllers about his own sister and brother-in-law for the next 40 years, including for decades after they had left Romania. On 14 August 1952, a year after Octav and Marcela's wedding, Marcela gave birth to a daughter, Camelia. The young family lived in an elegant flat in Bucharest situated in a quiet cul-de-sac where, among others, a former prime minister had lived (8, Intrarea Armasului).

In his various jobs in import-export, Botnar demonstrated exceptional skills. He earned a reputation for being highly motivated and for getting things done. Unfortunately, he was also accused of being authoritarian, conceited and arrogant, and of treating his colleagues gruffly and rudely. These complaints quickly made their way into the reports submitted by various informers to the secret police. In 1950, one informer wrote that he was "vain, extremely nervous, impulsive, proud, and someone who does not accept personal criticism".[110] He added for good measure that Botnar had a persecution complex and that his management methods were "brutal".

The backbiting worked. Within six years of returning to Romania as a hero of the anti-fascist struggle and the French Resistance, and with a glittering career ahead of him, Botnar was expelled from the Communist Party in May 1952. This was a severe blow for someone trying to make a living in the administration of a totalitarian one-party state. His foreign connections, especially to France where his mother and brothers lived, were used as a pretext for alleging that he was a foreign agent with cosmopolitan views. The regime would not let go of this obsession: after his reintegration to the Party in 1955, a report in 1957 advised that because he had relatives in the West he should not be allowed to travel to capitalist countries but only to "people's democracies", i.e. Communist ones.[111] Naturally such considerations trumped the recognition by the author of the same report that Botnar had considerable problem-solving abilities and analytical skills: his lack of subservience outweighed such qualifications.

Botnar's expulsion from the Party was part of a mini-purge which also included far more powerful figures than him. Ana Pauker, for instance, who was practically the leader of the Romanian Communist Party in the war years, was expelled from the Politburo that year. Indeed, all over Eastern Europe, anti-cosmopolitan purges were directed against former leading lights from the war, especially if they were Jewish. Botnar's former commander in the Resistance, Artur London, was famously a victim in the anti-Semitic Slánský trial in Czechoslovakia in 1952.[112] The standard accusation, made against Botnar and many others, was that he had shown favour to Yugoslavia and Tito, who had split with Stalin and the rest of the Communist bloc in 1948, and whose more liberal version of Communism attracted interest and threatened to undermine the bloc.

Botnar did not take this exclusion lying down. Instead, he wrote a long and detailed rebuttal of all the charges against him, some of which concerned events that had occurred years previously in the Resistance in and around Paris. He also took the unusual and courageous step of writing to the fearsome leader of the country and the head of the Communist Party, Gheorghe Gheorghiu-Dej, just as he had done four years previously. In his letter, Botnar claimed that many of his colleagues merited expulsion from the Party much more than he did. He insisted that he had been the victim of a smear campaign, that he had been unjustly accused, and that he had not been given an opportunity to reply to the charges against him. He also insisted that the letter confirming his credentials and his membership of the French Communist Party, signed by the veteran French Communist leader, Jacques Duclos, who was effectively second-in-command to Maurice Thorez, was worth more than the "unobjective references" now made about him by his former Resistance comrades and superiors, Cristina Boico and Boris Holban.

As in 1948, there is no record of Botnar receiving a reply from the Romanian dictator to the letter he sent in 1954. On the other hand, Botnar was shifted sideways but continued to work in import-export. In due course, his career started to progress again. He became Inspector of Goods at Fructexport, the state company which exported fruit and alcoholic drinks. However, he could not hold his tongue and always said what he thought. He was reported on for making less than respectful remarks about the Soviet Union, one of Romania's main clients for plum brandy, saying that Communist propaganda was wrong to claim that its economic system was superior to that of the West. He also attracted negative attention for reading Western newspapers every day, especially *Le Monde*. In spite of all this, Botnar's tenacity with the Party paid off and he was reinstated as a member in November 1955, having become Head of Department for the Office for the Control of Goods in 1954. Again this dealt with agricultural exports. By 1956, he had become Deputy Director of Cartimex, the exporting company which belonged to the Ministry of Foreign Trade and which exported Romanian handicrafts including rugs. His new post meant that he was once again, after years of confinement in Romania, able to travel abroad. He was to become Director of Cartimex in 1959.

Seen from the outside, the Botnars led a privileged life. They had a nice flat in central Bucharest; they partied with the country's elite including Securitate agents, police officers and state prosecutors; they had access to Western gadgets like tape recorders, portable radios, even Mont Blanc pens, things which were denied to the ordinary population, who lived in conditions of ever worsening poverty.

Under the surface, however, things were not going well in the Botnars' marriage. In 1956, according to statements Botnar later made to the Securitate, Marcela embarked on an affair with the head of the judicial police, General Alexandru (known as Lică) Ioanid (né Leibovici).[113] Ioanid had been a close friend of Botnar and therefore the affair was a double betrayal – by her and by him. Botnar was later to claim that Marcela had had other affairs, but that he had forgiven her each time to keep the family together for the sake of their daughter, Camelia.[114] He also later claimed that she had continued to see Ioanid after their affair had been discovered and after the inevitable row.

Botnar's friendship with Ioanid was special because the latter's powerful position within the Romanian power structure was useful to Botnar. Indeed, it was perhaps for this reason that Botnar had employed Ioanid's father in Cartimex, even though he was by then a pensioner. The father, who had changed his name from Leibovici to Ionaşcu, was put in charge of the library where foreign journals could be consulted by staff if they had clearance: Botnar regularly took *Le Monde* home to read, even though this was forbidden by the country's paranoid censorship rules. Botnar had also done Ioanid himself a few favours: he had had a fridge sent to him from Moscow and he had bought a radio for him in Athens, both items which were difficult to obtain in Romania itself.

In August 1957, when he learned about Marcela's infidelity, Botnar was due to join her and Camelia in the mountains for his daughter's fifth birthday (14 August). When he got to the resort, Breaza, Marcela's mother, who was looking after Camelia, told him that Marcela and Ioanid had left for Braşov (then known as Stalin City) together. Botnar drove straight to Braşov, where he confronted the two lovers in a hotel. The next day, the two men returned to Bucharest in the same car, quarrelling so violently that they nearly started punching each other in the car itself.

This all had a severe emotional effect on Botnar. A few years later, in prison, he was to recall this to a cellmate, who in reality was a Securitate informer, and say that he blamed Marcela's misbehaviour for his professional and personal problems. These included infidelity on his part as well.

"He reproaches his wife, wanton and unattached, with having destroyed his inner (spiritual) equilibrium, something that set him against those who showed him the slightest hostility, making him react violently and in an uncontrolled manner, which in the end led him to prison. He claimed he had been loyal for many years and that he would have never cheated on her if she hadn't brought him to a nervous deterioration, which had also physical consequences. He is determined to tell her everything, regretting that he would cause her suffering too; depending on her attitude towards his confession, he will decide on how to proceed."[115]

On an earlier occasion, Botnar had blamed Marcela's infidelities for his unguarded talk on sensitive political issues.[116] He also blamed her for a range of complaints including asthenia (with which he was formally diagnosed while in prison in 1961[117]) and impotence.[118] He was even given injections for this latter problem, using some product imported from France. When that did not work, the doctor at the clinic imaginatively suggested that he have an affair, advice which Botnar followed. He started a relationship with a woman called Popescu, an inspector at the National Bank, and apparently grew very close to her.[119] The doctor's advice worked and his libido returned.

The reason why he suffered from these various complaints was not, however, only because of his distress at Marcela's infidelity. Instead, another event intervened which severely destabilised both Octav and Marcela. In 1959, Botnar became General Director of Cartimex and the family moved into a flat in a leafy neighbourhood of villas in the North of Bucharest (12, Captain Demetriade Street, in what was then named the "Stalin" quarter of Bucharest) – a flat which had a little garden and allotment just across the quiet street. However, although they were therefore firmly integrated into the regime, disaster was just around the corner.

On 28 July 1959, six senior officials, including former police officers, carried out a spectacular bank robbery in central Bucharest. It was the biggest such heist ever in any Communist country and remains the subject of intense comment and speculation to this day. The gang took the equivalent of $250,000. This was a severe blow for the Botnars because the leader of the gang was none other than Alexandru Ioanid, his former friend and Marcela's former lover, who had been dismissed from his post as head of the judicial police at the beginning of the year.

The Botnars were troubled that the police would find out about their association with Ioanid. In fact, Marcela was so frightened that she fainted when she heard about the robbery.[120] For his part, Botnar was afraid that Ioanid might take revenge on him, and incriminate him somehow, in order to get his own back on him for their argument about Marcela, even though Botnar had nothing to do with the raid. Botnar even wondered whether Marcela herself might have been involved in it. He immediately therefore tried to pump others for information about the gang and the robbery, and this in turn prompted suspicions about him.[121]

Retribution was swift: the gang was tried the following year and its members, including Ioanid, executed. The only woman in the gang, Monica Sevianu, was given a 25-year prison sentence. The affair immediately generated intense comment and speculation. Because all the perpetrators were Jewish, many people suspected – as did Botnar at the time – that the robbery might have been a false flag operation set up to incriminate Jews, or at least that it would be exploited against them, as it certainly was. The regime alleged that the robbers had stolen the money to give to Zionist organisations, thereby turning it into a political crime. It did this by making a propaganda film about the robbery which bizarrely included a re-enactment of the raid staged by the perpetrators themselves, who had perhaps been told that their sentences would be commuted in return for taking part.

This accusation fed into the frenzy about "cosmopolitan forces" which gripped Communist regimes all over Eastern Europe in the 1950s. However, many in the population at large doubted this version of events because the cash stolen was in Romanian lei, which could not be exchanged for foreign currency and which could not, therefore, be used or sent abroad. People were also sceptical that such a daring robbery could have been carried off at all in a police state where everyone was under constant surveillance. Was the regime itself therefore somehow complicit? Ioanid's former position only added to speculation. Not only had he been a very senior police officer but he was related by marriage to the Interior Minister, General Alexandru Drăghici. Ioanid had been married to Drăghici's wife's sister, but he divorced her, perhaps because of his affair with Marcela Botnar.

The conspiracy theories went so far that some people questioned whether the robbery had even occurred at all, or whether the executions of the five guilty men were really carried out. It was speculated that the whole thing had been invented so that they could go underground with new identities and operate as Securitate agents abroad. The feverish theories continued to prosper after the fall of Communism. Two further films were made about it, one a documentary by Monica Sevianu's granddaughter, the other a feature film entitled *Closer to the Moon* and released in 2013 which tells the story of the robbery and of how the original 1960 film, *Reconstruction*, was made. The event continues to generate discussion here and there, some commentators even heralding the bank robbers as heroic resistants against Communist tyranny.[122]

Botnar's nervous enquiries about the fate of the robbers were ill-judged. People wondered why he was so interested in finding out secret information. Shortly after his appointment as Director of Cartimex, the secret police launched yet another investigation into him and amassed a great deal of unsubstantiated backbiting and smears from colleagues as "evidence". Some of this included his reaction to the Ioanid gang's heist.

Unfortunately for Botnar, one of these allegations stuck. He fell under the suspicion, in the delusional minds of those compiling his dossier, of having committed the catch-all crimes of economic sabotage and sedition. The extravagant allegation of sabotage in fact concerned something rather banal: a contract to sell rugs to a company in Hamburg, Atico, owned by an Iranian, Ezetolah Atighetchi, who had allegedly been a member of the French Communist Party and who therefore seemed a suitable business partner for a Romanian state enterprise. The contract involved producing Iranian-style rugs in Romania, bearing an inscription in Persian. It had originally been negotiated by Botnar's predecessor as Director and he finalised it when he replaced him.

The Securitate opened an investigation into the terms of the contract and, after seven months, decided to launch a prosecution. Allegations of graft were made against Botnar's predecessor as Director, and Botnar himself was said to have been complicit in this. The investigation documents[123] were signed off by two secret serviceman, Emil Macri and Aristotel Stamatoiu, who were both to attain the rank of general under the dictatorship of Nicolae

Ceauşescu in the 1980s. Macri, who became head of Economic Counter-Information in the Securitate, was involved in the repression in Timisoara which marked the end of the Ceauşescu regime in 1989, and he was prosecuted for genocide in 1990, while Stamatoiu became Chief of Romanian Counterintelligence. They were major henchmen of Communist persecution.

Based on the statement of three Securitate informers within Cartimex itself, the allegation was that the contract gave too much exclusivity to the Hamburg company; that the price negotiated was too low; that the production schedule was not sufficiently clear; and that the buyer had too much power to reject sub-standard goods. Botnar was also reproached for the fact that nowhere did it say "Made in Romania" on the rugs, whose Persian inscription instead implied they were Iranian. All this, it was alleged, caused losses of $55,000 to the national economy (in 1958).

The accusation that Botnar's deals were somehow directed against the state, or that they constituted deliberate economic sabotage, were of course the fruit of Romanian Communist paranoia; and the claim that he had sold the carpets for less than their value and then pocketed a commission was soon withdrawn. The Romanian goons did, however, add in for good measure some old gripes about how Botnar had been responsible for the incorrect storage of some plum brandy destined for export to the USSR, which had allegedly gone off as a result, as well as a host of other allegations dragged up from the past.

What seemed to carry the day in the minds of the spooks and gangsters who ran the Securitate – they returned obsessively to the subject – was Botnar's defiance in the face of power. When the auditors they sent turned up in his office, he taunted them, "Do you want to search my pockets as well?".[124] He displayed the same attitude when an auditor asked him to show him a document justifying the sale of the rugs to Atico, saying:

"Officially I do not provide you with any information in this particular problem, as I consider you have no right to ask for such papers. I know you act on the basis of reports provided by informers, produced by various rascals whom I fought every day in the company and whom I knew how to sort out."[125]

This was not the way you were supposed to speak to those in power in a Communist state, and recalled another occasion when Botnar had refused to submit to police inspection, saying that the Ministry of the Interior was full of people who had nothing useful to do, or when he had refused in 1948 to have his bags searched by his colleagues in Brussels.[126] Such disobedience was a sign of disloyalty. The informers also accused Botnar of making disparaging remarks about the Soviet Union and comparing it unfavourably to capitalist countries.[127] It mattered nothing that everyone agreed that these remarks had been made in private: Botnar was being accused of free thinking and of free speaking.

"(Botnar) is a very cautious and intelligent individual, who does not openly show himself to be against the regime. But, judging by his statements, he is not loyal to the regime, but on the contrary, hostile to it. OB has had hostile manifestations against the state organs, and based on the information we have, tried in some cases to render their work more difficult."[128]

Botnar was guilty of thoughtcrime. His fate as a Romanian Party cadre, and as a free man, was sealed.

CHAPTER 5

THE ROMANIAN GULAG

If you can wait and not be tired by waiting,
Or being hated, don't give way to hating...

On 26 April 1960, Botnar and four others were arrested, including his brother-in-law, Eugen Perian, Marcela's brother. Perian got caught up in the affair because he was accused of having divulged to Botnar various aspects of his work in the Securitate over the years. He was accused of discussing his espionage work in London and in Romania with Botnar; he would be sentenced to three years' imprisonment. (He was in fact released in 1962.) When the case came to trial, the court considered it an attenuating circumstance that Perian had helped expose his brother-in-law: he had indeed been the source of some of the compromising information about Botnar, having informed the police about his brother-in-law's views on the Soviet Union, Romania, Yugoslavia and the West.[129]

One of the other co-arrestees was Alexandru Isoveanu, the Head of Protocol at the Ministry of Foreign Trade, who, like Perian, was a Securitate agent. It was common for people in jobs involving contact with foreigners and trips abroad to work for the secret services. Isoveanu would fake admiration for the West to dupe others, including Botnar, into thinking that it was safe to speak openly with him. As was common practice, Isoveanu was put in a cell with an informer: the belief being that such detainees would open up to such "cellmates" more easily than to their interrogators. Isoveanu probably knew this and used his conversations with his "cellmate" to influence the investigation. From co-defendant, Isoveanu became an important witness for the prosecution against Botnar.

A third defendant was Ioan Pantazescu, a distant relative of Isoveanu and an employee at Cartimex. Botnar had tried to get information about Alexandru Ioanid from Pantazescu after the former's arrest, especially about whether he had said anything about him. Pantazescu did know some prosecutors and he did keep Botnar informed, whence his arrest. He also had a criminal record, having engaged in the trafficking of medicine.[130] He was to receive a harsh sentence. The fourth indictee was a corrupt police officer, Major Dumitru Arsenie, who had protected criminals and prostitutes in Craiova.[131] Botnar had also approached him for information about Ioanid and about other hostile complaints lodged against him. Arsenie denied everything and was let off.

Between his arrest in April 1960 and his conviction in May 1961, Botnar underwent over 60 interrogation sessions, half of which were carried out by Securitate officers and others by military prosecutors who were even more aggressive. The interrogations could last for 10 hours: the starting and finishing times are recorded in the official accounts of these sessions. Botnar did everything he could to resist this intense pressure and even fought back: he took the unusual step of writing to the Minister of the Interior, General Drăghici, one of the most brutal henchmen of the regime. He complained that he was being treated as a subversive and a reactionary, and that his impeccable Communist credentials were not being taken into account. The Minister did not reply to his letter.

Botnar then got an old friend from French Resistance days, Laurenţiu Marinescu, to write to the dictator of the country, Gheorghe Gheorghiu-Dej. Marinescu tried to reply to the accusations against Botnar, especially those alleging corruption. He told Dej that all these claims had been cooked up by a jealous subordinate, Constantin Merchea, who wanted Botnar's job and who needed to cover up his own mistakes. Botnar, indeed, could not stand this Merchea and Marinescu told Dej (perhaps on Botnar's prompting) that he had been a member of the Iron Guard, the wartime fascist movement in Romania. In particular, Marinescu denied in his letter that Botnar had sold the rugs for less than their market value and pocketed a commission instead, or that he had stolen company money.[132]

There is little doubt that Romania's endemic anti-Semitism played a role in these accusations, just as it did in similar purges conducted across Eastern Europe, where "cosmopolitan" elements were regarded with suspicion by the provincial thugs who became Communist leaders after the war. Whereas people like Botnar, who never paid much attention to his Jewish background, thought that they had earned their spurs by fighting in France or Spain, on their return home they discovered that their foreign contacts, and their knowledge of foreign languages, were regarded with suspicion and hatred by their doltish overlords. Indeed, quite apart from its ideological and conspiratorial delirium, the Communist regime in Romania, as in other Warsaw pact states, was mainly characterised by its stupidity – by the fact that the system rewarded and promoted talentless and brutish people, while repressing and punishing the most gifted and intelligent. This is a very human key to understanding the extreme dysfunctionality of Communist regimes.

Laurenţiu Marinescu argued in his letter to Dej that Botnar was already suffering from mental illness (perhaps depression) which he was combatting only thanks to "sedatives and bromides" and that imprisonment might hasten his death. Marinescu concluded his letter by tackling the issue of anti-Semitism head on:

"I am not a Jew, so as perhaps to have a race persecution complex, but I tell you with a clear conscience that this is a machination against an honest Jew and the person who carried it out did it to escape the responsibility for the losses he caused to the company.

In view of the above I ask you to order an investigation into
the case and to have those found guilty severely punished for
lying and influence peddling."

The letter was to no avail. Instead, the Securitate used informers'
reports to blacken Botnar's name. The informers included his own
secretary, who had been recruited by the Securitate's Third Directorate.
A total of 38 such notes were included in the dossier, giving an idea of
the high levels of espionage inside the Communist state. Everything was
reported, including fantastical allegations about orgies that supposedly
went on in the Botnars' flat and bank accounts in Paris where his secret
backhanders were supposedly being deposited. Denunciations were
included and the links to Ioanid amply dwelt on, as was his habit of
taking forbidden copies of *Le Monde* and *Le Figaro* from the Cartimex
library. Time and again Botnar was accused of speaking rudely to
other employees, telling them they were useless or stupid or lazy. For
instance, "Laura" told a Securitate officer in 1958 that:

"Comrade Botnar has not succeeded in making himself
respected by the work collective because he does not maintain
fair relations between himself and the employees.

With or without justification he uses a tone of voice
and expressions which are inappropriate for the director
of a company. He shouts and throws out insults ("useless",
"superficial", "lazy", "talking nonsense", "good for nothing")
at conscientious and mediocre employees, men and women,
old and young alike."[133]

The same report went on, however:

"But all the employees say that he has a good heart, that he
is helpful, that he helps a man in need, that he is sensitive to

people's troubles, that he fights to get and to justify the money needed for everyone's salary, and that he helps the sick."

The authorities also put informers into Botnar's cell with him. His dossier is full of their reports – 40 in total. Perhaps Botnar understood the trick; when questioned by the cellmate about his statements in favour of freedom of speech, for instance, Botnar cleverly cited the Soviet Union under Khruschev as an example to follow. He pointedly told him, "In the Soviet Union, words are no longer considered political acts, as opposed to deeds which can be considered treason or espionage."[134]

Botnar repeatedly said that everything could be sorted out if only he could get his message across to people higher up, like the Interior Minister, Drăghici, or his deputy Pintilie. Botnar may have been trying to name-drop when he said that he had alerted the Minister and the Vice-President of the Council (Deputy Prime Minister), Alexandru Bârlădeanu, about the machinations of his malicious subordinate, Merchea. Nearly 40 years later, when the Romanian dissident Ion Raţiu returned to his country and became an MP, he discussed Botnar with Bârlădeanu, who had survived the overthrow of the Communist regime and had become President of the Senate: Bârlădeanu told Raţiu that he remembered Botnar "with enormous admiration and affection" from his time at Cartimex and in Fructexport.[135]

Botnar was worried about the fact that lots of foreign books were found in his apartment when it was searched, including a *History of the World* in three volumes in French, of which Volume 3 was held to contain forbidden information about the Second World War.[136] He was also worried that he might have left a letter from his lover, Madame Popescu, in a book and that it might be found when the flat was searched. However, in spite of the intense pressure of the interrogations and his weakened physical state, he remained absolutely convinced – at least this is what he said to the cellmate informer – that the whole case against him was a stitch-up.

At one point, the interrogators had claimed that they had spoken to his brother Maurice to ask him why Botnar gave him his mother- in-law's address for correspondence. As we saw in the last chapter, he did this in order to protect his brother from getting into trouble with the French authorities over the Avramescu murder. He evidently feared that the French authorities would be intercepting his brother's mail. Botnar deduced that the same investigators must also have asked his brother about the alleged bribes he had been taking from the Iranian rug merchant, and that of course Maurice would have denied everything. In any case, he reasoned, his Iranian purchaser, Atighetchi, would have to be absolutely honest and honourable in order to do business in France. So, concluded Botnar triumphantly to his interrogators, the investigators themselves knew that the allegations were false. He remained determined to fight his corner to the bitter end and, even if he was convicted, to show the trial up to be a sham. An unknown hand, presumably that of a Securitate agent reading the report, wrote, "Damned cheek!" in the margin.[137]

Throughout all this, Botnar's worries, both personal and professional, took their toll. Botnar started to think about what would happen when he got out of prison. He told his cellmate informer that he would ask his brothers for financial help, and he even aired with him the possibility of emigrating to the Soviet Union.[138] Botnar was, for the second time in his life, preparing himself psychologically for the need to leave his home country.

At the end of the marathon of interrogations, the chief investigator concluded that Botnar was indeed a "hostile element" to the regime. He listed, at great length, all the evidence for this: Botnar had said in private that there was no freedom in Romania; that the regime used compliant but incompetent cronies; that it was guilty of creeping Stalinisation; that its elite was narrow-minded; that the Romanian media were catastrophic; that things were better in Yugoslavia; that the capitalist system was more effective than the Communist; that the USSR's seven-year plan was a bluff designed to bamboozle the West with figures that bore no relation to reality; and so on. All this was serious heresy in a country whose official ideology held – as many even in the West believed – that capitalism would soon collapse as a result of its so-called internal contradictions. Botnar had seen the truth and he had expressed it: what is striking is the courage with which he did so and his apparent lack of concern for the consequences. The ordinance recommending trial concluded:

> "The deeds of the defendant BOTNAR OCTAV of having indulged in libellous and defamatory manifestations towards the popular-democratic regime in RPR (People's Republic of Romania) makes up the constitutive elements of the crime of plotting against the social order, as per article 209/2/a of the Criminal Code of RPR."[139]

What the investigators had not succeeded in proving – as Botnar himself had predicted they would not – were the initial charges of incompetence or corruption. All the allegations about his having made a bad deal on the sale of carpets, or about taking backhanders from the deal, were abandoned. Instead, Botnar was prosecuted for words uttered in private, according to one of the now most notorious articles in the penal code of Communist Romania, Article 209.[140] This article was the purest – but by no means unique – expression of totalitarian tyranny because its second section made sedition, i.e. questioning the system, punishable by death in some cases. Botnar may well have recalled Kipling's reference to "the truth you've spoken, twisted by knaves to make a trap for fools".

Botnar was informed that the charges would be confirmed on the very day that the ordinance had been prepared (21 January 1960). Immediately noticing that he would not be tried for the thing he had originally been charged with – economic sabotage – he tried to press home his advantage by asking for two investigations, one into his economic activity at Cartimex, and the other into his colleagues (especially Merchea) who had accused him of taking bribes. Captain Nedelcu gave his reply in another, shorter ordinance, issued later the same day: the wheels of Romanian Communist "justice" certainly turned quickly when they needed to. It concluded:

"The analysis of the documents contained in the investigation's dossier shows the professional activity carried out in the economic field by BOTNAR OCTAV at Cartimex has been already investigated as per his request made on 21.01.60... It showed on one hand that the above named (Botnar) was not guilty of the crime of undermining the national economy according to Article 209/1 of the penal code, for which he was investigated, and on the other hand that through his activity he contributed sufficiently to fulfilling the objectives of the company's plan."[141]

For good measure, it also concluded that Comrade Merchea had been forced to withdraw his allegations against Botnar for bribe-taking.

The case came to trial before the Military Tribunal in Bucharest on 23 May 1961. Botnar denied that he had made the most of the alleged statements of which he was accused, for instance about the military superiority of the USA over socialist countries, but he did admit that he might have spoken freely on occasions on other matters.[142] Perian testified against his brother-in-law, alleging that he had insulted the regime, that he had said that Jews were discriminated against in Romania, that the Romanian leadership was incompetent, that the Romanian press told lies, and so on.[143]

Botnar's lawyers asked the court to consider four extra documents, including a medical certificate and documents relating to his activity at Cartimex, but this request was refused. His case was not helped, moreover, when his own lawyer told the tribunal that the accusations against his client had been proven.[144] This was common practice in such show trials. Invited to make a closing statement, Botnar told the court that he was not guilty of the deeds held against him, that the allegations were the result of machinations by some employees and collaborators of Cartimex, and he asked to be acquitted.

The court withdrew and reconvened two days later, on 25 May 1961, to pass sentence. The tribunal concluded that Botnar was guilty as charged for having said various things: praising Tito, criticising Romania and claiming that things were better in the West.

> "Considering that through all these actions the defendant created an unhealthy state of mind, thereby causing unrest which could have endangered the security of the state, which fitted into the crime of plotting against the social order, the court finds that that the constitutive elements of the crime of conspiracy, in accordance with the provisions of Article 209/2/a, are met."[145]

Botnar was sentenced to seven years' rigorous imprisonment, four years' strict (legal) incapacity and the confiscation of his estate. He also incurred 300 lei legal expenses.[146] On 8 August 1961, he sent an emotional handwritten appeal to the Military College of the Supreme Court. The letter was a combination of self-criticism and self-justification. He wrote that he sincerely regretted his acts; that he had not behaved properly during the trial; that he had underestimated the risk of endangering the regime by criticising it; that he was a good Communist who had in the past tried to do his best for the Party, and would do so in the future; and that he had worked well at Cartimex where he had increased its exports sixfold between 1957 and 1960, making it one of only 10 companies to have surpassed its plan. He appealed for at least partial clemency and especially for the seizure of his assets to be lifted, since otherwise his family, who would be deeply pained and discredited by his conviction, would have nothing to live on.[147]

The appeal was heard on 27 June 1962. It was alleged that not all the evidence had been heard and that the lower court had erred on a point of law. Arguments were also heard about the merits of the case – Botnar had been good at his job, he had not sabotaged the company but instead contributed to its success. The appeal recalled that the accusation that he had taken bribes, and that he had committed economic sabotage, had been dropped, and that his accuser, Merchea, had withdrawn his allegations. Evidence was produced that on occasions Botnar had praised the Romanian regime and Romanian products. It was also argued that Botnar's occasional indiscretions might have been caused by his personal problems. Some stress was laid on this argument about extenuating circumstances, to the extent of quoting a Soviet lawyer who had written about the emotional causes of crimes. It was also argued that clemency should be shown in view of Botnar's impeccable Communist credentials in pre-war Romania and wartime France. All this was to no avail: the appeal was turned down.

Two years later – but by then it was too late – Botnar's case was the subject of an initiative by the General Prosecutor of the People's Republic of Romania, who lodged an extraordinary appeal with the Supreme Court.[148] In it, he argued that the relevant article in the penal code on sedition had been misapplied in Botnar's case. The Prosecutor claimed that, at most, Botnar could have been prosecuted for libel or calumny, covered by a different article and with different penalties. Although this other article had not been on the statute book when the alleged deeds were committed, it was available to the court at the time of the trial. The Prosecutor therefore argued that Botnar's conviction should be quashed and the new article applied.

The Supreme Court heard this appeal in Botnar's absence

on 3 June 1963 (he had been in labour camp for two years by then) and turned it down.[149] The argument – that even libellous statements made without any criminal intent (*mens rea*) to change the social order nonetheless represented a danger to the state and should therefore be punished – represents a legal landmark in Romania's descent into full totalitarianism. Botnar's senior position in the company, and his good Communist past, actually made his loose talk even more dangerous, the Court reasoned.

> "The hold he had over his subordinates and other people due to his long membership of the Party since the days it was illegal, as well as his position, and also the fact that through the nature of his job he had links with people from capitalist countries, businessmen, representatives of various capitalist companies, were additional elements which confirmed the danger the deeds and the perpetrator represented for the security of the state."[150]

Following his conviction, Botnar was kept at the Uranus remand prison in Bucharest, where prisoners were three or four to a cell. From there he was sent to the prison at Jilava in the south of the country, where Marshal Antonescu had been executed in 1946. After that, he was sent first to the labour camp at Salcia, of which many internees said that the work regime was so harsh that it was a death camp, and thence to the labour camp in Periprava in the Danube Delta on the Black Sea and bordering Ukraine.

Botnar's trial and conviction had revealed to him the true nature of the regime he had hitherto supported. By now nearly 50 years old, he told his fellow prisoners – at least those whom he trusted – that he had been a fool. For the last 30 years, he had believed in Communism and in the role of the Communist Party, yet the very organisation in which he had put his faith, and whose instructions he had so faithfully followed, had turned viciously against him.[151] Not only had his experiences caused him to abandon his lifelong faith in Communism, he was now adamant that he wanted to leave the country. However, because he knew that he had many years ahead of him before he would be able to do that, he tried to make the most of them. He started to learn English again, just as he had done 20 years previously while in captivity in the German Stalag in Cambrai.

In Periprava labour camp, the work was hard. Prisoners were sent to cut reeds and to carry out other forms of manual labour – tilling vegetable plots, working in vineyards, digging irrigation canals. For this last task they had to move four cubic metres of earth per day, for which they received meagre rations: 1,000 calories a day including mouldy chocolate and rotten potatoes. Prisoners had their rations reduced if they did not work hard enough. They were woken at 5, they left the camp at 7, they walked to their place of work and laboured until 6 or 7 in the evening with just half an hour for a lunch break.[152] Prisons in Romania were notorious throughout the 1950s, when political terror started to bite; conditions were relaxed a little in the 1960s following Western pressure.

Botnar made few friends in the labour camp. One man he did get on with was Barbu Ollanescu-Orendi, a fellow convict who came from an upper-class family and who was in prison because his parents had hidden an anti-Communist partisan in their house. They had first met in Salcia and were then both transferred to Periprava. Ollanescu eventually came to the West in the 1970s and always regretted having failed to get back in touch with Botnar: he had liked and respected him immensely during their year together in prison. "Botnar was a driven man," Ollanescu recalls. "He always had to be doing something, he could never relax or sit around doing nothing. It is as if he had someone behind him, pushing him forwards."[153]

In Periprava, Botnar behaved with the same recalcitrance and courage which had characterised his time in civil life. He refused to follow several instructions from the guards, for instance in August 1962 when he disobeyed an order to go down into a canal to dig out mud because there was not sufficient protection. Several workers had been killed on the Danube-Black Sea canal project in similar circumstances when an unsecured bank collapsed. He was punished for this with five days' solitary confinement.[154] Like Ollanescu, he repeatedly stood up to the guards when fellow convicts preferred to keep their heads down. He often answered back to them and insisted on certain demands, such as having clean water. He was punished for failing to obey the myriad rules and regulations, such as the rule against looking through the peephole of one's cell or not wearing blindfold metal glasses when walking through the corridor. For such infractions he was given numerous spells in solitary confinement.

On one occasion, Botnar was nearly murdered by one of the prison guards. It was during the lunch break; he had walked some distance away from where the rest of the workers were sitting on the ground. The landscape was flat for miles around and there were no trees anywhere. The sun blazed down and the heat was intense. He started to construct a sort of wigwam out of reeds in order to have some shade. Suddenly, the sound of gunfire rang out as several shots were fired at him. The bullets landed so close to Botnar that he was grazed on the face by earth or shrapnel; he started to bleed. A guard had taken aim at him on the pretext that he was trying to escape: guards were rewarded with 10 days' holiday for shooting escapees, but in this case there was clearly no chance of running away in such a barren landscape. The guard was quickly overpowered by his colleagues. Throughout the entire business, which was over in a matter of seconds, Botnar carried on completely calmly eating his lunch, as if nothing had happened. The camp commander was called and the gun-toting guard was led away: he was never seen again.[155]

The full perversity of Romanian Communism reserved yet another twist for Botnar. In a move that demonstrates its Mafia-like practices, the Securitate tried to recruit him as a collaborator, having convicted him for being a danger to the state. The attempt began in May 1962, on his arrival at Periprava, where he was initially part of a new brigade working in the vineyards and harvesting reeds.[156] Because this brigade was full of "hostile elements", i.e. political prisoners like Botnar, and because it was new, the Securitate decided they needed an agent inside it. Botnar was chosen as a possible candidate. The procedure was cumbersome: others had to inform on the possible future recruit first, to check his suitability, and his correspondence was intercepted. The informers confirmed to their Securitate controllers that Botnar was determined to leave the country and emigrate to England, and that he was learning English for this purpose. Botnar was singled out as a possible recruit because, unlike the others, his political views were reasonable and not fanatical. So the decision was taken to try to enrol him as a spy.

The process involved hauling in prisoners for questioning about the achievements of the Communist regime. Botnar would be one of 10 or 15 prisoners thus interrogated. He was asked to collaborate and he agreed to send in reports on his fellow detainees. However, he refused to sign any pledge to that effect and said instead he would be judged by his acts. Rather amusingly, the views he attributed to the four people on whom he informed were very similar, if not identical, to his own – that things used to be better in Romania, that the leadership was incompetent, and so on. At no stage did he allege that his fellow prisoners were plotting anything serious and the guards probably knew about their views anyway. He may also have been just stringing the Securitate along. Eventually, his refusal to sign any sort of pledge caused the operation to be abandoned: the officer in charge of the regional section of the Ministry of the Interior ordered that the file be closed and classified as a failed attempt to recruit.

Botnar had been severely weakened by the harsh regime in

the labour camp and by various illnesses he had suffered in prison. The outlook was bleak. He was released from prison on 28 July 1964 under the terms of an amnesty decree, having served four years and three months.

Whilst Botnar had been incarcerated, Marcela and Camelia had lived alone without their husband and father. Marcela had followed advice from friends and had divorced Botnar during his imprisonment[157], taking back her maiden name Perian. However, it is clear that this was only for form's sake. She continued to behave as if she were still his wife, sending him parcels and the like. On the day of his release, she was sent a telegram saying that he would be home the next evening. She took the day off work to prepare for his return.

Emaciated and undernourished, and mentally and physically weakened, upon his release Botnar weighed just six stone (40 kg). Released political prisoners in Romania were only allowed to do manual work for the rest of their lives, and that was out of the question for Botnar in his state. He therefore faced the prospect of a lifetime of penury. Something had to be done.

For the second time in his life, Botnar was saved by his brothers. It will be recalled that Maurice, the doctor, had let his younger brother stay with him in Lyon when he left Romania in 1938. On his release from the Romanian prison camp in 1964, Maurice's French wife, Marguerite, visited Romania and gave the Botnars money. The Botnars regularly received parcels from Max and Maurice, as did everyone in Romania who had relatives abroad. Octav Botnar applied to emigrate on the basis that his brothers would be able to support him, and they clearly did.

In spite of the help Max was now able to offer on his release from prison in Romania, relations between Max and Octav were not good. The tensions between them were perhaps typical of those between an older and younger brother but they were aggravated by political differences. Max was right-wing, while his two brothers were Communists. While only a teenager, young Oswald had twice caused his older brother trouble because of his political activities. The first occasion was after Oswald had left Romania for Spain in 1938: Max was briefly arrested on his account, and had been able to get out of Romanian police custody only after paying a bribe.[158]

Later, his younger brother's political leanings had thwarted Max's plans to emigrate to America: the fact that Max had two Communist brothers caused the Americans to refuse him a visa. On the other hand, the tables were turned while Botnar was in prison in the 1960s: he was hauled in for interrogation on many occasions to be questioned about his relatives abroad, especially about Max. The Romanian authorities were paranoid about any foreign contacts and they knew that Max had been a British spy. This was very suspicious in their eyes. The fools had evidently forgotten that Britain had been on the same side as their beloved Soviet Union during the war.

A row in 1947, after Botnar's first wife returned to Paris without him, caused a breach in relations between Max and his brother which lasted for 10 years. Botnar recalled that, when they met again for the first time in a decade, in 1957, Max had been patronising, laughing at him for calling himself a "director" (of Cartimex) and implying that he, Max, was more of a businessman than Botnar would ever be. He boasted to his younger brother about how rich he had become – and gave him several thousand German Marks to prove it.[159]

Nevertheless, in 1965, Max Bunford – by now a wealthy plutocrat in London, and having anglicised his name from Bundorf – decided to let bygones be bygones and once again assist his brother.

The Securitate files contain the transcript of a telephone conversation in January 1965 which makes it clear not only that Max was in charge of getting his brother out of Romania, but also that he had little or no confidence in Botnar's own organisational abilities. The two brothers always spoke in their native German:

Max:	*Have you filled in the application?*
Octav:	Yes.
Max:	*Have you done it already or are you going to do it?*
Octav:	I did it a month ago.
Max:	*Good. Don't do anything. Leave the application to take its course.*
Octav:	All right.
Max:	*Do absolutely nothing.*
Octav:	All right.
Max:	*Do you understand?*
Octav:	Completely.
Max:	*Don't worry about anything else, you only have to obtain the exit visa, that is all.*
Octav:	Yes.
Max:	*I will deal with the rest myself.*
Octav:	You'll deal with it?
Max:	*Yes, of course, I deal with it all the time.*
Octav:	All right. All right. I will wait.
Max:	*Is there a problem?*
Octav:	It's fine. I'll wait. Thank you very much.
Max:	*Don't you do anything, even if it takes time. It doesn't matter how long it takes. I deal with it. I have always dealt with it.*
Octav:	Yes. Very good… Things will take a long time.
Max:	*I know, I have been giving a hand for the last four years, you understand?*
Octav:	Yes, I know. If you can…
Max:	*Everything that can be done will be done. Do not do anything yourself. Do you have everything you need to survive?*
Octav:	Yes, yes, I have. I don't need anything. Thank you for calling. I was a little disoriented by all these questions.
Max:	*That's why I rang*[160]

After his release from prison, Botnar's brother-in-law and co-defendant, Eugen Perian, now also a free man, continued to inform on him. A note from April 1965 records how Botnar told Perian that he had not changed his convictions; that the things for which he was convicted were now being said by the regime itself; that he remained a Communist and would rejoin the French Communist Party once he got to the West; and that, without any prospects in Romania, all he wanted was to emigrate. The officer writing up Perian's note concluded that Botnar had no desire to take revenge on anyone, that he only wanted to join his brothers who had promised to help, and to lead a peaceful life from then on.[161] Did Botnar tell Perian these things deliberately, in the knowledge that they would be passed on to Perian's Securitate controllers, in order to smooth the process?

Max Bunford then arranged, by paying a large bribe, for his brother and Marcela to leave Communist Romania and come to the West. A London-based lawyer secretly handled such transactions, which was a common practice. Both Israel and West Germany also made large payments to the Romanian state, over many decades, to enable respectively Jews and ethnic Germans to leave the country. Botnar undoubtedly benefited from this programme.

Marcela and Octav Botnar were allowed to leave Romania on 28 July 1965, on a plane from Băneasa airport to Tel Aviv.[162] They spent several months in Israel, which Botnar did not like, before travelling to Düsseldorf in West Germany, where they acquired German citizenship: the Federal Republic of Germany was happy to give passports to native German speakers from Eastern Europe.

Botnar was never to return to Romania again.

CHAPTER 6

A FRESH START

Yours is the Earth and everything that's in it...

The lives of Max Bunford and Octav Botnar had followed very different trajectories. Young Oswald (Octav) left Romania altogether in 1938 for France; Max started up a business in Czernowitz and dreamt of emigrating to America. During the war, Max set up a spy network, based in Istanbul, on the back of the business activities which he ran out of that city. In the period 1943 to 1944, Max travelled into occupied Europe from Istanbul on no fewer than 18 occasions. He collected information on the Holocaust and set up a courier network within occupied Europe. He smuggled radio transmitters into Germany, while also dealing in diamonds, medicine, nylon stockings and spirits. He even managed to get a mole into the German army's transportation branch and was thus able to communicate information about the movements of German military units and equipment across Europe to the British and to Isaac Berman, head of a Zionist spy network in Istanbul, who would later go on to become Speaker of the Knesset.[163] Bunford was also involved in helping Zionists exfiltrate Jews from occupied Europe into British mandate Palestine.[164] Isaac Berman described Max Bundorf as "one of the heroes of World War II."

In reward for his extraordinary work supplying military intelligence, Max had been granted British citizenship. He was able to draw on his wartime contacts to start businesses in Britain and in Europe. One of his contacts was Gerd Stieler von Heydekampf, an engineer who had become chairman of the Tanks Commission under Hitler and who joined the NSU motor company after the war.

NSU had been founded in the late 19th Century and was based

near Stuttgart. The factory originally made knitting machines before progressing to bicycles, motorbikes and then cars – a rather Darwinian progression. There is some dispute about the origins of the name NSU and, by the 1950s if not before, the meaning of the abbreviation had been largely forgotten. Max had built a close relationship with NSU. He now took advantage of that relationship to get a job at NSU in Germany for his recuperating brother. This was to be the modest beginning of Botnar's remarkable career in the motor industry.

Max's relationship with NSU had been so close that he had on his own account acquired the NSU distributorships for both France and the United Kingdom. When it became clear after a few months that Botnar was in fact doing a good job in Germany, Max asked his brother to move to Britain to sort out his NSU distributorship there. So it was that, in June 1966, Botnar moved his family to the UK. Already aged 52, and with little direct experience, Botnar became part of the British motor industry – an industry he was subsequently to transform.

The NSU franchise in Britain was held through a dedicated company called NSU (GB) Limited. Having recently relocated from Hammersmith in West London to Shoreham – the port in West Sussex through which its cars were imported – the business was not in good shape, with poor sales and weak credit control.

NSU (GB) Limited employed about 125 people, many of whom were locals who had joined at the time of the relocation from London. Botnar was introduced as a "management consultant from Germany", and threw himself heart and soul into the new challenge, even though he hardly spoke any English.

For the first few years in his newly adopted country, Botnar took an interpreter with him when travelling around Britain visiting dealerships. Mike Hoppis, the interpreter, was in fact the company's After-Sales Manager, and was a Greek Cypriot with whom Botnar would speak in French. Hoppis would translate into English for the benefit of the dealers. In spite of this considerable linguistic handicap, Botnar was quickly very successful in England, thanks to the hands-on hard work and inexhaustible energy which became his most famous hallmarks.

When Botnar had arrived at NSU (GB), the company was run by a former Major-General in the British Army. Botnar discovered that the business was not only ill-managed but it was also over-staffed. The Major-General soon left, Botnar becoming Chief Executive. He rapidly developed the dealer network, reduced the workforce and improved the company's ability to collect monies owing to it. Within three years, NSU (GB) was selling 15,000 cars a year, including the new and revolutionary Wankel rotary-engined Ro 80. It was a first demonstration of Botnar's extraordinary ability that NSU sold more Ro 80s in the UK than in Germany itself, the country where it was being built. This achievement was even more remarkable given that the car was only available in Britain in its original left-hand drive form. Botnar was also endlessly – remorselessly – inventive. One of the NSU models, the Prinz, was an air-cooled rear-engined car like the Volkswagen Beetle or the Porsche 911. This meant that the cars had no radiator at the front, only headlights, giving them an unusual appearance. The customers did not like this and the cars did not sell well. On the verge of despair, one of the salesmen explained the problem to his boss. The next morning, Botnar said he had been thinking about the problem all night and had come up with a solution. "We will put a metal grille on the front of the car and the customers will think it is a radiator."[165] A company in Worthing made the grilles and they were stuck onto the cars in the NSU workshop. The ruse worked.

In addition to the UK distribution rights for NSU, Max Bunford owned the franchise in France for the little-known Datsun brand and, in 1968, had started, in a limited way, to import Datsun cars into the UK.[166] A company had been set up for this purpose – Nissan-Datsun (U.K. Concessionaires) Limited – although the staff, offices and infrastructure of NSU (GB) were effectively used to operate the Datsun concession as an adjunct to NSU.

Things changed in 1969 when, in Germany, the newly-merged Volkswagen-Audi also acquired NSU. As a result, the UK importer of Volkswagen, the Thomas Tilling Group, took over the NSU concession in Britain as well, along with many of the NSU (GB) staff and NSU (GB) dealers.

This left Nissan-Datsun (U.K. Concessionaires) exposed and vulnerable. There were difficulties with the franchise in France and a formal agreement for the UK had not been signed with Nissan Motor Company (NMC). Some 2,000 Datsun cars were standing on the dockside in Amsterdam, unpaid-for and starting to rust.

Although he had been instrumental in the successful development of NSU (GB), Botnar had simply been an adviser to the business and was not part of the sale of the company. He decided to form his own company and to negotiate directly with NMC to obtain the distribution rights for Datsun cars in Britain.

While the handover to Thomas Tilling was taking place, Botnar approached a number of the key staff in the NSU (GB) team to join him in his new venture. Many had little hesitation in joining him. A number, however, chose to go with the Thomas Tilling Group. Several of these then asked to work for him later on, when it was clear he was going to make another success of his new venture. Although he took them in, Botnar never forgot their initial choice and remembered it as a sign of disloyalty.

Botnar incorporated Moorcrest Motor Co. Ltd. on 20 October 1970 and flew to Tokyo to negotiate a long-term, stand-alone distribution relationship with NMC. On 3 December 1970, Moorcrest changed its name to Datsun UK Limited. One month later, on 1 January 1971, a formal Distribution Agreement between Nissan Motor Company and Datsun UK Limited was signed.

Botnar's initial working directors, whom he also made shareholders in the company, were Michael Hunt and Frank Shannon.

Hunt had impressed Botnar at NSU (GB) with his talent for collecting debts owed to the company. He had worked in Northern Rhodesia (now Zambia) a few years earlier and was thinking of returning there, but Botnar persuaded him that he and his family would be better staying in Britain.

Shannon had qualified as an accountant and had also worked at NSU (GB) but had gone over to the Thomas Tilling Group, considering his prospects would be better served by a bigger company rather than with Botnar. He had subsequently changed his mind.

Botnar, Hunt and Shannon worked as a team in the early years of Datsun UK, but the three of them did not socialise and remained business associates only. Their ages, backgrounds, education, attitudes to and experiences of life were entirely disparate. It would be 20 years, for instance, before Hunt learned that Max Bunford and Botnar were in fact brothers.

Botnar's acquisition of the Datsun franchise led to another major row with his brother. Max alleged that Botnar had negotiated with the Japanese behind his back. The row was so intense that Botnar blamed it for the heart attack he had in June 1970. Conveniently, he attributed no importance to his chain smoking up to that point.

Botnar denied that he had tricked his brother and put down his version of events in writing decades later during legal tussles with the Inland Revenue. In a 120-page Witness Statement prepared in September 1996 for an appeal in the Commissioners v. Botnar case, he insisted that not only had his brother agreed that he would take over the franchise, as NMC insisted had to be the case, but also that he had paid him compensation.[167]

In spite of the row, Botnar had a strong sense of duty and family loyalty and, after Max's death in 1984, he never spoke ill of his brother to Max's children, Amalie and Dominic. On the contrary, Dominic often felt that Botnar's kindness to him was a way of tacitly making up for the differences he had had with his father.

In later years, Botnar advised Dominic to study in the United States after leaving Eton College and gave him an introduction to the world of banking. He also kept an avuncular eye on Maurice's two granddaughters in Spain, who had sadly lost their mother, Maurice's daughter, at a very early age to cancer.

Acquiring the Datsun franchise posed challenges for Botnar. Although cars had been made in Japan since before the First World War, awareness of Japanese models in the UK and Europe was extremely limited. Datsun enjoyed no brand recognition: the press used to joke that people mistook the name for a dachshund. It was believed that they were prone to rust and that they handled badly. They certainly looked rather odd, and had unfashionable names like Violet and Cherry. Despite this, Datsun cars possessed the two desirable characteristics which were essential for cars sold on the Japanese market. Built in a country with few outlets for service and repair and with no indigenous fuel supplies, Datsuns boasted unfailing reliability and outstanding fuel economy.

Botnar also pioneered the concept of the fully equipped yet competitively priced car. He ordered cars from Japan with reclining seats, heated rear window, radio, clock, cigar lighter, etc. as standard. Botnar understood that the perceived value of these extras was higher than their actual cost. He could, for example, pay £200 extra to NMC for additional features and then charge the customer £500 for them. On top of this, he would also order some additional cars to which he would add even more extras when they arrived in Britain – pop-up sunroofs, for instance – for which again he would be able to charge. His perception of the car market was that a desire for comfort and prestige had to be aroused in the customer in order to increase sales.

Botnar's ingenuity would develop as the company progressed, and he adopted various means to create the impression that the breadth of his product range was wider than in reality it was. He would, for instance, create the illusion of a model having received a major facelift, when in fact it had simply been modified cosmetically, often almost at his own hands.

Botnar threw himself into his work with the exceptional zeal which was his hallmark. His irrepressible energy was to change radically not only the way cars were sold but also the way they were made. He worked long hours and expected from his employees the same full commitment that he himself gave to the company.

One of his earliest insights was that dealers simply wanted to make money, and did not need to feel part of a hierarchical management structure. He put in place a single-tiered operation with direct contact between the dealers and the Datsun UK office. Dealers were given high margins and profits were heavily reinvested.

Botnar pioneered the concept of lean management. Having started Datsun UK with 20 employees, the company would eventually grow to just 250 staff members at a time when its competitors Renault, Peugeot, Citroën and Volkswagen had almost 1,000 employees each in the UK.[168] Indeed, the head office staff numbers of Datsun UK were the smallest of any major car distributor in the UK, recording by far the best figures in the industry of sales turnover and profits per employee.

Datsun UK also avoided the use of outside suppliers. Wherever possible, everything was done "in-house". Initially, all the company's publicity material was produced by just one person, using a single-colour A4 Rotaprint machine, a plate maker and a darkroom which had been converted from a ladies' toilet. In due course, these primitive resources were replaced by a four-colour Heidelberg printing press in an impressive purpose-built wing of the building. The company also built a parts supply service, using its own lorries, as well as a fleet of delivery transporters, and it provided its own insurances and warranties.

Botnar was also conscious of presenting the right image. When he set up Datsun UK, he had decided that he needed a London business address. He had approached a prominent Romanian expatriate and noted anti-Communist, Ion Raţiu, who had an office to let on Piccadilly

Circus. Ratiu was a flamboyant character who always wore a bow tie and who spoke such impeccable English that one could tell immediately he was a foreigner. He regarded himself as the head of the Romanian anti-Communist diaspora in Britain. Ratiu recalled 30 years later, "He (Botnar) wanted really a postal address in London rather than an office. He already had everything else organised. He came into my office with an assistant and we talked, we talked in English all the time, and I showed him the little office that I had available. He liked it and we made a deal there and then."[169]

Even though Botnar did not initially tell Ratiu he was from Czernowitz or that he spoke Romanian, it was the beginning of a long friendship which would last the rest of his life; the Ratius and the Botnars would often holiday together. In 1998, the Communist regime having collapsed and Ratiu by then having become a member of the Romanian parliament, this old friend was to be one of the first speakers at Botnar's memorial ceremony.

Having recruited some of the old NSU dealers who had been sidelined after the merger with Volkswagen, Botnar also targeted independent, privately-owned used car dealers, such dealerships gaining prestige by being able to sell new cars, often for the first time. The basic reliability of Datsuns made the cars popular with independent dealers because they did not need to stock so many spare parts or have big workshops to repair the cars, in contrast to dealers in other, less reliable cars like those made by British Leyland.

The single-tier system enabled the dealers – often very small family businesses with modest facilities – to be in direct contact with the head office. This was in contrast to the system operated by Ford, British Leyland and Vauxhall who had a two-tier system of main dealers who supplied smaller retail dealers, and where margins had to be shared. Botnar's dealers had an 18.5 per cent margin – a much higher percentage than the industry enjoys today. This enabled them to make a great deal of money very quickly, much of which was reinvested.

They also asked Datsun UK for yet more cars to sell.

As part of the initial distribution agreement with Nissan, Botnar had agreed to annual sales targets of 4,000 and 5,000 cars for the years 1971 and 1972 respectively. Nevertheless, his pioneering sales formula immediately proved such a winner that those targets were exceeded spectacularly, actual sales in 1971 being 6,900 cars, and in 1972 30,500 cars.

As 1972 drew to a close, Botnar realised that he was on the right track, and that his approach to selling cars was working. He was already in profit, and he knew that there was much more to come. After decades of struggle and difficulty it seemed as though a rosy future was almost guaranteed. However, something was about to happen which would change his life forever.

CHAPTER 7

CAMELIA

Or watch the things you gave your life to, broken...

Two days before Christmas 1972, the Botnars heard an unexpected knock on the door of their London flat. Rather than carol singers, a policeman was standing outside. He delivered the devastating news that their daughter, Camelia, had been killed in a car accident. She was just 20 years old. Marcela later recalled, "It was one of those moments that is frozen in your head forever. I didn't believe what the policeman was saying – no mother could understand that her child had gone without warning. If she had been ill, if it had not been so sudden and unexpected, I think it might have been easier to bear."[170] Botnar turned to Marcela and said in despair, "What are we going to do now?" In his grief, it was Ion Rațiu to whom Botnar turned at that moment, telephoning and asking his friend to accompany him to Wiltshire to identify the body.

Camelia had been born in Bucharest in 1952, and was to be the Botnars' only child. Marcela had miscarried a baby boy before Camelia was born and had had abortions later, a very common practice in Romania until 1967, after which abortion was severely restricted.[171] On the day of Camelia's birth, Botnar had not been allowed into the hospital – men were not welcome in maternity wards in those days – so with characteristic determination and contempt for authority, he shinned up a drainpipe and waved in through the second-floor window instead.[172]

Camelia's childhood had not been easy. Her father had been sent to labour camp when she was eight. He had been away for four years, missing the formative years of her childhood and early adolescence. She was often left alone in the flat with little to amuse her but books. Then the family left Romania, the country of her birth, in 1965, when she was 13. Having studied at the French lycée in Bucharest, she spoke perfect French. The Botnars therefore decided to send her to school in Paris, in the care of her uncle Maurice, while they moved to London where Botnar took up his new job with NSU. This meant that Camelia was plunged into a foreign country and an alien environment at a tender age. This time she was separated from both her parents, just as she had been separated from her father during his imprisonment.

Paris had effectively become the family home of the Botnar/ Bundorf family – Botnar always regarded the city as his favourite. Max Bunford, his eldest brother, had lived there for many years and kept a flat in Paris long after he acquired British citizenship. Botnar's other brother, Maurice, had married Marguerite Polinard in Lyon in 1937, having graduated in medicine at the University of Lyon that year, and in 1939 he had enrolled in the same 22nd RMVE regiment of foreign fighters in the French army as his brother Oswald (Octav). Also like his younger brother, he had joined the Resistance, enrolling in the *Forces Françaises de l'Intérieur* (FFI – French Interior Force) in Lyon in 1942. Since the war he had lived in Paris, becoming a French national in 1946.

Maurice and Marguerite Bundorf lived in the 15th arrondissement (rue du Commerce) where Maurice also had his surgery. They had a reputation for being a kind and considerate couple, especially towards his working class patients to whom, it was said, he showed great understanding when it came to settling fees.[173] A Communist all his life, Maurice shared the political persuasion of Oswald (Octav) but not of their eldest brother, Max. The sons' mother, Amalia, had also moved to Paris from Czernowitz after the war and she would die there. All of them – Max, his first wife Zoé (Zenaida/ Zina), Amalia, Maurice, Maurice's daughter Michèle, Octav, Marcela and Camelia – are now buried in the same cemetery at Passy, just behind the Trocadéro.

Camelia attended the Lycée Victor Duruy in the 7th arrondissement, near Les Invalides, before rejoining her parents in London in 1969, when she enrolled for her sixth form studies at the French lycée in South Kensington, opposite the Natural History Museum. By this time, she had blossomed from a schoolgirl into a young woman. Camelia Botnar was beautiful, intelligent and very strong-willed. A close friend remembers her very well, 45 years after her death.[174] "She was drop-dead gorgeous," recalls Catherine Laylle (now Lady Meyer). "She had thick blonde hair, she was very self-confident and grown-up. She was very bright and very opinionated. We were constantly together, giggling. I was in awe of her." Photographs of Camelia indeed show a very self-possessed, beautiful young lady who dressed stylishly and who had a mature, frank and intelligent look. She had several boyfriends long before many of her contemporaries even started going out with boys. She bore a strong resemblance to Jane Fonda and led the sort of enviable life one would expect of a sophisticated and good-looking girl whose parents lived comfortably.

In 1971, for instance, shortly after her parents bought a holiday house in Javea, south of Valencia in Spain, she and Catherine Laylle set off for a summer holiday, driven by a chauffeur provided by Botnar. They stopped off in Paris on the way. Overnight the car was broken into and all their suitcases were stolen. Furious with the driver for his negligence, they ditched him and proceeded on their way without him – and without any belongings. None of this prevented them having a wonderful and carefree time in the empty house, nor from driving back to London on their own at the end of the holiday.

In many ways, Camelia was like her father. She was left-wing but hated Communism and Communists; she read a lot. She was, also like her father, not religious: Botnar was convinced that there was no after-life and he never entertained religious feelings of any kind. She did, however, have a philosophical streak. Aged 15, in Paris in March 1968, she penned the following thoughtful words, in flawless French, about the possibility of change in politics. In her essay, she expresses her premonition of the whirlwind of revolution which was about to hit her home city two months later:

"This morning, I awoke tired. Moreover, the gloomy morning, this insignificant but obstinate drizzle, this low sky, grey and heavy, end up insinuating thoughts of escape into my mind.

Once outside, the sight of preoccupied passers-by and of dustbins piled up on the pavements reminded me that for weeks a general strike has been trying in vain to find 'the best' for thousands of people's lives. Nonetheless, there is no atmosphere of decision or of will in Paris. Instead, people seem resigned... The workers will bury themselves once more in their life without satisfactions and without reward... I feel that they will lose this chance to obtain their demands, and all because of a few obscure violent occurrences and of the thoughtless suspicion of the workers towards the younger generation...

What is missing today, when all seems to point to great changes, is an ideal which has come from a new ideology.

What is superfluous is the invasion of new political or ideological tendencies in conflict with one another.

There is something bitter in the air, and I, in my corner, feel powerless. 'Change the world, it needs it,' said Bertolt Brecht. Imperative but impersonal.

And under this low, grey and heavy sky even my thoughts of escape lose themselves in a black desert... If, for lack of dreaming about a better world, one no longer knows what to dream about, if there are no more illusions into which to seek refuge, the world and the universe become poor places in which to welcome new generations, new children, new adolescents who need to dream.

The future seems bleak: human beings, with their wretched wills, will destroy all hope."[175]

In short, Camelia was a genuine *soixante-huitard*, not in the sense of having been an activist during the events of May 1968 but instead in that she was a young person who wanted social change and who was alive at that emblematic time. Those heady days were identified with the sexual revolution. Camelia was determined to be a free woman.

Unfortunately, as was perhaps inevitable for two strong-willed personalities, especially when both showed a cussed defiance of authority, Camelia and her father had a difficult relationship. She called him a bully to her friends and referred to him as only "he" in her conversations with them.[176] She had never forgiven him for a cruel remark he had made on the day of his release from prison: she had been a little girl when he had last seen her, four years previously, and by the time he returned home she had become a precociously well-developed teenager.[177] He had disapproved of her clothes and had said so to Marcela, in harsh words she never forgot.

Such difficulties were no doubt fairly typical of those between certain kinds of fathers and certain kinds of daughters. Although her parents accorded her a good deal of liberty – they bought her a flat in Paris, for instance, so that she could study at university there after she left the French lycée in London – Botnar sometimes resented the way that she used that liberty. In particular, he disapproved of one of her boyfriends, Yves Fletcher, to whom Catherine Laylle had introduced her in Paris and with whom she fell in love.

In 1972, Camelia invited Yves Fletcher to spend Christmas with her. This caused ructions with her father and there was a row. On Saturday 23 December, she and her boyfriend left her parents' flat in Gloucester Road under a cloud and headed out towards Stonehenge. Darkness fell early. Shortly before Marlborough, on the Bath Road (A4), on a bend in the road near the then Golden Arrow Café (where there is still a garage and now an Indian restaurant) their car hit a Jaguar in a head-on collision. Camelia took the full force of the crash and was killed instantly. Fletcher was seriously injured with multiple cuts and both legs broken. Firemen had to cut Camelia's body from the wreckage, although her mother would later testify that there was not so much as a scratch on her: she had died from a broken neck. The wife of the driver of the Jaguar was also injured and taken to hospital.[178]

For the funeral, Marcela chose the clothes in which Camelia was buried, a tan suede outfit which had been one of her favourites. A crucifix was put around her neck and an Orthodox priest officiated at the burial in Gunnersbury cemetery, West London, even though Botnar was an atheist and Marcela non-practising. Marcela was to visit the cemetery almost every Friday over the coming decades; Botnar suppressed his grief, buried himself in his work and seldom went to the grave. After his death, Camelia's body was exhumed and transferred to the Passy cemetery in Paris, where she is now buried together with her parents.

That question Botnar put to Marcela on the night of Camelia's death – "What are we going to do now?" – should be understood quite literally, not rhetorically. For Botnar, doing things was a way of dealing with life and, even more so, with the sort of profound despair which comes from losing one's only child. He once said, "There is nothing to life but work,"[179] and he now channelled his energies into his job even more intensely than before. Botnar never rested and he used to say, "I don't like weekends."[180] Even on holiday in Spain, he would devote any spare time to watering the garden or to giving instructions to the gardeners about where to plant things.

In fact, "doing" was the key to Botnar's very existence and, as we have seen, he was convinced that anyone can do anything if only he puts his mind to it. Marcela found his workaholism difficult because it meant that she was often at home alone with her grief.

However, there was little she could do to control her husband, especially since he himself could not bear to be reminded of his loss. Catherine Laylle, Camelia's friend, recalls how after Camelia's death, on her visits to her late friend's mother, Marcela would tell her to leave the flat before Botnar came home so that he would not have to confront a living reminder of his dead daughter.

Camelia's death is therefore in large part the key to both Botnar's subsequent spectacular success in business and his unparalleled commitment to philanthropy. Botnar threw himself even deeper into his work after Camelia's death. It certainly explains what was to become his greatest legacy, his gigantic charitable giving. Botnar was determined that his daughter's name should live on, and that something good should come out of her death. He decided to create first one Foundation bearing her name, and then several others over the years, and to erect several buildings, especially hospitals, through which her memory would live on. However, as we shall see in a later chapter, much of his charitable giving was done with maximum discretion, as Botnar never sought publicity. The result was that relatively few people knew about it at all.

CHAPTER 8

THE RISE AND RISE OF DATSUN UK

If you can fill the unforgiving minute
With sixty seconds' worth of distance run...

In October 1973, one of the worst fires ever seen in West Sussex broke out at Datsun UK's parts warehouse, eventually destroying both building and contents. As ever, Botnar was on the spot, thinking of ways by which he could keep the business running. He noticed the Parts Manager was one of a group of people who were standing watching the conflagration. "What are you doing?" he asked incredulously. "Watching the fire," came the answer. "Don't worry about the fire," Botnar replied. "I'll watch it for you. Go and order replacements." Within days, planeloads of parts were winging their way to Britain from across the globe.

A devastating fire was not the only significant development of 1973. At the start of the year, the United Kingdom had become part of the European Economic Community (EEC). With trade barriers down, there was an immediate and sharp rise in import penetration of the UK car market by European car makers. In 1971, the European share of the market had been 21.6 per cent. By 1980, that would rise to 34.1 per cent. From a much lower base, the Japanese, and in particular Datsun[181], were creating a further substantial dent in the British market.

Meanwhile, British manufacturers, notably British Leyland Motor Corporation, were suffering. British Leyland was a ramshackle conglomerate which, in 1968, at the urging of Prime Minister Harold Wilson's Labour Government, had created a merger which amalgamated all of Britain's motor industry businesses into a single company. It manufactured cars, buses and trucks under numerous brands and at 40 separate plants spread throughout Britain. Beset by strikes, it was poorly managed and hopelessly under-capitalised. Unsurprisingly, the cars it manufactured were unreliable. Despite this, it still had a third of the UK market in cars. However, the group was losing money, and insolvency was looming. As British Leyland was one of Britain's biggest employers, the UK Government considered it had no alternative other than to step in and attempt to save it. In 1975, in his second term of office, Harold Wilson did so by nationalising the company.

The creation of British Leyland and the company's subsequent nationalisation are considered by many to have been an unmitigated disaster. The sprawling group lacked the resources to modernise in order to compete with traditional international car companies like Ford and General Motors, and there were the additional and growing threats from Europe and Japan. Although Austin-Morris and Jaguar-Rover-Triumph were spun off into separate divisions, as were bus and truck manufacture, British Leyland was plagued by poor industrial relations and product unreliability. With some exceptions, its vehicle designs were unimaginative and dated, and the company's market share continued inexorably to decline.

Meanwhile, although the UK Government could do little to stem the flow of European imports, a very different view was taken in relation to the Japanese. The overall case for protection against Japanese imports was in reality weak, with the trade balance in fact being in the UK's favour. Nevertheless, some sectors of the economy were viewed as being particularly "sensitive", the car industry being one such, with motor vehicles representing about 25 per cent of all UK imports from Japan at the time. In 1974, the Society of Motor Manufacturers and Traders (SMMT) approached the Government for assistance to protect the domestic industry from intensifying import penetration from all car manufacturing countries, but especially Japan. It was impossible to ignore the growing clamour for protection which Japanese manufacturers were facing not just from Britain, but from around the world. At the same time, the Japanese themselves were known to be extremely worried over the possibility of direct action by governments and of the long-term consequences of protection.

The Japanese listened carefully to the entreaties made to them by the governments of those countries most affected. In 1975, Harold Wilson managed to secure a "prediction" from the Japanese Government that during the remainder of the year their exports of cars to the United Kingdom would decline, and indicated that Japanese cars would be "exported in an orderly way during 1976". The actual results for 1976 told a rather different story, as a result of Datsun UK's continued success. In 1976, new registrations of Japanese cars increased by no less than 31 per cent year-on-year.

At the invitation of a Japanese consortium made up of Nissan, Mitsubishi, Honda and Kansai Paint, British Leyland engineers toured car factories in Japan in the summer of 1975. This was the first visit to Japan by British car manufacturers since British Motor Corporation had provided model designs, equipment, and advisers to, ironically, Nissan in 1950.

The detailed engineers' report of that visit reflected the shifting fortunes of the two national industries over the 25 years since. It catalogued the institutional virtues of Japanese manufacturers and the advanced productivity of the Japanese plants by comparison with their British counterparts.

Notwithstanding this evidence that greater productivity and efficiency, rather than dumping, were the explanation for Japanese competitiveness, formal discussions on import restrictions began in 1975 between the SMMT and the Japan Automobile Manufacturers Association (JAMA). These resulted in a voluntary reduction in exports to the UK under Voluntary Export Restraints (VERs) which were implemented in 1977 and, although these were initially negotiated for a five-year period only, restrictions remained in place until December 1999.

Botnar's hugely successful development of Datsun UK was about to be reflected in the share of the resulting quota he gained. JAMA agreed to confine sales within the limits of current market shares, leaving Datsun UK with 6 per cent of the entire UK market, which represented 60 per cent of all Japanese car sales in Britain. Even working within these limits, in 1977 Botnar was able to sell 82,000 cars and a year later this figure had risen to more than 100,000. In the same period (1978), Toyota sold 28,000 cars in Britain, and Honda only 19,500.

In addition to Botnar's innovative approach to selling, other elements played an important role in the success of Datsun UK. For instance, Botnar recognised the importance of communications technology and data management, and used highly innovative schemes to embrace it.

To co-ordinate the unloading, transporting and selling of the cars, Datsun UK set up one of the first remote computer links in Britain, enabling information to be transmitted instantly from the docks in Middlesbrough, where the cars were unloaded, to Worthing head office on the South Coast. This opened the way for a unique system of forward-selling. As soon as the cars arrived in the UK, the chassis number was noted for the purposes of invoicing, and the car sent off to the dealer who had forward-ordered it. Signed cheques for the cars which dealers had ordered had been handed over when the order was placed, and these were cashed when the car had left the docks.

This had huge benefits for cash flow. Though the cars arrived in Britain just one month after they were shipped, Datsun UK was not required to pay for them until 90 days after lading in Japan – by which time the cars had already been sold.

The company's ability to monitor and to marshal cars was ground-breaking. It could locate in real time every car for which it was responsible, and could do so from any one of the company's linked information terminals. Today, such communication is commonplace; at the time it was revolutionary.

Data management was constantly improved. From the mid-1980s, the computer department produced a daily report, known as "the yellow pages" because Botnar had them printed on yellow paper so that they would be instantly recognisable. This report listed the daily sales performance of every dealer in the country, of which there were by then several hundred. It also showed orders for up to three months ahead. It was common at the daily lunch meetings for each dealer's performance to be carefully scrutinised and discussed, based on the information gleaned from these yellow pages. In due course, all sales activity and profits for each new and used vehicle sold by Botnar's dealer network became available on screen and in real time. Each morning, Botnar would first undertake a strenuous physical workout before arriving at the office around 9.30am to pore over these figures. He would see who was selling what and how quickly. Then he would get on the phone to his various employees and the dealers themselves to see what could be done better. He got into the very guts of the whole process. "Why are the dealers in Leicester taking 37 minutes to wash a car but the dealers in London an hour and half ?" he would ask.[182]

Paul Yallop, who worked in the computer department, recalls how advanced the information processing was for its day. He credits Botnar for giving the computer technicians challenges they had not thought of themselves. As with the intricacies of car sales and car production, he was a seemingly inexhaustible source of initiative in information technology as well. "Octav Botnar always came up with ideas," Yallop recalls.[183] "He would never accept anything as it was. He was always convinced there was a better way of doing things, and he set about finding it. He questioned everything. You could never pull the wool over his eyes."

A very important additional factor in the success of Datsun UK was the provision of finance, providing hire purchase facilities to its customers, lending them the money on favourable terms to buy a car. It was the first company to offer finance as a parallel service, and customers could buy a car with only a small deposit. Originally started in the early 1980s on a 50:50 basis with Lloyds & Scottish Finance Ltd., this part of the business would later be conducted by Datsun Finance alone (later, Nissan Finance; later still, AFS Financial Services). This quickly developed into a vast financial operation. Botnar correctly perceived that hire purchase for cars was rather like credit cards: the loans were profitable yet low-risk. They were in any case secured against the car, and people tended to give priority to paying off the HP on their cars, without which they often could not survive. The default rate was therefore very low. Moreover, by providing easy finance, Datsun UK was able to increase the number of cars sold. At that stage, such wholesale ownership packages were unique – today they are commonplace.

The more the business grew, the more internal financing became key, for instance to pay for increased stockholdings by dealers. Not only could funds be invested in the dealerships, but the cars themselves, by virtue of inflation, also became more expensive. Dealers could be given greater flexibility, especially during peak periods. This all meant that very early on, Datsun UK, and later Nissan UK, controlled the whole "food chain" of car sales – import, distribution, marketing, sales, hire purchase, the supply of parts, insurance and guarantee. Each stage generated a profit.

Botnar believed strongly that people were his greatest asset and he took a keen interest in recruitment. He held that the best judges of a candidate were his or her future colleagues. People applying for a job were therefore typically invited to spend a whole day at the company, so that they could get a good idea of how the business worked and so that their possible future colleagues could get a good idea of them. One recruit, Tony Stone, who started to work for Datsun UK in 1972, went home after his interview to find a message from the Finance Director, who told him to come straight back to the office. Stone returned and Botnar himself burst into the room. "I have two questions," he said. "The other two candidates say they need 18 months to install the computer system. You say you can do it in six. How?" Stone explained how. "Second question: the other candidates want £3,000 and you want £3,200. Why?" Stone shot back, "Because I can do the work quicker than they can." "I like this guy," Botnar said, turning to his Finance Director. "Give him the money."[184]

Similarly, during interviews at which dealership managers were being recruited, Botnar would hover just outside the office and occasionally peer in to make a gesture to the person conducting the interview – thumbs up, or a slashing motion with the forefinger across the throat – to indicate to his staff whether or not he approved of the candidate. He was happy to give vent to his own prejudices: for instance, any candidate with a beard was generally sent packing.[185]

Once employed, people were treated generously provided that they worked hard. Just as Botnar was to become a major philanthropist, giving gigantic sums to large hospital and other humanitarian projects in the United Kingdom and abroad, so he was generous too on an individual level. He personally reviewed the salaries and bonuses of everyone who worked at head office, often finding out about their personal circumstances to see if they were in particular need. Bonuses were paid twice a year, in December and July (at least until 1987, when a new senior manager from Ford persuaded Botnar that once a year was enough) and these bonuses were typically between one and two months' additional pay. Naturally this was greatly appreciated by everyone who worked at the company. Brian

Groves, who became Marketing Director of Datsun UK in 1974, remembers him as "magnanimous, considerate, kind and friendly".[186] "Everyone was treated equally and fairly in the company," he added. "He was a very kind and considerate man. Datsun/Nissan was a lovely place to work – for those who were interested, there was a squash court, a hairdresser and a chiropodist." Botnar even engaged a physiotherapist who was available to treat the men who carried out manual work in the warehouse. Tony Stone described Datsun UK as akin to "one big family, with Octav Botnar as the *paterfamilias*".[187]

Those who knew Botnar well often remarked on this generosity. One of his colleagues, Richard Smith, recalls that Botnar gave him a dressing-down just before the directors' lunch. Smith had just taken over responsibility for a region where a dealer had said he would pay his overdue car stock invoice after his fortnight's holiday. Botnar blew up about this and called Smith stupid. Smith slunk down to the staff canteen, not wanting to subject himself to more public humiliation, but the waiter was sent to summon him back up to the boardroom. No doubt because he felt remorse at having been so sharp, Botnar asked Smith about a new dealership he had discovered for sale in Torquay. "How much is it?" he asked. "£395,000," replied Smith. "I will buy it for you," said Botnar, and he did. Smith now owns a string of such dealerships along the South Coast and makes millions of pounds a year. Smith later opined that, "While he was a very hard taskmaster on the outside he was truly a very generous and thoughtful person on the inside. A very misunderstood gentleman greatly missed."[188]

Sometimes Botnar's generosity led to amusing situations. Ion Raţiu recalled how, on a safari in Kenya, he had taken a long time to get a photograph of himself with a Maasai tribesman in full regalia. When they had finished, he tried to press what Raţiu described as a very large bank note into the Maasai's hands for his trouble. The warrior would have nothing of it: he wanted real money, a coin. It was only after much haggling, in which Botnar vainly struggled to persuade the tribesman to take the larger sum, that he reluctantly gave in and handed him a coin.[189]

According to his merchant banker, Otto Bruderer, Botnar's generosity was inspired by his view that you had to take a punt on people's goodwill. He applied this policy even to complete strangers. One day, in later life, after he had left the United Kingdom for Switzerland, Botnar saw a farmer in a field cutting hay with a scythe. "Haven't you got a machine to do that?" he asked the farmer, who replied that it cost 20,000 Swiss francs which he did not have. "If I give you the money for a tractor, will you bring me fresh vegetables every day?" Botnar immediately suggested. The farmer gladly agreed, Botnar gave him the money – and he never saw him again. However, Botnar did not care about the man's bad faith. Instead, he regarded it as part of life. He felt that it was essential to give people the benefit of the doubt, in the hope that the gamble would pay off. He believed in a humanist version of Pascal's wager, that you gained more by believing in people and being right than you did by not believing and being wrong. "I learned in the war," Botnar told Bruderer, "that you can survive only if you trust people."[190]

The result was that Botnar was a brilliant motivator. All those who knew him attest to this rare quality. Some of the motivation came from his own infectious energy. Brian Groves remembers fondly how Botnar "was a little dynamo, he made things happen."[191] Otto Bruderer independently uses a similar metaphor: "It was as if he had a nuclear reactor in his body. He was the most energetic person I have met in my life."[192] Botnar could not abide a single second being wasted. He expected everyone else to do the same.

Botnar's ability to motivate came from his liberal use of incentives. For example, one young salesman, Barry Clarke, who joined NSU in 1965 shortly before Botnar became Chief Executive, initially had to sell 15 cars a day. One day, Botnar saw him cycling to work in the rain. Later that day, he came to see Clarke and told him to sell not 15 cars a day but 20, or 100 a week, and said that he would get use of the company van to drive to work if he succeeded.

Clarke agreed but, the next day, found that his two colleagues were no longer there. When he queried this, Botnar said he had moved them to other jobs. Clarke protested. Botnar replied that Clarke had agreed to the new target and that he had given his word in return for the use of the van. Clarke could not think of a response to this, except to say that there was no petrol in the van: Botnar immediately agreed to give him four gallons a week.

Later in the year, Botnar summarily moved Clarke to a new job in sales and increased his target from 100 to 150 cars a week, double the initial amount of 15 a day. He promised Clarke an even bigger company car if he succeeded – and he did. Clarke recalls, "Mr Botnar's philosophy in business was the carrot and the stick and it certainly worked for me and for many, many other people. He helped us achieve success in our lives and we will never forget him... At times he was a hard taskmaster but Datsun and Nissan UK were the great success stories of the British motor industry and it was a wonderful privilege to be with Mr Botnar from the start."[193]

Time and again, indeed, people would testify to Botnar's ability to get people to do things of which they initially thought they were incapable – in short, to his leadership qualities. Dawn Lawson, his secretary for 17 years, says, "His philosophy was to employ few people but to motivate them with good pay. He also liked to multitask people – to make them do things they had never done before." Brian Groves, for instance, who was Director of Marketing, had originally been a journalist. When he protested in his recruitment interview that he knew nothing about marketing, Botnar insisted that he should try and that he would succeed. He did.

Botnar's employees agree that he was a frequent source of original ideas. "When he asked you what you thought of something," Brian Groves recalls, "you always knew that he had already thought about the matter himself and that he had his own firm views. You had to give the right answer. He motivated you to do the thing he asked." Nobody wanted to fail. Otto Bruderer concurs: "Octav Botnar made me a tougher, higher-reaching and harder-working professional."[194] His niece, Amalie, also said the same thing after her uncle died: "He was someone who was always there to advise me no matter how busy he was. To steer me and push me towards goals I never thought I could reach."[195]

Another employee told Ion Rațiu, as they were standing outside a skyscraper hotel in Tokyo, "I work for Botnar. If he tells me that we must climb this tower, I'll go. I know it's impossible but I'll go with him."[196] Indeed Botnar himself occasionally used such climbing metaphors: he once shocked Otto Bruderer with an audacious but calculated demand he made during a very delicate negotiation, and just as the deal was about to be clinched. It appeared to put the whole agreement in jeopardy, but the strategy paid off. Bruderer took him aside afterwards and asked why he had done it. "Where I come from," Botnar replied, "mountains do not have summits."[197] It was maybe not a very good metaphor (they do) but the point was clear.

A good example of how Botnar motivated his employees to achieve the impossible was when the company moved into its new offices in Worthing in 1975. The construction work dragged on and so Botnar forced the issue by unilaterally proclaiming a date for the opening ceremony, 25 October. It required huge effort to get the building ready on time. Improvisation was the name of the game. The Sales Director put a nice sheen on the new reception desk in the main entrance hall with wood varnish from his boat; the Data Processing Manager had to get the plaque ready for the unveiling ceremony.

On the morning of the opening, however, he realised there was no curtain for this purpose. One employee volunteered that his wife was good with a sewing machine and that she had an old skirt she could use; she was promptly set to work. Another was despatched post-haste to the local department store, where he negotiated the purchase of a short display curtain rail he had seen in the shop window: it was just the right size. However, because the brackets could not be drilled into the marble walls – where they would leave a lasting mark – they had to be stuck on with Araldite, which normally takes 24 hours to set. The guest of honour, Tadahiro Iwakoshi, the then President of Nissan Motor Company, was due to perform the ceremony in a couple of hours, but was asked politely not to pull too sharply on the cord. In the end, everything went off without a hitch.[198] The sense of exhilaration felt at having snatched victory from the jaws of defeat, and of having done so with inventiveness and humour, only encouraged Datsun UK employees to try to do so again.

By contrast, if employees were not up to scratch, they were sacked without ceremony, or at least banished to the warehouse until, like a courtier, they were later forgiven and brought back into favour. Sue Parmenter, a former secretary, chuckles as she remembers that, on occasions, employees would arrive at work to find their desk had disappeared, a sign that they had been dismissed without notice or that their job had changed. Botnar was acutely aware of the need to focus on making the business work, even if this meant appearing to be ruthless.

On one occasion, he gave Brian Groves, his Director of Marketing, a huge new task. Groves reminded Botnar that he was going on holiday the very next day. "Then how will you do it?" asked Botnar. Groves did it by sending his family ahead to start the holiday without him whilst he tackled the task at hand. Having done so, he caught up with the family.

When a senior employee went on holiday at a particularly busy time when all hands were required on deck, upon his return he discovered he had been sacked. Botnar also did not like his own sales staff getting too close to the dealers because he knew that it meant that they were treating the dealers too leniently and that the dealers were taking them for a ride. If a dealer told Botnar he liked one of his staff, it was curtains for the employee concerned. On two occasions, he sacked all his sales staff for that very reason.[199]

Because he wanted everyone to aim high, Botnar became notorious for openly criticising employees, including company directors, to their faces and in front of others, when he thought they had done a bad job. The daily directors' lunch, in reality a marathon board meeting, was an occasion when Botnar could dish out the criticism in generous helpings. "Those lunches resembled jousting competitions," recalls Richard Smith, a Nissan UK director. Botnar would fire off instructions left, right and centre. Some resented this; others understood that it was just his manner. Although he could certainly use harsh words, his gruff talk was not an expression of nastiness but instead a result of the way he used the English language. It was also the consequence of his overriding conviction, which he kept until the end of his life, that anyone can do anything if only he applies himself to it.

Botnar's relentless energy meant that waking hours had to be spent working. What else was there? When he organised dealer trips to Tokyo, he would spend the flight walking up and down the aisle selling to the dealers; he never wasted a single moment. He was always focused on the essentials and was convinced that you could never ask for too much in a negotiation. He believed that a good deal was one in which both sides felt that they could have done better. He had a knack for homing in on the critical elements and for going for the jugular when others were flailing around on side issues.[200]

Perhaps surprisingly for a man of German/Jewish/Central European origin, he possessed many of the qualities associated with a British eccentric: quirkiness, a wicked sense of humour, and great originality combined with a complete lack of pomposity. With this drive always to improve everything, Botnar was a somewhat maniacal micro-manager. He would, for instance, go into the parts department and show the men working there new ways to pack boxes. He knew from having built up the business with his own hands that careless packing wasted materials and increased the cost of transport. On one occasion, someone said that the company car park was too small for the growing workforce and that it should be extended: later that day, Botnar was seen down in the parking lot measuring out exactly how much space each car needed. He would often rearrange the furniture in people's offices, telling them where to put their desks or their filing cabinets.

Botnar did not like to leave things to chance. Having trained as a radio operator in the Resistance, he retained an interest in technology and covert operations. He bought in Japan a special device, a pen which had a radio transmitter hidden in it, which he would leave on the desk at meetings he was not attending, with the knowledge of the Nissan UK negotiator. This would enable Botnar to monitor the meeting if necessary. He also did not like disorder. One day, Botnar came into the room where the typing pool secretaries worked: one of them recalls how her desk was covered with in-trays and out-trays and the paraphernalia of office life. Botnar calmly brushed the whole lot onto the floor with a backward movement of his forearm. "You need only one pen and one piece of paper," he said, and left the room. He was very particular about details: at one point, he had two assistants in his office, a man and a woman, Dawn Lawson. The man's desk was a little bigger. "Change your desk," Botnar told Lawson, who protested that she did not mind. "No, change it," he insisted. "Your desks should be the same size."[201]

He was a manic user of the phone. He knew most of the dealers personally and especially liked the down-to-earth, no-nonsense approach of the ones in the North of England. They, however, were rather afraid of him: he would ring them up and get them to accept huge targets for sales. He also ensured that every telephone in the headquarters in Worthing had an earpiece: he would walk around the offices, to see what everyone was doing, and would occasionally pick up the earpiece to listen in to the conversation his employees were having. If he thought the employee was not negotiating the right sort of deal, he would give liberal advice in a loud voice, sometimes even grabbing the receiver and taking over the conversation himself.

In the days before mobile phones, the staff at Worthing knew there would be a blissful two hours of silence while he was in his car driving down from London. That came to an end, however, in the 1980s, when everyone – and especially Mr Botnar – acquired a mobile. Initially, the coverage was patchy and so the signal would often be lost as he drove through the countryside. This made Botnar so furious that he bought a second mobile with a different network. In the last years of his life, after 1991, when he was no longer able to return to the UK and had to work from his home in Switzerland, he would spend up to 10 hours a day on the phone, sometimes conducting board meetings with the directors seated around the table and Botnar's disembodied voice commanding the proceedings from a speakerphone in the middle of the table. The only person who could get Botnar off the phone, it has been said, was the company's local solicitor in Worthing, Frank Haddock. Haddock had a pre-war radio in his office and the telephone itself was not much younger. When he had had enough, he would put the receiver near the radio to create noisy interference. "Very sorry, Mr Botnar, we seem to have a bad line," he would say, and hang up.[202]

Botnar spent a lot of money entertaining the dealers and their wives and giving them lavish trips abroad. The company would throw gala parties for them at which famous entertainers would be invited to perform: Sammy Davis Jr, Bob Monkhouse, Petula Clark, Lenny Henry, Ronnie Corbett, Larry Grayson, Bob Hope, Dionne Warwick, Victor Borge and the like. On one occasion in March

1984, the dealers' annual bash had been arranged to take place at the Loews (now Fairmont) hotel in Monaco. By coincidence, Botnar's brother Max had died a few days previously and the funeral was held on the morning of the event. It was a surreal and sad juxtaposition of engagements for Botnar that day.

In the initial agreement with Nissan, Botnar had been allocated sales targets of 4,000, then 5,000, then 5,500 cars for the years 1971, 1972 and 1973 respectively. Datsun UK's pioneering formula had proved such a winner that those targets were exceeded spectacularly, actual sales in those three years in fact being 6,900, 30,500 and 60,500. Botnar was so successful during his first three years that NMC amended the clause in Datsun UK's distribution agreement, extending the renewal period from three years to five, to be renewed automatically provided that Datsun UK had achieved agreed sales targets.

All of this was achieved despite the almost continuously rising yen during the 1980s, meaning that Nissan UK's transfer price was always under pressure. There was never any fat margin upon which Botnar could rely. He worked hard to get the best deal from Japan, and just as hard to get his dealers to perform.

In this he took great care to recruit good dealers, and Datsun UK's independent network of dealers increased from a handful in number in 1971 to over 400 by 1983. In addition, between 1971 and the end of 1983, Datsun UK itself opened an additional 23 retail sites, mostly in major conurbations. These were operated by a wholly owned subsidiary called Datsun Retail Limited.

During the period 1982-1990, 1,013,847 Nissan cars were registered in Britain, making Nissan UK (as the company became) the first importer to sell more than a million cars. (The name Datsun UK was changed to Nissan UK on 2 January 1984.) The closest in terms of numbers was Volkswagen Audi (UK), which sold 975,281 cars over the same period. Volkswagen Audi (UK)'s corresponding turnover of £6.7 billion over those eight years was actually greater than Nissan UK's by some £1.1 billion, because the average unit price of cars was higher. In terms of market share in Britain, Volkswagen Audi (UK) and Nissan UK delivered very similar numbers throughout the 1980s. The next biggest was Renault, with 647,000 vehicles and £4.3 billion turnover in the period 1982-1990.

During the same period, Toyota's sales numbers were only 32 per cent of Nissan UK's but, with a higher average unit price, Toyota's turnover was about half that of Nissan UK's. Throughout this time, the Japanese importers were operating under the terms of the quota which restrained imports. Japanese sales were limited to a share of the British market of approximately 11 per cent, with each importer able to sell a fixed allowance within that 11 per cent, being the share of sales they had at the time of the agreement's implementation in 1978. Should any importer not sell the whole of its stake, any shortfall was then distributed amongst the others in the following year.

Crucially, cars representing the allotted share were not actually allowed to leave Japan until New Year's Day each year. Given that they would take a month to be transported by sea, importers of Japanese cars were very short of stock at the beginning of the year. This meant that a month's sales were lost annually which, following on from the traditionally slow sales month of December, resulted in Japanese importers really only selling cars for 10 months each year.

Notwithstanding all the challenges faced, between 1982 and 1990, Nissan UK declared profits before tax of £558 million. Expressed as a percentage of sales this was 11.2 per cent – four times higher than the average of all importers, and twice that of Toyota GB, the next most profitable. If one were to consolidate the profits during the same period with those of sister company AFGH, declared profits before tax rose to £777million. This compared to the total combined figure for all other importers during the same period of £617 million. In other words, Botnar made and declared more profits than all other car importers added together.

TAX PAID BY COMPANIES WITHIN THE NISSAN UK GROUP COMPARED WITH ALL OTHER CAR IMPORTERS: 1987-1991[203]

	Turnover (£m)	Tax paid (£m)	Tax paid as %
Nissan UK Group	5,934	235	3.96
Volkswagen/Audi	4,946	41	0.82
Mercedes Benz	3,794	5	0.13
Renault	3,222	0	0.00
Volvo	3,170	59	1.86
Toyota	2,121	40	1.88
Citroën	1,981	6	0.30
Honda	1,571	16	1.01
Fiat	1,506	0	0.00
Mazda	1,064	21	1.97
Mitsubishi	741	19	2.56
Other Japanese (total)	636	11	1.72
Other European (total)	11,011	88	0.80
Nissan UK Group	5,934	235	3.96
All Japanese (other than Nissan UK)	6,133	107	1.74
Nissan UK Group	5,934	235	3.96
All European	29,630	199	0.67

Although he had long since changed his name to Botnar, his 1966 French Carte du Combattant was issued in the name Oswald Bundorf.

Camelia Botnar was beautiful, intelligent and strong-willed.

Lord Stokes (above right) had what the Financial Times described as "the toughest job held by any boss in Britain" when he was asked to turn round the British-owned car industry in 1968. The British Leyland Chairman is pictured here at the 1972 London Motor Show being introduced to the Japanese opposition – a Datsun.

A 1970 photograph of what is represented as a Datsun dealership. In reality, it is the NSU yard at Shoreham (note the NSUs in the background), with images of Datsun cars pasted into the foreground. This was Botnar's attempt to impress.

The first Datsun House, an office building on East Worthing seafront. Botnar is pictured outside with an unidentified Nissan official.

Meeting the press. Botnar (centre) talks to Courtenay Edwards, motoring correspondent of The Sunday Telegraph (left), with Marketing Director Brian Groves (right) and Public Relations Director Maxwell Boyd (far right).

The state-of-the-art headquarters in Worthing into which Nissan UK moved in 1975 (offices above; warehousing opposite below). The guest of honour at the opening, Tadahiro Iwakoshi, President of Nissan Motor Company (opposite above), was asked not to pull too sharply on the cord at the unveiling of the commemorative plaque as the curtain rail had been stuck on with glue only that morning.

Botnar greets NMC's President Yutaka Kume (far left) and Chairman Takashi Ishihara (far right) at Nissan UK headquarters in Worthing.

Botnar in serious conversation with Chancellor of the Exchequer Sir Geoffrey Howe.

Datsun UK was self-sufficient at every opportunity. All its printed materials were produced in-house using the Company's four-colour Heidelberg printing press.

Botnar (centre) took NMC executives Kawai (far left) and Shiro Ozawa (far right) – then responsible for NMC's business in Europe and the Middle East – to see major South London Datsun dealer, Ancaster Garages. Owner Harold Cole (left) and his son Robert (right).

Nissan Motor Car Carrier's Kyushu Maru. This box-like ship was part of a specialised fleet owned and operated by Nissan to transport its cars across the globe.

CHAPTER 9

THATCHER'S FLAGSHIP

If you can talk with crowds and keep your virtue,
Or walk with Kings – nor lose the common touch...

In early 1980, less than a year after Margaret Thatcher had been elected Prime Minister – a change of government which heralded a revolutionary decade in British politics – the strength of Nissan sales in the UK, the constraining effect of import quotas, and the potential for even greater sales all prompted Octav Botnar to approach Takashi Ishihara, president of Nissan Motor Company, with an idea. Botnar's proposal was to make a major contribution to the success of the Conservative Government's free market policies, both in Britain and around the globe.

Botnar's idea was that Nissan should build a car factory in Britain to supply not just Britain but the rest of the Europe as well. Given that Britain had languished for decades in industrial decline, and that the car industry was among the worst sector affected by the abusive power of the unions, this was a very radical proposal. Yet Botnar's suggestion, which was given strong support by the Conservative Government and eventually taken up by the Japanese, made a substantial contribution to the success of the radical reforms which successive Thatcher Governments implemented in the British economy. Botnar's initiative therefore has a historical significance far greater than the simple issue of where to build a car factory.

What Botnar had correctly spotted was not just a market opportunity for Nissan, based on his assessment of the demands of the British car market and on the ability of the Japanese to meet them. To be sure, his decision was market-driven: Botnar knew that the UK market offered the potential of much greater demand for Nissan cars than that which Nissan UK was currently able to supply, given that its sales were constrained by quotas. Should Nissan build a car factory in the UK it could supply, quota free, both the British and continental European markets. However, Botnar also understood the politics. He correctly perceived that the objectives of the new British Government and NMC coincided – that, as he put it in a later letter, "the interests of Nissan and the (British) Government for this project are identical."[204] Nissan needed to sell cars, and Her Majesty's Government needed to show that it had cleaned out the Augean stables of Britain's industrial relations, and especially the car industry, in order to haul the country out of the socialist morass into which it had slid in the 1960s and 1970s.

The proposal was radical because British Leyland, the national car producer, was a symbol of all that was most catastrophic about British industry in general. Like many of the country's employers at the time, it was heavily unionised: one of the most notorious union leaders was the British Leyland employee, Derek Robinson, known as "Red Robbo". British Leyland continued to suck in ever larger amounts of taxpayers' money in subsidies and it became a byword for the sort of lame duck industries that were soon to be allowed to wither on the vine in accordance with the new tenets of Thatcherism. Indeed in the year the Conservatives were elected, British Leyland's total production was 500,000 (when Nissan UK was selling 100,000 cars a year, artificially capped at that level) and it continued to fall in the early 1980s, reaching a dismal 374,000 in May 1981.

British Leyland tried to fight against foreign imports by exploiting a sort of economic jingoism. The slogan used by the government was "Buy British, " even though the company did not even practice this itself, since many of the primary materials for its own cars were sourced abroad. After Britain joined the European Economic Community in 1973, European cars started to flood into the country: they had 21.6 per cent of the market in 1971 but 34.1 per cent in 1980. In 1974, the Society of Motor Manufacturers and Traders (SMMT) successfully lobbied the government for protection from these imports. There was not much anyone could do about the European competition but Japanese cars were a different matter. By 1975 an agreement was reached between the SMMT and its Japanese counterpart to limit imports of Japanese cars into Britain. Datsun UK was given 6 per cent of the UK market (60 per cent of all Japanese car sales in Britain): Datsun UK sold between 80,000 and 100,000 cars a year in the late 1970s, as against 28,000 Toyotas and 19,500 Hondas.

The Thatcher Government, elected in 1979, rejected such protectionist arguments. It decided instead to adopt precisely the opposite policy from its predecessors: it was prepared to facilitate foreign producers, partly as a way of bypassing the problems of their British competitors and of forcing them to adapt to more modern practices and industrial relations. What Botnar had understood was that Nissan could help the British Government rid itself of British Leyland.

Previous Governments had already agreed to bring Honda into the UK to co-manufacture British Leyland cars. So the principle of Japanese car manufacturers operating in Britain had already been accepted. In reality, however, the Honda deal was something of a facade, since it essentially involved the Japanese manufacturer sending kits to Britain for assembly and collecting a commission for each car thus produced.

Botnar strongly advised Nissan not to follow the Honda example. He told Nissan Motor Company that British Leyland was situated in the wrong part of the country, that the workforce was left wing, demoralised and of low quality, and that its interests and those of Nissan were opposite. He strongly urged NMC, in February 1980, to push instead for a greenfield site, geographically far away from the industrial problems associated with the mammoth national car giant in Oxford and the Midlands.

Botnar argued in his correspondence with Nissan in Japan that previous British Governments had pushed British Leyland into a downward spiral by injecting it with ever larger sums of taxpayers' money, and that the result was that few Europeans would contemplate buying British cars any more because "the quality and reliability of British products has been totally destroyed over the last 20 years". They would, however, he claimed, contemplate buying Japanese ones made in the UK, and so the market opportunities were very considerable.

On 31 July 1980, a meeting was held at the UK Department of Industry in London, hosted by the Minister of State, Lord Trenchard, to discuss the project. It was attended by the Vice President of Nissan Motor Company, Masataka Okuma, Octav Botnar and others. Okuma told the British officials that Botnar had recommended the UK as the best place for NMC to choose if it wanted to manufacture cars in Europe.[205] He said that Nissan was giving serious thought to the possibility of UK investment, although nothing had yet been decided. There were many complicated problems to address and Nissan was also looking at other EC countries such as Spain, but the problem in that case was a relatively small domestic market and a need, therefore, for the majority of production to be exported. The UK was a good candidate because it was politically stable, had a good industrial base, secure oil supplies and good quality labour.

There were, however, difficult problems in respect of labour relations: both Lord Trenchard and Okuma raised this issue. Trenchard pointed out that such problems tended to be concentrated in large organisations and in declining industries, and that new legislation was in hand relating to secondary picketing and closed shops. He also pointed out that rising unemployment was "influencing trade union opinion more powerfully". Okuma was not entirely persuaded by Trenchard's assurances, and asked about the prospect of public sector strikes affecting things like electricity supply. He also asked about "wildcat" strikes and whether it was possible to establish a single union operation.

Okuma also indicated that Nissan was interested to learn what level of financial assistance might be made available. He said that the first step was to decide whether Nissan should proceed to a detailed study and that, should this be decided, an outline programme for investment would be prepared and presented to the Department of Industry for further discussion.

In contrast to the hard work which Botnar subsequently had to do to convince the Japanese, his plan won the immediate support of the new Thatcher Government, and in particular of Trenchard's replacement as Minister of State at the Department of Industry, Norman (later Lord) Tebbit. Botnar and Okuma met him to discuss the project on 27 January 1981, an indication of the national importance of the project.

As Botnar made clear in the letter he sent to Tebbit to prepare the meeting, the possibility of building a factory in Britain would not have existed without the exceptional track record of Datsun UK's car sales in that country over the previous decade.[206] One of the first things that Botnar requested of Tebbit was that the quotas be increased so that an even larger market base for the new factory could be ensured. The current quotas, he argued, were stifling the dealer network which would soon be too small to handle the volume of cars to be produced in the new factory.

The prospect of Nissan – one of the oldest and largest car producers in the world – deciding to expand from its base abroad to build its first foreign car manufacturing factory in the UK, on the basis of market profitability alone, chimed in perfectly with the key tenets of the new Government's creed. (In 1983, Nissan Motor Company would open a manufacturing facility at Smyrna, Tennessee, USA in the form of a truck assembly plant. But Sunderland was to be its first car production facility outside of Japan.) Tebbit, the emblematic Thatcherite minister who would be in charge of ensuring the success of what was to be the largest inward investment project anywhere in Europe at the time, thought it was an excellent plan. Years later, in his memoirs, he called it "the most important foreign investment in the United Kingdom certainly since the Second World War". He subsequently said, "I have no doubt that Mr Botnar played a key role in stimulating the interest of Nissan in making such an investment, and in encouraging the company to commit itself to the project."[207] Tebbit felt that Botnar was repaying a debt to a country that had given him sanctuary and which had helped liberate Europe from Nazism.[208]

Norman Tebbit describes in his memoirs how difficult it was to keep the overall project secret until it was ready to be announced, and how delicate the negotiations were.[209] He knew that there would be hostility from different quarters, including from Conservative friends of British Leyland and of course from the Labour opposition which still had a very statist mindset. Yet he was eager to announce what appeared to be good news as soon as possible. Two days after his meeting with Botnar and Okuma, he rose to address the House of Commons, on 29 January 1981. He was prepared for a fight: being Tebbit, he positively relished the prospect. He said:

"The Nissan Motor Company has approached Her Majesty's Government to seek their views upon the company's intention, subject to a feasibility study, to establish a substantial car manufacturing operation in the United Kingdom. The Government have given a warm welcome to Nissan's proposal and are prepared in principle to give them their approval and support.

Nissan's proposals are to start building a car manufacturing plant, including an engine manufacturing facility, in a development area or special development area in 1982 and to begin production at the end of 1984, reaching the full figure of 200,000 cars a year by 1986.

It is Nissan's intention to achieve a very high local content involving United Kingdom and other EEC suppliers. The local content at the start of production would be 60 per cent, and the company's objective would be to increase this to 80 per cent as soon as possible after full production is reached. The company is confident of achieving a high level of exports from the United Kingdom.

The feasibility study is expected to last four months and to cover a range of matters, including location. Two matters of special importance in Nissan's decision will be the competitiveness of local component manufacturers and the prospects of establishing a good structure for industrial relations.

The Government wish the company well, and hope that the study will reach a satisfactory outcome."[210]

The opposition Tebbit had anticipated manifested itself immediately. A veteran Labour politician, Stanley Orme, Member of Parliament for Salford West and the Shadow Secretary of State for Industry, rose to say he thought the whole plan was useless and that it would have a detrimental effect on the British motor industry. He listed, in the form of a series of questions, all the possible objections one could have to the plan. Tebbit shot back, "I think that those looking for jobs from foreign investment coming into Britain will be deeply shocked and dismayed by the churlish reception to this good news that I have been able to give to the House." He later added wryly that he assumed that Mr Orme's constituents would be pleased to hear that their MP had effectively ruled out their town from hosting the new plant.[211]

In spite of the Government's enthusiasm, the Japanese remained undecided. There were internal disagreements within NMC: some executives were nervous about the risk. The Japanese are cautious people and there were no other similar Japanese factories anywhere in Europe. Nissan did not want to go first and so it took time for the company to agree. Unlike Botnar, they were risk-averse. He often criticised them for that, even though his experience in working with them led him to become interested in Japanese culture and to respect the esteem in which they held trust and long-term relationship. His appreciation of their qualities did not blind him to their weaknesses, including in business and industry. He was aware of these at a time when many in the West put the Japanese economic model on a pedestal and considered it to be the best in the world. Botnar was not surprised when the Japanese economy started to nose-dive in the 1990s.

The aversion to risk was partly due to the fact that, like other Japanese companies, Nissan was notoriously hierarchical. Employees wore name badges indicating also their date of hire, and more junior employees had to wait for their seniors to speak first before voicing their opinion. Loyalty and reliability were rewarded more than enterprise or merit.[212] There is no doubt that Nissan opted for Britain in the end, in spite of its doubts, because its market share was already higher there, thanks to Nissan UK, than anywhere else in the world. There were some 500,000 Nissan cars on British roads in 1980.

A taskforce was set up which discussed employment and industrial relations, financial assistance, environmental protection and local content. NMC initiated a detailed feasibility study based on an assembly plant with a capacity of 5,000 cars per month from one shift working, which could be doubled later. A pressing plant would be part of the facility from its initiation, with engines, axles, suspensions and instruments initially being imported from Japan. One or two basic models would be produced – front wheel drive cars with good fuel economy, suitable for the fleet market and previously introduced in Japan.

In private to Nissan, Tebbit hinted that the workforce was likely to be less prone to drink in the North-East than in other parts of the country (an interesting opinion, at odds with that region's reputation). When NMC asked about industrial relations, he again adopted a hands-off attitude, saying that this was their business. But he did offer some advice: any meetings of workers should be conducted in company time, and on the company's premises, so as to avoid the presence of outside agitators. This had been a long-running problem dogging British industrial relations for decades.

The Japanese still needed a good deal of prodding. Mrs Thatcher herself flew to Tokyo to meet Nissan in September 1982 to try to convince the company that Britain was very interested in the proposed factory.[213] Still the Japanese demurred.

In October 1983, NMC President Takashi Ishihara and NMC Chairman Katsuji Kawamata sent a special emissary to visit Botnar. Teiichi Hara explained that he had been sent to give Mr Botnar an outline of the potential Nissan project as it was then being negotiated with the British Government. He said that he had also come:

"to get an assurance from Mr Botnar that he can sell an additional 100,000 Nissan cars to be produced in UK, for without such an assurance it would be difficult for Nissan to make its final decision on this project, and Mr Kawamata feels that only Mr Botnar can do it".[214]

In other words, for the factory project to proceed, Botnar needed to guarantee that, in addition to the 100,000 cars a year which Nissan UK was already selling, he would guarantee to sell all the 100,000 cars a year which Nissan would build in Britain, i.e. a total of 200,000 cars a year. This was a considerable challenge and required significant levels of expertise and investment.

Botnar accepted that it would be possible to guarantee the additional sales, provided that he could build up his dealer network by appointing new dealers. With this proviso, he agreed to provide the guarantee and the two men signed a formal commitment in October 1983. However, Botnar also required that his company be allowed to import an additional number of cars, over and above the national quota, before the factory opened. This was so that his dealer network could get up to speed before the cars started to roll off the production line in the UK, building up the market for the cars which were to be made in Britain. In the event, this increase in the quota was never agreed and yet nonetheless Botnar managed to increase the dealer network and sell the additional cars anyway once production started.

It had taken three years of intensive negotiation to get this far. Not only would the deal never have been done without the success of Nissan UK stretching back many years, but also it depended upon Nissan UK's agreement to intensify its sales in the future, even though this required massive investment in new dealerships but with no new cars to sell until the factory commenced production.

However, even at this stage, the Japanese would commit only to an assembly plant, leaving open the possibility – or not – of building a fully-fledged manufacturing plant. Tebbit, who by then had been promoted to Secretary of State for Trade and Industry, addressed the House of Commons on 1 February 1984:

"I am pleased to inform the House that the Government and Nissan have reached an understanding on the basis for a Nissan car plant in the United Kingdom. The President of Nissan, Mr. Takashi Ishihara, and I have signed heads of agreement today.

Subject to a satisfactory outcome of negotiations with United Kingdom trade unions and local authorities, Nissan will proceed with the construction of a car plant on a greenfield site of substantial acreage – probably around 800 acres – within a development or special development area.

The first phase will be a pilot plant, to begin production in 1986, providing an assembly capacity of 24,000 cars a year based on imported kits. These will be treated as though they were built-up imports in the context of the discussions between the Society of Motor Manufacturers and Traders and the Japan Automobile Manufacturers Association, both of whom have given their agreement to this arrangement.

During this phase Nissan intends to gain experience of general operating conditions in the United Kingdom, to develop effective relationships with local component manufacturers and establish the prospects for further development.

Nissan will decide, not later than 1987, whether to proceed to phase 2 which will provide capacity for 100,000 units on a full manufacturing basis. If Nissan decides to proceed to phase 2, production would start by 1990 at 60 per cent local content on an ex-works price basis. Full production would be reached in 1991, with 80 per cent local content being achieved and maintained from the middle of 1991.

In addition to regional development grants, the Government will also be ready to provide selective assistance of up to £35 million if Nissan proceeds to phase 2; that is equivalent to 10 per cent of the total capital costs of both phases. In phase 1, the plant will employ directly between 400 and 500 people, and in phase 2 about 2,700 people, but particularly in phase 2 the potential total direct and indirect employment will be considerably greater.

This project represents an important opportunity to create fresh investment and jobs in the motor industry. It will introduce a major, efficient new domestic customer for the United Kingdom components sector; and it represents a constructive step forward in the dialogue between Europe and Japan on trade and investment. For those reasons I am sure

that the House will join me in welcoming the Nissan project to
the United Kingdom." [215]

In due course, and thanks to the intensive investment programme
by Nissan UK and its sister company AFG in new dealerships, NMC did
eventually move to Phase 2. The deal was therefore concluded thanks to
a triangular discussion between Botnar, NMC in Japan and the British
Government. Each of the three parties was crucial to the deal; but the
initiative was Botnar's.

Tebbit later commented that his role as minister had been
that of a facilitator, bringing people together who otherwise
might not have been able to cooperate, but that he had not been
a manager.[216] There is no denying that the British Government
emphatically wanted the project to succeed. Indeed, Tebbit's role
in dealing with the opposition was key. He repeatedly told the
House of Commons, in the face of accusatory questioning from
Labour MPs, that the market would decide the fate of the industry
and that only the clients of the future factory would guarantee
the jobs there. When opponents appealed to patriotic sentiment to
argue against the Japanese, Tebbit responded with a characteristic
killer retort, "Surely it is better for the British to buy Japanese cars
made by British workers than to buy German cars manufactured
by Turks."

So when NMC finally agreed to go ahead with the full factory,
the decision was trumpeted as a victory for the Government's new
business-friendly policies. Nissan's decision appeared to confirm the
position for which the Conservative Government had fought for so
long, namely that state subsidies were not only not the solution to
the problems of the British motor industry. Instead, they were part
of the problem. In addition to the obvious benefit of showing that
jobs would be created, a new car plant built by a foreign company
would be an emblem of the new direction the British and eventually

world motor industry should take. So indeed it proved: ever since the mid-1980s, car manufacture has ceased to be dominated by national champions and has instead become a business of multi-nationals involved in ever more complicated forms of international crossover ownership. Nissan's great Japanese rivals, Honda and Toyota, would later follow its lead and set up their own factories in Swindon and Derbyshire. The Conservative Government, which delighted in presenting itself not only as business-friendly but also as being in the avant-garde of a new industrial and even social revolution, wanted the Nissan plant to show that Britain had turned the corner away from its bad industrial relations and that it was now capable of attracting investment from around the world.

Nissan's decision therefore chimed in with – and reinforced – the euphoric mood in the heyday of Thatcherism. When the factory finally opened in 1986, on the site of a former RAF airfield in Washington, a suburb of Sunderland in Tyne & Wear in the depressed North-East of England, it was a national event which made the headlines. This was the radical Prime Minister's second term, she having been triumphantly re-elected in 1983 after the Falklands War; 1984 was the year of the year-long miners' strike, one of the most vicious social conflicts anywhere in post-war Europe, a conflict which was eventually won, at huge apparent political and economic cost, by the Government; and it was during the period 1983-1987 that the most radical steps were undertaken. These included such flagship projects as the privatisation of the national telephone monopoly, British Telecom, as well as other industrial giants like British Aerospace.

However, in some respects the opening of the Nissan factory in Sunderland trumped even these achievements. Certainly, it has been described, many years later, as "Thatcher's greatest legacy" by the very un-Thatcherite BBC.[217] One of the civil servants involved in the deal gave his view thus:

"Sir Robin Mountfield, the civil servant in charge of the negotiations, told BBC Radio 4's *Where Did It All Go Right?* that this was 'one of the few occasions where Government intervention has had a beneficial effect at relatively minor cost in improving not only the volume of UK car manufacturing, but setting a sort of gold standard for manufacturing technology right through the engineering sector'.

Industry experts believe that investment, and the improvements it stimulated, saved British manufacturing.

'If those things were not done at that time, getting the inward investment, getting Japanese companies here, we would have been wiped out from the point of view of manufacturing. I mean there would have been nothing left here,' according to Lord Bhattacharyya, who advised both Mrs Thatcher and Tony Blair."[218]

Because she had herself also lobbied Nissan in Tokyo, Margaret Thatcher was invited to open the Sunderland plant, in an official ceremony held on 8 September 1986. Botnar was there on the dais alongside Mrs Thatcher. His old friend Takashi Ishihara, by now the Chairman of Nissan Motor Company, paid him a heartfelt tribute in his speech saying that, without Botnar, Nissan would not have built the factory. The event was trumpeted as regenerating a part of the country whose shipbuilding and coal mining industries had been decimated and where there was no history of car manufacture at all.

The site chosen for the factory was the 800-acre former airfield of RAF Usworth, at Washington, Tyne & Wear. It was just five miles from the Port of Tyne, through which Nissan could easily import components and export finished cars. The site had good road connections and was also close to Newcastle airport. It truly was a depressed area: when the company first advertised 450 jobs, it received 25,000 applications.

The factory proved to be an enormous success over the long term. In 2016, as UK car production reached levels not seen for more than 15 years, the Sunderland factory was the biggest and most productive car plant in the UK. With this success came political clout, as was visible in the aftermath of the Brexit referendum of June 2016, when Nissan was very quickly able to get assurances from the British Government that its interests would be protected after the UK left the EU.[219] Journalists and opposition politicians suspected some sort of behind-the-scenes deal between the Government and the car manufacturer, possibly involving secret guarantees.[220] The speculation was that Nissan had effectively blackmailed the Government by threatening to close the plant if it did not get what it wanted. The power of the auto giants has long been recognised, as these quotes from *The Nissan Enigma* (1992)[221] clearly demonstrate:

"Japanese auto firms are now the only genuinely global ones… The decision making power now established in the hands of these titans of late-twentieth-century capitalism can make or break notions of local, or even national, political independence."

Botnar had achieved spectacular triumphs with the success of Nissan UK. Paradoxically, his greatest success – the construction of the Nissan factory in Britain – marked the beginning of the end of his relationship with Nissan in Japan. Once again in Botnar's life, success was to be the prelude to disaster.

CHAPTER 10

THE BREAKDOWN OF THE RELATIONSHIP WITH THE JAPANESE

If all men count with you, but none too much...

Botnar had worked closely with the Japanese since the early 1970s. In 1975, Datsun UK had relocated to Durrington, Worthing, to occupy a new purpose-built headquarters which brought together, side-by-side, administration, training school and parts warehouse. The offices were contained within a state-of-the-art marble-clad building. Its upper floors commanded spectacular views to the South Downs one way, and out to the sea the other. Directly alongside the offices, and connected to them, was the huge parts warehouse.

The opening ceremony was carried out by Tadahiro Iwakoshi, the then President of Nissan Motor Company, on 20 October 1975. Iwakoshi's presence in Britain for the opening of the new building had been a matter of great significance and prestige for Nissan UK and for Botnar personally. The top brass of NMC had very high status in Japan and were quite inaccessible. Iwakoshi's presence had reflected NMC's high regard for Botnar and his company and it marked the start of a golden period in the relationship between NMC and Nissan UK.

When Iwakoshi stood down in 1977, Botnar found himself holding a number of the Japanese senior management in high regard, notably Chairman Katsuji Kawamata, the new President, Takashi Ishihara, and Executive Vice President, Masataka Okuma. Kawamata and Ishihara likewise respected Botnar, and they depended upon his abilities and his advice. This was a powerful and mutually profitable relationship. Botnar and Ishihara had an understanding between themselves that any major operational difficulty could be referred directly to Ishihara himself, who would resolve the matter personally. Botnar never abused this facility, and the procedure was rarely called upon. However, when it was, Ishihara always took immediate action. Their relationship could not have been closer nor more effective.

In March 1986, Kawamata died. Ishihara had stepped up to the Chairman's role the previous year, and away from day-to-day operational matters. A year earlier, in response to NMC's domestic sales dropping year-on-year for more than a decade, a management reshuffle had taken place. Yutaka Kume, an engineer who had been with the company for almost 40 years, had been made President.

Kume appointed Yoshikazu Kawana to head up the European operations. At this stage, all had appeared to be well, with the Japanese continuing to value Botnar's contribution. This was hardly surprising, for in 1985 Nissan UK had sold no fewer than 105,000 cars. Nevertheless, the agreement to build the factory, although in most respects a highly positive development, also created conditions which led to the eventual collapse of the collaboration between Botnar's Nissan UK and NMC.

In 1981, once NMC had accepted the principle of building a factory in Britain, talks had been held in London concerning the acquisition by NMC of Datsun UK. Botnar and NMC's Executive Vice President, Masataka Okuma, met at the newly-constructed Inn on the Park hotel (now the Four Seasons Hotel) over two days in November 1981, the result of which was an agreed memorandum.

Okuma had begun by making clear that, should NMC decide to build a manufacturing/assembly plant in the UK, it would be essential for NMC to control Datsun UK. Botnar had responded by referring to the principles he had outlined in his letter to Okuma dated 1 June 1981, in particular that the shareholders of Datsun UK recognised and agreed that it was in the long-term interests of all parties for NMC to acquire control of Datsun UK, and that all shareholders had in principle to agree to sell their shares to NMC.

Both sides agreed that 100 per cent of the shares in Datsun UK must be acquired, the acquisition to commence with production of cars in the UK. It was agreed that the price of the shares would be based on the company's audited balance sheet as at 31 July 1981, with adjustments linked to the precise acquisition date, based on changes to the net asset value of the company and to the value of Datsun UK's real estate.

Book value would be confirmed by physical stocktaking, which would be the basis of valuation of all assets except real estate and Datsun UK's investment in subsidiaries. Each party would appoint "an internationally reputed specialised valuation company" to check and confirm all assets. The results of the independent valuation would not be binding on either party but would form the basis for negotiation.

The additional matter of goodwill was also dealt with expressly in the memorandum, with both sides agreeing that this was the most difficult item to value. Goodwill is the element of a deal which compensates the seller for the loss of future profit. (In the 1980s, a company might typically be valued by at least seven or eight times annual earnings.) Okuma stated that this should be based on an assessment of a reasonable net profit after tax ratio to turnover, and that goodwill should represent the purchase of a number of years of such profits. The appropriate number of years would be proposed by the valuation company.

Okuma also stated that NMC wished only to acquire Datsun UK's distribution network and parts operation. However, Botnar pointed out that related companies such as Datsun Finance, Datsun Fleet and Leasing and Datsun Parts Transport were vertically integrated with the business and were an essential part of it.

Negotiations took a long time and it was not until May 1985, more than three years later, that NMC and Botnar signed a letter of intent for the sale and acquisition of what by then had become Nissan UK. The shares were to be acquired in two stages. The first, which was to take place "no later than 31 July 1986", would involve 26 per cent of the shares. The remaining 74 per cent would then be acquired by mutual agreement, but no later than 31 July 1988.

NMC had said initially that it wanted to acquire only the distribution of vehicles and parts. Nevertheless, when Botnar had said that the subsidiaries formed an essential part of the whole operation, NMC agreed that it would make sense to acquire them too, but that they would have to be valued separately from the core business. Botnar told them that if they decided they did not want to acquire the subsidiaries, then these could easily be hived off in whole or in part but continue to maintain the service they offered to Datsun UK if required.

In November 1985, four years almost exactly to the day of the initial agreement, a memorandum of understanding was signed which confirmed the letter of intent which had been signed six months earlier. Nissan UK and NMC had agreed on all the underlying conditions of a sale to NMC. All that remained was "How much?" and "How would NMC finance it?" Botnar had built a very valuable business, and its cash purchase was well beyond the means of even NMC. NMC sought assistance, and brought in Mitsui & Co, one of Japan's *sogo shosha*, its huge international trading conglomerates.

One condition of the November 1985 memorandum was a reconfirmation that Nissan UK upgrade the dealer network to cater for the much greater number of cars it had committed to sell in 1983 as a condition of the factory's construction. Botnar embarked on a rapid programme of dealership acquisition and development. He realised that there were many cities and towns, up and down the country, where Nissan was not adequately represented. Initially, Botnar acquired some 80 extra dealerships which continued to be run as though they were independent businesses, but with the full financial backing of Nissan UK. Even this was not enough.

Botnar therefore set about creating a parallel and overlapping network of wholly-owned dealers under the brand name Automotive & Financial Group. This new structure acquired dealerships with great rapidity – some eight sites a month over a three-year period. Location was key: two-thirds of the sites acquired in this period were in places where there had previously been no Nissan dealership at all. Between 1985 and 1988, 280 such sites were bought, either by converting existing garages or by building new ones. The purchases were often undertaken at breakneck speed: having decided on a site, the staff would grab the local solicitor, jump into a helicopter, and the deal would be signed that afternoon.

Eventually AFG would employ some 4,000 people. Its sister company, Automotive Financial Services, provided consumer credit for new and used cars and working capital to the dealerships. By the late 1980s, Datsun Finance Ltd. and then AFS had lent some £1.5 billion to 500,000 customers. AFG became the largest motor retailing company in the UK and one of the largest in Europe. The 1981 agreement had left it open whether NMC would buy the dealerships as well, or just the distribution of vehicles and parts, and in any case these other parts of the business (dealerships and finance) were to be valued separately from the core distribution of Nissan UK.

Botnar invested heavily in the AFG dealerships, especially in their physical size, so that they would have the space to sell a higher volume of new and used vehicles. The sale and re-sale of cars, often through the same dealer, represented repeated opportunities for profit – a car would be sold, for example, first to a company fleet, then a year later to a young professional, then later on again to a first-time buyer. At every stage the dealership could make a profit. However, it was difficult to find people of the right calibre to manage dealerships. Many salesmen, who were often young, did not have the required combination of management and entrepreneurial skills coupled with experience. To succeed as a car dealer, one needed to have an intimacy with the business plus good general financial and management skills. The difference between success and failure lies in small but important judgements like buying at the right time and valuing part-exchange vehicles correctly, as well as managing a team of sales, service and administrative staff.

During this period, external factors intervened which complicated the relationship between Botnar and the Japanese. This was Japan's heyday. Her industry seemed unstoppable and her economic model commanded respect and envy around the world. As a result of the country's impressive economic performance, and especially after the Plaza Agreement of September 1985 – at which the US, Japan, Britain, France and West Germany agreed to force down the value of the dollar – the yen rose sharply on international markets, gaining over 50 per cent against the US dollar in two years. This pushed up the price of Japanese exports sharply.

However Botnar was a tough negotiator and operated Nissan UK with maximum economy and efficiency. As a result, UK sales continued to be very healthy in spite of the difficult foreign exchange environment. Profits were £44 million in the year to July 1986 and £65 million the following year (on sales of £796 million). As the negotiations between Botnar and the Japanese over the fate of his companies dragged on, and as deadlines were missed, he began to believe that NMC thought that Nissan UK's profits were merely a reflection of the superiority of its cars and had nothing to do with his business skills or with the conglomerate that he had built up around the core business.

This perception was odd in view of the fact that Nissan's market share in Japan itself had fallen every year since the 1970s. By 1988, the original 1986 deadline having been missed, Nissan UK and NMC came to widely different views about the value of the business, and Botnar's old contacts were no longer in charge.

The merchant bank which Nissan UK had engaged valued the company at £750 million, while the Japanese claimed it was worth only £330 million.[222] The huge gap between the two valuations incensed Botnar. By November 1987, Botnar came to the conclusion that the

Japanese were either unwilling or unable to buy the whole of his business and so he suggested that the deal be confined to distribution alone. He offered to sell NMC the core distribution business alone for £390 million, whilst retaining the network of owned dealers (AFG), the financial group, and the car transport unit, which comprised 30 car transporters and 15 parts trucks. NMC declined this pared-down alternative. They wanted control of the whole business but they did not want to pay a market price.

The negotiations dragged on. Botnar considered that his intimate knowledge of the market, his micro-managing, his energetic encouragement of the dealers, and the investment and infrastructure he had devoted to expanding the dealerships, to bringing them up to the highest standards and also to boost second-hand car sales, were all the keys to Nissan UK's success. He was convinced that the sale of a huge network of dealerships was not just a transaction of property rights or legal franchises. It was also the sale of a large amount of accumulated knowledge and logistical practice, involving very detailed ordering and delivery procedures; a huge financial services operation for hire-purchase; business savvy; and a network of personal relations.

It was clear that there was a chasm between the two sides, which Botnar eventually concluded could not be bridged. He remembered the matter of Nissan Suisse, which he had bought as Datsun Suisse in 1978. Between then and the time he sold it, he had trebled its market share, and under Botnar, Nissan Suisse was turning in annual profits of around 10 million Swiss francs. Botnar nevertheless sold the company back to NMC in November 1984 for its net asset value alone, something that was never contemplated for Nissan UK. Within three years of NMC's ownership, Nissan Suisse had lost market share to such an extent that it was being overtaken by minor competitors. Worse, far from being profitable, it was now incurring losses.

In November 1988, Botnar wrote a long letter to the President of Nissan Motor Company, Yutaka Kume, explaining the position. He began by expressing disappointment that, whilst Mr Ishihara had in the past always been prepared to listen to his concerns personally and to act on them directly, Kume had delegated that responsibility to others. Those people, instead of resolving problems, appeared intent on creating difficulties, an unhappy state of affairs.

He reminded Kume of the history of Nissan UK and its outstanding success, which had been achieved in the face of great difficulty. He pointed out the scale of the investment which Nissan UK had been asked to make in the dealer network, which was already selling huge additional numbers of Nissan cars. He criticised the naivety of senior NMC managers in imagining that they were able to take over and run a business as complex as Nissan UK with little training or preparation, and with no understanding of either the company or the market in which it operated:

"Suddenly Nissan presented itself as being ready to take over Nissan UK within a few months, with no training of any staff, no preparation, no knowledge of the company or the market and with no interest in the effect such a takeover would have on the management and staff of Nissan UK or the dealer body, and regardless of the fact that relations between Nissan UK staff and the dealer body had greatly deteriorated in recent years.

We were amazed at how Nissan personnel could have acquired the intricate know-how and expertise necessary for running a complex business like Nissan UK, without having any knowledge of the business. Yet the whole problem as far as the Nissan delegates were concerned was to find out the purchase price – everything else was no problem...

The Nissan delegates were very interested in Nissan UK's overall profitability, but although we tried to explain the business to them, they were not interested and seemed not to understand that the profit shown on the balance sheet is not generated only from new car sales, but mainly from returns on retained dividends, the finance business, transport, accessories, property rental and retail activities etc...

Such a level of crass and mindless behaviour is really unbelievable in a company of purported international standing..."

Botnar concluded his letter by saying:

"As far as the UK is concerned, we would ask you not to worry. We are doing everything necessary and possible to develop the business in view of the expansion of the UK plant. We are also ready to repeat that we are not considering selling the company. Should the situation ever change in the future, Nissan would have first refusal. I trust that this letter will not offend you or anyone else at Nissan. Although some issues may be unpleasant to face, my only intention in writing is to try to explain a very complex situation and series of events with the objective of being of help to Nissan."

Botnar's forthright language did not go down well in Japan, whose companies very much stood on ceremony. Nevertheless, it was accepted that all understandings about the acquisition of Nissan UK would be removed from the table and negotiations would cease. Instead, it was proposed that a meeting take place between Botnar and Yoshikazu Kawana, Nissan's European head, with the professed objective of re-establishing the formerly good relationship between the two companies.

In spite of these promises, from that point on NMC started to restrict the model mix which was made available to Nissan UK, resulting in an increasingly narrow product range.

At the same time, differential pricing became more and more evident, with NMC offering better prices to European countries where NMC itself owned the Nissan concession. The price difference between cars offered to the UK and those offered to, say, Germany or the Netherlands averaged 19-24 per cent.

In May 1989, against the background of disagreements over transfer pricing and the sale of Nissan UK as a whole, *The Sunday Times* published its first Rich List. Botnar was listed as the ninth richest person in Britain, with a fortune estimated at £1 billion, which made him richer than people like Sir James Goldsmith, Robert Maxwell or Alan Sugar, and only slightly behind John Paul Getty II. The newspaper had incorrectly attributed money held in trust for charity as Botnar's personal wealth. Botnar threatened to sue and the newspaper published a retraction. The damage was however done: the idea that Botnar had gigantic personal disposable wealth only poured fuel on to the already smouldering resentment which the bosses of NMC felt against him.

In 1989, price increases from NMC were accompanied by unexplained failures to supply. In July, the month before Nissan UK would expect to make 22 per cent of its annual sales because of the annual August 1st registration plate letter change, NMC inflicted a 50 per cent volume reduction on Nissan UK.[223] Nissan dealerships throughout Britain lost thousands of sales worth tens of millions of pounds.

In August 1989, the disagreement over the sale of Nissan UK unresolved, Botnar transferred a large part of the shares in AFGH (the holding company which owned the dealerships and the financial services) to Union Bank of Switzerland. This so-called "sale" of AFGH to UBS, which nonetheless left him in operational control of the company, was a major blow to the Japanese. They perceived that Botnar had outwitted them and that some 200 dealerships had at a stroke been taken out of any potential deal.

Botnar reasoned that, as he had invested £350 million into building up the dealership network, and in giving it the physical facilities it needed to do the job, he had every right to maintain control of it and to get a good price for the company in the case of a sale. Not only was Botnar's dealership network the largest car retailing group in the UK, and one of the largest in Europe; the finance part of the business was also one of the UK's biggest finance companies.[224] These were all legally separate entities from Nissan UK but inseparable from the core business. Indeed, they were the keys to its phenomenal success.

In October 1989, Botnar led a Nissan UK team which flew to Tokyo intending to address the overall problem. He received assurances that NMC remained committed to working with Nissan UK, and that its plans were still based on the achievement of sales in Britain of 200,000 units per year, a fact which was subsequently reconfirmed in writing to Botnar in February 1990.

Notwithstanding reassurances, the team came away from Japan with a firm belief that the Japanese were trying to undermine Nissan UK entirely. Botnar wrote to Kume again, expressing the view that NMC's tactics were designed to make trading conditions for him unacceptable and the franchise so unprofitable that he would be forced into relinquishing Nissan altogether. Botnar told Kume that he found this disturbing as he had done so much to support the establishment of a factory in Britain, with his sales commitment making the factory possible.

Matters got progressively worse, culminating in a surprise announcement in November 1990 that Nissan Europe was to set up a London office, pointedly making no reference to Nissan UK. As part of its strategy to sideline Nissan UK, NMC therefore set up its own administration and PR office in Britain. This was an open declaration of war.

The problems with over-pricing continued during 1990, this

time focusing on the price at which Nissan UK was expected to buy the Primera, the new model being built at the plant in Washington. For the launch of the Primera in September 1990 – the pricing of this car had been one of the issues over which Botnar was that year in conflict with the Japanese – Nissan UK and the Japanese-owned Nissan Europe (together with Nissan Motor Manufacturing UK, the Japanese- owned company created to manage the Sunderland factory) each sent out separate invitations to the launch press conference. It required considerable effort on Nissan UK's part to clear up the confusion.

The press spoke openly of "a full-scale power struggle over the UK concession"[225] and the bust-up between the two companies was common knowledge.

During the run-up to the opening of the factory in Washington, NMC had engaged the advisory services of former Labour Party Transport Minister Richard Marsh, by then a crossbench peer. In determining how to get rid of Botnar, Nissan had sought advice from Marsh and from the public relations consultancy, Grayling, of which Marsh was then Chairman. Thus was conceived "Project T – Public relations strategy", which included the following elements:

"Attack and destroy the image Botnar has been projecting, especially in recent weeks, of a successful and philanthropic British businessman being victimised by a Japanese car giant."

Displaying NMC's envy of Nissan UK's success, the file continued:

"… NMC's profitability has been lowered, whilst NUK group has been maintaining its profitability, thereby resulting in an unjust distribution of profits."

At the meeting of the NMC Management Council on 27 August 1990, PR consultants Grayling insisted that it was essential to "take the initiative in the communication war" with the goal of destroying Botnar's reputation. Teams of people were set up to handle the expected volume of calls from the press and to coordinate NMC's message.

Against this backdrop, in a letter dated 27 December 1990, NMC's European head, Yoshikazu Kawana, wrote to Botnar stating that Nissan UK's distribution franchise was being terminated. He cited as justification alleged breaches of the distribution agreement by Nissan UK. The letter to Botnar was sent by fax which, because it was the Christmas break, meant that it arrived in an office in Worthing where no one was working. At the same time, though, press releases announcing the termination were sent to journalists, also by fax. Jim North, a director of Nissan UK, planning to catch up on some work between Christmas and New Year, happened to be in the office on 27 December when he was surprised to receive a telephone call from the *Financial Times*. He was even more surprised when he was asked for his views on the termination, about which he of course knew nothing, as did no one else at Nissan UK.

The termination was to take effect 12 months later, at midnight on 31 December 1991. Nissan UK, the most rewarding partner NMC had ever had, was being presented with just one year to redeploy £350 million of investment and to safeguard the jobs of Botnar's 4,000 employees.

The unilateral cancellation of the franchise was a terrible blow. Botnar protested that it was contrary to the terms of the agreement signed in 1971 and updated in 1972, which provided for a five-year notice period. Both these agreements, moreover, had been solemnly reaffirmed to Botnar in a letter sent by the President of NMC, Yutaka Kume, on 10 February 1987, in which he wrote:

"It has never been the intention of Nissan Motor Company to cancel the sole and exclusive rights of Nissan UK Ltd to import, sell and distribute Nissan products and vehicles in the United Kingdom of Great Britain and Northern Ireland. We therefore confirm herewith that the Memorandum of Distribution Agreement between Nissan UK (formerly Datsun UK) and Nissan Motor Company dated 1st January 1971 and as amended by letter from Nissan Motor Company to Nissan UK on 6th December 1972, remains valid."

Within days, NMC began to unveil its plans, advertising for staff and independent dealers to join them. Simultaneously, the Japanese banks which were part of the banking syndicate which provided the £500 million line of credit to Nissan UK's finance company unexpectedly and unilaterally withdrew. Even though the banks in question had been minor contributors only, the syndicate required unanimity of support. The Japanese banks' withdrawal therefore caused the syndicate to collapse. This deliberate act was calculated to deliver a mortal blow to Nissan UK. However, Botnar managed to raise capital elsewhere, and NMC's plans were thus thwarted.

Botnar was then approached by representatives of Mitsui & Co., which was to have provided NMC with the finance needed to buy Nissan UK a few years earlier. They urged Botnar to reach a "compromise" with NMC – that was, they claimed, the Japanese way of dealing with such situations. Botnar was having none of it.

In March 1991, Botnar was approached once again by NMC itself, with a new offer to buy the business. The intent was serious but the proposed purchase price was not. NMC had calculated that Nissan's independent dealers, starved of product, would switch automatically to the new operation, and at no cost to NMC. With that part of the equation "in the bank", as they thought, the only thing in which they were truly interested was AFGH's network of dealers which, deprived too of cars to sell, would be valued as a much less attractive business. NMC expected to pick up the business – the product of 20 years' painstaking work – for a song. Realising that this was the plan, Botnar rejected the approach.

NMC deployed a further tactic. By inventing a "need" to contact warranty holders, NMC persuaded the Driver and Vehicle Licensing Centre in Swansea to provide NMC with the names and addresses of all 400,000 customers of Nissan UK. At a stroke, and at almost no cost, NMC had acquired a marketing database which Nissan UK had built – once again over 20 years, and at a cost of tens of millions of pounds.

On 10 May 1991, NMC petitioned the Japan Commercial Arbitration Association (JCAA) for arbitration, seeking to confirm the cancellation of Nissan UK's distribution rights, prohibit Nissan UK from using Nissan trademarks and, adding insult to injury, to have Nissan UK pay the cost of the arbitration.

In its Petition for Arbitration, NMC cast aspersions on Botnar's past. The petition contained these words:

"With reference to Mr Botnar, with the exception of his age (reported as approximately 80 years old), few details of his life are clear. Even in the press in the United Kingdom, he is treated as quite an enigmatic figure. His place of birth, identity and career all remain unclear to the press. If we rely on press information, all that we know about Mr Botnar is that he holds a passport from the former East Germany, that he has residences in both Switzerland and Spain. There is little evidence of what Mr Botnar did during and prior to World War II. Mr Botnar has relatively few public documents or records."[226]

It would be difficult to pile more untruths and innuendos into so few sentences. NMC had been a major business partner of

Botnar's since the original Memorandum of Distribution Agreement was signed on 1 January 1971. Now the company was claiming, after working closely with him for 20 years, that he was a shadowy figure about whom no one knew anything. NMC had had plenty of time to find out such things if it had had any genuine worries.

The allegation that Botnar had something to hide about his wartime or pre-war record cut to the quick. A very private man, he had indeed never discussed his Resistance exploits. Now, his natural reticence was being cynically exploited to destroy him. The truth was being shamelessly turned on its head. Later that year, Botnar wrote to several of his former Resistance comrades – Boris Holban, Irma Mico and Georges Filip-Lefort, who were all still alive and living in France – to ask them to send written affidavits confirming the truth about what he had done during the war. This they did, and in glowing terms (quoted in Chapter 3), but Botnar chose never to make those statements public.

NMC made another, even more serious, allegation within its petition. It suggested that Nissan UK was involved in tax fraud. NMC wrote that the corporate structures of Nissan UK had "been concealed for tax evasion purposes".[227] It also alleged that Nissan UK had become involved in vessel chartering for the purposes of creating "a structure whereby Nissan UK could transfer money equivalent to the excess charged for transportation charges to bank accounts in a tax haven".

The so-called "T-file", outlining NMC's strategy, also said that "relevant Government departments" should be briefed as part of the PR strategy. Putting two and two together, the suspicion arises that these "departments" included the Inland Revenue, and that Nissan Motor Company therefore communicated its allegations to the British taxman.

There had been a change of government in Britain at this time, Mrs Thatcher having been ousted by an internal party coup in November 1990 and replaced by John Major. Botnar's old friends from the inner Thatcher circle were no longer in power. Yet NMC, already one of the biggest manufacturers in the United Kingdom, retained huge leverage over the British Government.

The text of the Petition for Arbitration perhaps inadvertently let slip one of the psychological reasons for the falling-out between Nissan UK and NMC: "Regarding the UK manufacturing project, Mr Botnar aggressively provided instructions and comments with Nissan as if he were a co-promoter of the project." In other words, NMC was accusing Botnar of insubordination, just as he had been accused by his enemies in Communist Romania. NMC viewed Botnar as someone they could not control – which was indeed the case – and who did not respect their sense of protocol. Botnar had fallen foul of exactly the same sort of petty resentment which had sealed his downfall in Romania in 1960.

Having received the letter terminating the franchise at the end of December 1990, Botnar immediately set about developing a strategy to save his business. The strategy had two prongs. First, legal proceedings would be initiated against NMC.

On 4 January 1991, a press release was issued in which Nissan UK announced that its solicitors, Herbert Smith, had advised the company that the termination of the franchise was null and void and that Nissan UK would therefore commence proceedings against NMC. The release contained a statement by Botnar himself:

"These developments are extremely regrettable, particularly when one considers what has been achieved over the last twenty years by co-operation and by working towards a common objective. However, Nissan Japan's policies over the past few years, including its failure to respond to opportunities to buy the Company at a fair price, and the service of its invalid notice are an attempt to obtain the benefit of our efforts at no cost."[228]

Nissan UK sought to have the dispute litigated in the English courts. Botnar reasoned that £350 million had been invested into the British dealership network, and that therefore the English courts had jurisdiction. Botnar had great faith in the English commercial court system, believing it to be a fair and independent tribunal. He was bitterly disappointed when the court determined that it did not have jurisdiction, and that instead his dispute with the Japanese would have to be resolved by arbitration.

Nissan UK nonetheless sought a temporary injunction, requiring NMC to continue to supply it with cars until such time as the question of termination of the agreement could be resolved by arbitration. However, the High Court determined that it could not grant such an injunction, on the grounds that the relationship between the two companies appeared to have broken down completely, and that NMC had sufficient financial resources to settle a subsequent award for damages, however large that might be. This decision was confirmed by the Court of Appeal.

At the same time, NMC and its European subsidiaries also took Nissan UK to court to try to prevent the company from using the Nissan name any more.

Thus began a time-consuming and hugely expensive legal battle, fought on ground which was not of Botnar's choosing and where the only certainty was eye-watering legal bills. The odds throughout were stacked against Botnar, and victories were not only modest but few and far between. As luck would have it, one of the rare victories was not managed by Botnar, so distracted was he on other matters, but instead by Nissan UK's sales director, Jim North.

Car production had started in Sunderland in 1986 and, in the early years, only one model, the by then aging Bluebird, was built there. By April 1990, the Bluebird was due to be replaced by a new model, the Primera, to be shown at the Birmingham Motor Show in September 1990. Towards the end of the Bluebird's production at Sunderland, the factory had been struggling to dispose of what had become an outdated and unsaleable model. Nissan UK found it increasingly difficult to sell Bluebirds even though it managed to sell 40,000 of them in 1988. In October 1989, What Car? rated the Bluebird worst in five critical tests out of seven – on performance, handling, safety, cost and overall verdict – against comparable models from Volvo, Peugeot and Ford etc.[229]

In the absence of assistance from distributors in other countries, Nissan UK was asked whether it would take the entirety of the final production, as no-one else would help. Botnar agreed to do this but on condition of the receipt of substantial incentives. After several months of hard negotiation, NMC agreed to pay Nissan UK £6 million if it took all of the unwanted Bluebirds. Botnar was true to his word, not only taking all of the Bluebirds but making sure that his dealers sold them. However, by September 1990, when NMC was due to pay the £6 million as agreed, no monies were forthcoming.

Nissan UK sued for breach of contract, the case eventually coming to court in 1993. By then, Botnar was not only hugely distracted but was living in Switzerland and in any case unable to attend the hearings. Jim North took responsibity for the litigation, his legal team being led by Anthony (later Lord) Grabiner QC. Referring to Botnar's absence, the High Court judge remarked wryly that this was a case of "Hamlet without the Prince". Nissan UK won the case hands down and NMC was ordered to pay the £6 million with interest.[230] Botnar was certain that, had he been allowed to litigate in Britain, the English commercial courts would have dealt with him in a way that arbitration in Japan never did.

With the legal challenge to Nissan's termination notice in place, Botnar's second course of action was immediately to plan for life after Nissan. The massive conglomerate he had built up, its thousands of employees and the independent dealer network needed a replacement franchise to secure a successful future. Through contacts within UBS

Phillips & Drew, discussions commenced early in 1991 with Fiat in Turin, the giant Italian motor manufacturer. The interests of both Fiat and the Botnar Group coincided. Discussions moved fast, with a letter of intent planned for signature by 28 February 1991, and a timetable of objectives outlined after that. Both parties were highly sensitive to the risk of the discussions leaking, hence the need for speed. In addition, codenames were adopted, with the project given the name Foenix, in anticipation of the Botnar Group's re-emergence from the ashes of Nissan UK.

Botnar was a hard negotiator. He was often ready to appear to jeopardise a deal that was about to be signed by demanding a better one. So it was that, in June 1991 – the original optimistic deadlines having slipped – Botnar started to play hardball with the Italians. "These lengthy negotiations have had a very negative effect which may reflect on future relations between the companies and have dampened the enthusiasm of Botnar Group personnel involved in the discussions."[231]

It worked. The deal was soon hammered out, with Fiat even offering Botnar a seat on its board, an offer he declined. On 25 June 1991, Botnar signed a Memorandum of Understanding with Fiat. The same day, in preparation for the transition to Fiat, Nissan UK had announced a drastic reduction in the dealer price of Nissan cars. The plan was to reinvigorate sales for dealers suffering as a result of the Nissan termination, and to facilitate the clearance of Nissan stock ready for the introduction of Fiat. The Memorandum was to be sent to Turin for counter-signature by the Fiat board the following day.

The Memorandum provided for "the assumption by Botnar Group of the full and exclusive responsibility, for the United Kingdom, of import, distribution and sale of new Fiat, Lancia, Alfa Romeo, Maserati and other marques of motor cars and of light commercial vehicles manufactured by FIAT AUTO Group and of the original spare parts relating thereto..." The existing dealership network of

Fiat/Lancia and Alfa Romeo would be integrated into the Botnar Group's distribution and retail sale organisation.

The Fiat deal would unquestionably have dealt a body blow to NMC's plans. Hoewever, Nissan UK was about to find itself plunged into controversy by an event which ultimately killed it off. The Memorandum of Understanding signed by Botnar on 25 June 1991 contained the following words:

"The public announcement of the AGREEMENT will be subject to the approval of both parties and will, in all circumstances, be made in such positive manner as to guarantee the best positive public impact of the transaction and as to foster the good image of Fiat, Lancia and Alfa Romeo products, as well as the good image and reputation of FIAT AUTO and BG (Botnar Group)."

This sentence showed the importance for both parties of the image they would present to the world. For the deal to succeed, both sides needed to be seen in the best possible light, and this need was formally expressed as part of the agreement. However, early in the morning of 26 June 1991, the day after Botnar had signed his copy of the Memorandum, the offices of Nissan UK and AFGH and the private homes of Botnar, and many others connected to his companies, were the subject of the largest Inland Revenue raid in history. The damage to Botnar's image was to prove fatal to the Fiat deal.

CHAPTER 11

A KNOCK ON THE DOOR

If you can meet with Triumph and Disaster
And treat those two impostors just the same...

At 7am on the morning of Wednesday 26 June 1991, without warning, a series of raids took place in Sussex, Surrey, London and Hampshire. 135 officers of the Inland Revenue raided the homes of the directors of Nissan UK and the Company's offices as part of what had been christened *Operation Bluebird* in allusion to the Nissan car.

No one at the company had a clue as to what was happening nor, it seemed, did many of the Revenue officers who appeared not to know what they were looking for. However, in an orchestrated effort to maximise publicity, and create the impression that the Inland Revenue had good reason to believe that serious tax evasion had taken place, the media was tipped off in advance. A helicopter was hovering overhead, television cameras and reporters were waiting on the steps of the offices as staff arrived for work. The Inland Revenue's Head of Public Relations was on site, talking freely to the journalists. When the Revenue was later challenged about the tip-off to the media, officer David Hugo denied that the Revenue was responsible. His explanation for their presence at the start of the raid was, "The press just follow our cars around, that's all."[232]

The officers exercised little discretion in conducting the search, seizing documents from organisations which were not covered by the search warrant. As a result, large amounts of material were seized unlawfully. So indiscriminate was the seizure that old magazines and brochures, the instruction manuals for the heating system and the company's Christmas card list were all taken away. Botnar's medical records were taken, as were files relating to the possible deal with Fiat, and to the dispute with NMC. In fact, many carried recent dates, and fell outside the scope of the warrant. When one of the officers pointed out that papers were not needed because they were from 1990, his colleague just said, "Take everything."

Equipped with six rental vans and dozens of packing containers, the Revenue loaded a vast volume of paperwork into the vans and took it all to their office in Bristol. The vans had not been positioned in front of the loading doors at the side of the building, which would have been the sensible position from which to effect a wholesale removal of files. Here, they would have been out of sight. Instead, the vans were parked at the front entrance of the building, requiring heavy containers to be carried awkwardly down a flight of marble steps in full view of waiting cameras. It was to be many months before any of these papers were returned to their owners, rendering the continued running of a number of businesses extremely difficult.

The Revenue's Head of Public Relations went on record as saying, "This is the biggest operation of this kind we have ever done and we only do it when we expect a serious fraud has taken place." The warrant had been sought under Section 20 (c) of the 1970 Taxes Management Act, requiring the Revenue to have satisfied a circuit judge that it had "reasonable grounds for suspecting tax offences involving serious fraud".

Officers also raided the homes of directors – including Botnar's in Worthing and London – and former directors, and the company's auditors. Botnar was just getting up when officers turned up at his home. Their early arrival reminded him of the night-time knock on the door favoured by Eastern European secret services. He put on his dressing gown, told the taxmen to go about their business, and had his breakfast as usual before being driven down the hill to the office. Officials also turned up at the Botnars' London flat, where Marcela was staying. TV crews even accompanied them, which meant that there were so many people on the doorstep when Marcela answered the door that they could not all get into the flat at once.

Inland Revenue officers Tom Cawdron and Robert Brown led the raids and were responsible for the information lodged in support of the applications for the warrants. Years later, in October 1997, *The Sunday Times* published, under the title "Exposed: the bullying tactics of the taxman", an article which quoted Cawdron and Brown extensively. "They portrayed the Revenue as a ruthless, confrontational agency, prepared to use underhand, even sinister tactics, to extract taxes," wrote the journalist, Paul Ham.[233] Dawn raids, such as the one on Nissan UK were, they said, "routine", as were random audits on innocent members of the public.

Both Brown and Cawdron had by then left the Revenue to work for accountancy firms, advising private clients on the Revenue's investigation methods and how to deal with them. In 1996, Brown had the gall to write to Botnar's solicitor, Mark Spragg, to suggest that Spragg put clients his way so that he and his new firm could provide services including "detailed knowledge of how the Revenue conducts and proceeds with its criminal work as well as really uptodate *(sic)* practical experience of how the Special Compliance Office approaches its investigation work".[234]

The Nissan UK warrant was one of the widest in scope ever issued in English law and, with the benefit of hindsight, should have been challenged immediately in the High Court as defective. The company did not realise this at the time, and the Revenue was thus able to embark on a "fishing expedition" of a scale hitherto unseen.

Botnar remained calm, as is evident from a photograph taken of him in the middle of the raid, which is reproduced in the photographic pages of this book. He has all the confidence of a man with nothing to hide.

On the occasion of a subsequent raid, in October 1991, Botnar reacted in a similar way. Two Revenue officials turned up at the Worthing offices saying they had come to see him, and went straight up to his office on the fourth floor without waiting to be announced. As they were on their way up, the receptionist rang Botnar's office to warn they were on their way. Cool as a cucumber, Botnar calmly walked out of the office and took the service lift down as the officials were coming up in the directors' lift. It was like the early scene in the film, To Catch a Thief, in which John Robie, a former cat burglar and ex-member of the French Resistance played by Cary Grant, similarly gives the police the slip by walking out of his own house and getting on a bus after performing a clever ruse to distract them. Botnar quietly made his way into the huge warehouse, where he prudently dawdled until the men from the Revenue had gone away. On another occasion, he taunted them by saying, "Do you want to search my pockets as well?" – exactly the phrase he had used in Romania in 1959.

The event made front-page news, the media tip-off having worked and in spite of the fact that the war in Yugoslavia had broken out on the same day as the raid. Botnar immediately denounced a conspiracy. He accused the Inland Revenue of acting on behalf of the Japanese to torpedo his imminent deal with Fiat. Using language which implicitly accused the Revenue of behaving like the Mafia, he told the Daily Mail:

> "I am at a delicate stage in securing a major deal for the future. What has happened could wreck everything. It's a sting."[235]

The Mail added a sub-headline to make sure that its readers got the message: "Angry Founder Accuses Rivals of Trying to Wreck Business." Although both NMC and the Inland Revenue denied that the raid had anything to do with the dispute between Nissan UK and

Nissan in Japan, parts of the press did not buy that line. On the contrary, *The Daily Telegraph* wrote, "It is understood that a document lodged by NMC in Japan in its legal battle to end the distribution agreement with Nissan UK makes allegations about the way Nissan UK organises its tax affairs."[236] Meanwhile, on its inside page "City Comment", the *Telegraph* explained its scepticism over the whole matter:

> "On May 14, Nissan Motor submitted its petition for arbitration… It is a strange document, full of unsubstantiated allegations and bizarre assertions. It would not get past the door of an English courtroom. It is certainly no basis for the commercially catastrophic raids of yesterday. If the reasons for the Revenue raid are clear to those behind it, they are in a minority. Nissan UK is a large but simple business, buying cars from Nissan Motor and selling them to dealers, some of which it owns. The accounts contain no black holes and corporation tax is paid according to profit."[237]

The day after the raid, Inland Revenue officials visited various dealers, encouraging them to say that Nissan UK had given under-the-counter cash payments, which it had not. An order was sought by the Revenue which froze Nissan UK's bank accounts. Until this was lifted, thanks to an intervention before the courts by the company's local solicitor, Nissan UK could not trade. One of the directors, Richard Smith, who tried to go into the office as usual, was turned away by the police at the cordon. The tax officials later showed him what they claimed were invoices issued by Nissan UK's shipping agent which they said proved a scam: the Revenue's argument was to be that Nissan UK had been involved in a major tax fraud involving a corrupt and bogus shipping agent issuing inflated bills. However, when the matter subsequently came to trial, no such invoices were ever produced.

A week later, still in the dark, Nissan UK's accountants, Grant

Thornton, met the Inland Revenue to offer cooperation in resolving whatever it was that was going on, but expressing concern at the consequences of disruption for the future of the company and its employees. They wanted to resolve matters swiftly so that Nissan UK could get back to dealing with the challenge of replacing the Nissan franchise. They explained that what had been a difficult situation anyway, given the arbitrary termination of the distribution agreement, had now – thanks to the Inland Revenue – become an impossible one. Thousands of jobs were at stake.

The Inland Revenue was not only uncooperative, its Director General went as far as to say, at a meeting in July 1991, that that the jobs of 4,000 people (all of whom were taxpayers of course) were "irrelevant."[238] Within the coming months, as a direct result of the Revenue's actions, all but a handful of those people were made redundant.

Although Fiat had been deeply unsettled by the raid, there was a slim possibility that they might be persuaded back to the table if another route could be found. Nissan UK's sister company, Automotive Financial Group Holdings Limited (AFGH) was not part of the Inland Revenue investigations. If this fact could be confirmed by the Revenue itself, Fiat's deal could go ahead based on a distribution agreement with AFGH rather than Nissan UK. However, the Revenue procrastinated, delaying clearance for so long that Fiat was forever lost as an alternative.

In September, three months after the raid, two of Nissan UK's professional advisers, an accountant and a solicitor, met Revenue officer David Hugo to ascertain the nature of the Revenue's concerns. Hugo said that there were three areas of interest – stock relief, transport and currency. He added that the advisers were unlikely to be impressed with what the Revenue had in relation to transport and currency. That left stock relief, a matter which had been investigated by the Revenue in the 1980s and which had been settled with a legally binding agreement.

Nevertheless, on 2 October 1991, a partner of Kidsons Impey, Nissan UK's auditors; a partner of Grant Thornton, Nissan UK's former tax advisers; and a former Nissan UK director who left more than five years earlier and who had since been living in the United States, were charged in relation to alleged false claims for tax relief on £14.5 million of stock in the years 1980 and 1981, i.e. a decade previously.

Not only were Nissan UK's professional advisers unimpressed by the quality of the Inland Revenue's analysis, so too was the stipendiary magistrate who found himself presiding over a committal hearing in Worthing. This was the Revenue's first attempt to prosecute and it failed. The magistrate refused to commit the men for trial, and dismissed the charges. "I do not consider that there is sufficient evidence for a jury to commit. The prosecution have not put forward a prima facie case. I cannot commit this case for trial at Crown Court and, therefore, all three defendants are to be dismissed." Costs were awarded against the Inland Revenue.

This failed prosecution showed that the Revenue was itself uncertain of exactly what tax fraud it thought had been committed. A few weeks after the September 1991 meeting with David Hugo, two representatives of KPMG Peat Marwick, acting on behalf of Nissan UK – one of whom used to be a senior officer of the Inland Revenue – held a further two-day meeting with the Inland Revenue Enquiry Branch to establish the nature of the investigations which were being pursued. By now it was five months since the documents had been seized.

KPMG reported back that the Revenue was considering allegations under a number of broad headings, and was alleging a substantial underpayment of tax. It was suggested that monies had been diverted to overseas territories to the personal benefit of the directors of Nissan UK. However, the Inland Revenue could show KPMG no evidence to substantiate these allegations.

Having seized voluminous quantities of paperwork from Nissan UK and its associated companies, the Inland Revenue proceeded to conduct interviews with hundreds of people all over the country – directors and former directors of the companies, employees and ex-employees, dealers, former dealers, dock workers. They called on employees at home in the evenings, an intimidating experience. Few stones were left unturned in an exercise which proved just as indiscriminate as the raid itself. Revenue officers visited no fewer than seven countries in their pursuit of evidence on which to construct a case against Nissan UK.

In November 1991 two Revenue officers travelled to Japan to take witness statements. They were received by officials from the National Tax Administration (NTA), the Revenue's counterpart agency in Japan. From unused material from subsequent legal proceedings (see following chapter) it transpired that the Inland Revenue had been told they would be unable to visit NMC or to take statements from any of its employees or officers. The unused material also contained a statement drafted by the Revenue in advance, which they had hoped to ask Masataka Okuma, NMC's Executive Vice President, to sign, to try to use as evidence. Despite the Revenue's endeavours, it was clear that the NTA was under strict instructions not to give access to NMC.

As Christmas 1991 approached, therefore, the Revenue had not managed to put together a case in the six months since the raid, despite their allegations of serious tax fraud.

Botnar's reaction was characteristic. He determined to fight the Inland Revenue, come what may. When one of the barristers instructed by his solicitors suggested that the Revenue could probably be bought off with an offer of a cash settlement, he would not contemplate it. He could not agree to make a payment when he considered the company owed the Revenue nothing. At the time of the raid he had said: "I am interested that what I have built up does not go to pieces, so I am fighting. That is my character. I cannot alter it at my age."[239] (He was 77 at the time of the raid.)

With the Inland Revenue and an international car giant now at loggerheads with a man who had faced the brutality of the Nazis in France and the Communists in Romania and who had an uncompromising sense of justice and fair play, the stage was set for a struggle. This struggle was to last for the rest of Botnar's life.

CHAPTER 12

THE CHARITIES

And stoop and build 'em up...

Botnar's decision to fight the Inland Revenue tooth and nail cannot be understood without reference to the way he had lived his whole life. As we have seen, he had picked himself up out of several very difficult situations – his first imprisonment in Romania in 1932, his imprisonment by the Germans in 1940, his life under the German occupation of France and his engagement in the Resistance, his difficulties with the Romanian regime, his early marital problems, his five years of detention and hard labour from 1960, his decision to leave Romania, his new life in Britain and of course the death of his daughter.

Botnar was therefore clearly a fighter. However, he was not only that. Having spent his life taking up arms against a sea of troubles, Octav Botnar had decided, in the years after the death of Camelia, to help other people learn to do the same. He had therefore embarked, later in the 1970s, on a massive programme of charitable giving, spurred on by his innate generosity and by the determination that some good should come out of his daughter's death and that her name should live on. Most of this charitable giving had taken place out of the limelight and few people knew about it: he certainly never sought publicity for his giving. The fact that he had given away so much money and done it so discreetly made it difficult to believe the Revenue's claim that he was, in reality, a tax dodger and swindler on a gigantic scale.

Botnar's first major charitable act had been to create the Camelia Botnar Foundation in 1979 and to which he gave a handsome endowment. Its funds, some £70 million by the early 1990s, came from shares in Datsun (later Nissan) UK and sister company Automotive & Financial Group Holdings (AFGH), and from donations made by a charitable trust which he had created in Liechtenstein in 1974, and which was itself endowed with the bulk of Botnar's own shares.

The Camelia Botnar Foundation bought Ivory's House in Cowfold, West Sussex, a large and charming arts and crafts manor house designed by the renowned architect, Walter Brierley, dubbed "the Yorkshire Lutyens", and set in a 500-acre estate including farms and stables. The house had been built by a family which had grown rich on sugar but which had fallen on hard times: many years later, it was discovered that this Hornung family were Transylvanian Saxons who originally hailed from Brașov in Romania. Botnar chose this beautiful spot for the Foundation which bears his daughter's name and whose goal is to take young people, mainly young men but also now women, away from a life of crime, or from a difficult family or social situation, and to teach them a manual skill and to live and look after themselves independently. Botnar was always convinced that people should learn to do things with their own hands.

Today the Camelia Botnar Foundation offers residential courses for disadvantaged young people in metalwork, carpentry, catering, estate management, painting and decorating, building, pottery and horticulture. The teaching ethic there reflects Botnar's own convictions: students are taught to start making things themselves very early on, within the first day or so of their apprenticeship. The Foundation thinks – like Botnar – that it is a waste of time to spend days or weeks teaching someone how to operate, say, a lathe, without immediately giving him a goal which he can achieve with it. The objects made in the workshops – whether items of furniture, decorative metal pieces, plants grown by the horticulturalists, sculptures, crockery or whatever – are then sold in the adjacent and very large Garden Centre.

The quality of the apprentices' work is exceptional and the

Foundation's workshops are regularly commissioned to produce custom-made items. Some of this work is on public display at, for instance, the Nuffield Orthopaedic Centre, Oxford. (See illustrations within the photographic pages.) In past years, a number of the Foundation's male apprentices have won awards for the quality of their work. More recently, in 2017, Mahum Bahti, a 20-year-old Camelia Botnar Foundation apprentice, became the first woman in 30 years to be crowned winner of the Young Craftsman of the Year competition at the prestigious South of England Show.

Highly motivated by their work, the teachers of the various disciplines request that the sales staff quickly communicate back to the workshop whenever an item has been sold. This is so that the apprentice can feel for himself or herself, as quickly as possible, that the product of his or her labour has been worthwhile. The apprentices are typically enrolled at an age between 16 and 19, often after referral from social services agencies, and they stay for around two years. The Foundation pays them for their work, making a small deduction from their wages which is paid into a savings account so that they have a small nest egg to assist them in their transition to the next stage of their lives. "We teach them to get up in the morning and go to work," says Paul Yallop, the Foundation's General Manager. "We want them to be proud of themselves. Motivating is what we do."[240] Motivating is what Octav Botnar did too.

Shortly after setting up the Camelia Botnar Foundation in Cowfold, Botnar also started to fund a day centre in Worthing for physically and mentally handicapped children. Originally a self-help group, in 1979 it became the Datsun Foundation and later the Nissan Foundation. In due course, it was renamed the Camelia Botnar Children's Centre, providing pre-school development, free of charge, for thousands of families with children with special needs. The donations were considerable: during the period 1979-1993, for instance, Botnar gave £3 million to this local centre, i.e. well over £200,000 per year.

Botnar enjoyed giving money away. He also enjoyed making decisions quickly. In 1989, the Head of Accident and Emergency at Worthing Hospital came to see Botnar in his office to explain the need for a CT scanner. Although such scanners are now widely available, at the time they were in their infancy and scarce. Botnar nevertheless agreed to fund it on the spot. Over the coming years, he gave more than £500,000 to Worthing Hospital for various items.

Because of his persistent high blood pressure – he had suffered a heart attack in 1970 – Botnar was often in contact with doctors and hospitals. Medical causes therefore attracted a large proportion of his charitable giving, and he had a very special *modus operandi* when presented with requests for funding. He liked to scrutinise such requests carefully and, being an astute businessman, could quickly tell a good proposal from a bad one. If a request passed his tests, he would support it enthusiastically.

Professor Roger Greenhalgh, one of Britain's leading heart surgeons, recalls how Botnar came to see him for a generalised arterial condition:

"We scanned his arteries there and then… the team assembled to give him the results. Octav Botnar then checked these results against his own checklist and pronounced them correct. 'You are the best,' he said. 'In Switzerland, a famous specialist admitted me to hospital for 14 days and did angiograms. You did it in 45 minutes without angiogram and no waste of my time. I shall invite you to dinner and you bring a list of your research wishes."[241]

The professor gladly accepted the dinner invitation. After the other guests left around midnight, Greenhalgh gave Botnar a list of various projects, each one with a costing, in the hope that Botnar might agree to fund one of them. "Instead," recalled Greenhalgh, "he totalled the list to approximately £900,000. 'I will give you a million pounds,' he said and enjoyed my shock! 'I make you a millionaire right now,' he said."

In response, Greenhalgh set up the Camelia Botnar Arterial Research Foundation in November 1985 at Charing Cross Hospital, to which Botnar gave a further million in less than a decade. On one occasion, he asked Greenhalgh how much he had ever been paid for one consultation and offered to beat the figure. He gave him £35,000.

The work of this Foundation has been internationally recognised, with a number of medical practices discovered or encouraged by work funded by the Foundation, for instance on aortic aneurysm (the life-threatening swelling of the body's principal artery). Endovascular repair, the elective correction which the Foundation pioneered, has become the international standard. Greenhalgh said that Botnar "would love to know that his philanthropy achieved that success. Octav Botnar was a quite unique man in my experience. It has been a great privilege to have met this special man and to have been a very small part of his dreams for a better tomorrow."[242]

Over the period 1984-1994, Botnar pursued his interest in heart-related medicine by giving £1.7 million to the Cardiology department of the Hammersmith & Acton Hospitals, where he had been treated by Professor Celia Oakley, who was considered one of the most outstanding clinical cardiologists of her day.[243] The money was used by the hospital for laboratories and equipment, and for research into heart disease. He gave £1.5 million to the St George's Hospital Blood Pressure Research Trust between 1988 and 1991, where his contact was Professor Graham MacGregor, to whom he had been referred from Charing Cross for severely raised blood pressure due to the narrowing of a kidney artery and his previous history of coronary heart disease. This donation was used for equipment and staff and for research into the implications for blood pressure of a high intake of salt in the diet.

Professor MacGregor is now one of the leading authorities in the United Kingdom on the role played by salt and sugar in causing heart disease. He recalled after Botnar's death how, unlike most patients in his position, Botnar had refused to sit back and take things more easily. "He was determined not to be ill and to fight back, which he did with great courage… He was a remarkable and generous man, I feel proud to have known him."[244]

Botnar would often take a keen interest in the workings of the hospitals to which he was referred. On one occasion when Botnar visited Professor MacGregor, he had to make his way through a picket line of striking nurses. When he got into the Blood Pressure Unit, however, Botnar found that all its nurses were working normally. He asked why this was and was told that these nurses were paid out of the Unit's research budget. He immediately decided to donate money to the Unit in order to give the nurses more security and, of course, to promote the research itself. Having made an initial large donation before he left the UK in 1991, the companies and trusts he left behind would continue to be major donors to this research in his final years and after his death. Graham MacGregor is unambiguous about the role played by Botnar's donations: "Without his money, we would never have done what we have done on salt. What we have done in the UK is a model for the world. I owe him a great debt of gratitude."[245]

In the late 1980s, through his contacts in the Conservative Party, where he had made friends with numerous ministers, Botnar was made aware of the Wishing Well Appeal for the famous Great Ormond Street Children's Hospital in London. The head of the Appeal, Marion Allford, brought such a high level of professionalism to the fund-raising process that she was interviewed on the BBC about her strategy and later went on to write books on the subject. One of her key stratagems was to attract major gifts first, by identifying potential large donors, and then to move to the public phase of the appeal once the private part had secured big donations.

Marion Allford decided to approach Botnar through Cecil

Parkinson, one of the most prominent ministers in the Thatcher cabinet. Botnar looked carefully at the Great Ormond Street proposal and decided that it was not detailed enough.[246] Asked to go away and re-do their homework, the campaigners came back with a much better structured plan, with precise costings for a vital laboratory building in nearby Lamb's Conduit Street. Botnar responded by sending a cheque for £8 million. His offer was so generous that, being on its own many multiples of the donations of £1 million each which the Appeal had by then secured from a handful of major donors, it was accommodated outside the Wishing Well Appeal itself. Cecil Parkinson could hardly control himself for joy. "Dear Octav," he wrote to him, "I was stunned to hear of your astounding generosity. I can only add that, never in my wildest dreams did I believe that any one person would be so generous." Parkinson said that he would pass on the news to the Prime Minister (Mrs Thatcher) even though "I know that you hate publicity."[247]

This last sentence is important. Through Nissan UK, Botnar would, over time, give away well in excess of £100 million to a very wide range of causes in the UK – hospitals, foundations for children and young people, artistic ventures – and to causes in Romania and Israel. However, he always made his gifts with maximum discretion. Recognition was generally not requested, except for some of the bigger projects which bore the name of his daughter Camelia. The rare exceptions which do bear his name were named after his death.

This initial donation to Great Ormond Street went to the construction of the Camelia Botnar Laboratories which are also used by the University College London/Great Ormond Street Institute of Child Health. Marcela attended and spoke at the opening ceremony in 1996, when she unveiled a bust of Camelia by Anthony Stones, the then President of the Society of Portrait Sculptors. The bust is still there today. The laboratories were billed at the time as "the best of their kind in Europe".[248] Twenty years on and the importance and relevance of these laboratories has not diminished. The Camelia Botnar Laboratories provide the infrastructure for the university and the hospital to work together, the hospital patients providing new challenges to the doctors, and the researchers seeking new ways to respond to them. The interaction between the two is crucial. Great Ormond Street treats children with especially rare diseases, including very rare genetic disorders, and is a hospital of tertiary referral, i.e. it is where patients are sent when other hospitals cannot treat them. For this reason, its researchers and doctors are very often confronted with new challenges. In cancer alone, in 2016, there were no fewer than 25 different research projects being conducted in the Camelia Botnar Laboratories.

It is difficult to overstate the importance of such infrastructure projects for hospitals. The creation of wards and laboratories is the *sine qua non* for all medical activity. Buildings have a deep influence on human behaviour. Robert Creighton, then Chief Executive of Great Ormond Street, said in 1998 that Botnar's donations had been used to build "the very best laboratories in the country, and I would perhaps guess anywhere in the world, certainly the very best dedicated to paediatric pathology. These are the Camelia Botnar Laboratories, a superb building which has enhanced the conditions of our pathologists out of all recognition... Every child who passes through the hospital needs the services of these laboratories, and the progress which we make through research there extends the influence of these laboratories throughout the country and throughout the world."[249]

This was not the only donation Botnar made to Great Ormond Street. He gave a further £6 million in the last years of his life, bringing the total to £14 million. This made him at that time the biggest individual donor in the hospital's history, maybe surpassing even the author J. M. Barrie, who left all the royalties from Peter Pan to the hospital in 1929 (and whose royalties, the sum of which is kept secret, were extended by an Act of Parliament after the usual 50-year period in order to secure the legacy as a source of income for Great Ormond Street). The second donation paid for the building of the Octav Botnar Wing, next to the Camelia Botnar Laboratories, a six-storey building which houses an orthopaedic inpatient unit, a medical day centre and the Harris International Patient Centre.

This second donation also meant that Botnar continued his support for the hospital, and for other causes in Britain, throughout the period in which the British tax authorities were accusing him of decades of tax fraud. Sir Anthony Tippet, the former Royal Navy Admiral who was General Manager (later Chief Executive) of Great Ormond Street Children's Hospital from 1987-95, was one of Botnar's greatest supporters, even during the darkest days of the Inland Revenue investigation.

Another major target of Botnar's generosity came about, like Great Ormond Street, as a result of his association with Conservative Government ministers. Because of his key role in persuading Nissan Motor Company to build its factory in Britain, Botnar had, as we have seen, come into contact with Norman Tebbit. In October 1984, Norman Tebbit's wife, Margaret, was badly injured by the bomb planted by the Irish Republican Army in a bathroom at the Grand Hotel in Brighton, where the Conservative Party was holding its annual conference. Five people were killed and more than 30 injured. The Prime Minister, most of the Cabinet and several MPs were staying in the hotel; Margaret Tebbit was left permanently disabled and has been in a wheelchair ever since.

As a result of having to care for his wife, Norman Tebbit became involved with the orthotics unit which was then being developed at the Nuffield Orthopaedics Centre in Oxford. Orthotics is that branch of medical practice devoted to the creation of orthoses, an externally applied device used to modify the structural and functional characteristics of the neuromuscular and skeletal system. In plain language, it involves the manufacture of braces and prosthetics for the arms or legs, which help people who have suffered injury or illnesses like multiple sclerosis.

Tebbit decided to ask Botnar whether he could help the Nuffield. From an initial £100,000 given in 1988 to help rebuild the orthotics centre, Botnar's donations to the Nuffield were to mushroom and become larger even than those made to Great Ormond Street. After Botnar had left the UK, Tebbit flew to see him in Switzerland to discuss various matters including the fight with the Inland Revenue. He updated him on the Nuffield's ongoing development plans and Botnar decided to give £5 million, which was paid between 1996 and 1998. These gifts were therefore also made long after the raid and the battle with the Revenue. Botnar, and the trust set up after he died, the Marcela Trust based in the United Kingdom, were in the end to give £20 million in total to the Nuffield Orthopaedic Centre. These huge donations made it possible to rebuild the main hospital and create the Botnar Research Centre, which hosts Oxford University's Institute of Musculoskeletal Sciences, itself part of the Nuffield Department of Orthopaedics, Rheumatology and Musculoskeletal Sciences, as well as other new hospital buildings. In fact, it is no exaggeration to say that Botnar saved the hospital with his gift in the mid-Nineties. In the view of the person who ran the appeal, Jeanette Franklin MBE:

"When the Appeal was launched to fund-raise for a new children's ward and two adult wards, the Nuffield Orthopaedic Centre's buildings were very old and in serious decline. The buildings had become cramped and very expensive to maintain. There is no doubt that the expertise and skill of the clinicians would have been lost, as they would have moved to more modern hospitals, with better facilities, if the new hospital had not been built. It is entirely due to the first generous major gift of £5 million from Mr Botnar which stopped the decline and saved the Nuffield Orthopaedic Centre, now one of the five Centres of Excellence in the country."[250]

The creation of the Botnar Research Centre built on this impressive history and made it possible for Oxford medical students to conduct their research in the hospital itself, part of a wider trend among Oxford medics. According to Professor Andrew Carr, the director of the Institute of Musculoskeletal Sciences, "Before Botnar, we had 20 staff and three or four researchers. Now we have 500 staff and a hundred D. Phil. students. You can't do quality research without adequate resources."[251] The creation of the Botnar Centre also had a magnetic effect on other bodies: the Kennedy Institute of Rheumatology, for instance, would have undoubtedly gone to Cambridge had it not been for the Botnar Centre at Oxford. "The combined setup is now the biggest research unit in the world for musculoskeletal diseases," Professor Carr points out.

Professor Carr's current work is in tissue engineering, the science of creating functional constructs that restore, maintain, or improve damaged tissues or whole organs. At the Botnar Centre, he has developed a brand of tissue engineering implant, called Biopatch, which, inspired by spiders' webs, will cause damaged tendon tissue to re-grow, a technique which in due course will revolutionise shoulder repair operations. Currently, such operations can fail because the tendons do not re-grow, causing patients to spend the rest of their lives in pain.

Professor Carr's department has also developed at the Botnar Centre very sophisticated monitoring technology for trainee and practising surgeons which, inspired by the technology used to monitor and advise Formula One drivers, and with the use of monitors and sensors placed on the trainee's body, helps the future surgeon to train and practise before performing an actual operation. As with the cancer research being conducted in the Camelia Botnar

Laboratories at Great Ormond Street, these are deeply impressive medical research programmes which make a radical difference to medical science and to ordinary people's lives.

In 1997, Lord Tebbit had to do battle to defend both himself and Botnar after the latter had agreed to give £5 million to the Nuffield. A Mr Englefield wrote to the Editor of the *Daily Telegraph* casting aspersions on Tebbit's integrity and implying that there was some sort of sleaze behind the fact that the Nuffield, a charity which Tebbit chaired, was accepting money from a man to whose business success Tebbit had contributed when a minister. True to form, Tebbit relished the opportunity for a fight. He replied the next day with a letter of his own to the same paper, defending Botnar for his run-in with the Inland Revenue, saying that the tax issue had been settled, which it had been by then, and concluding with a classic twist of the knife by the "Chingford skinhead":

"I am not a mean-spirited man and I recognise the strength with which Mr Englefield holds his views. I am sure therefore that some arrangement could be made under which Mr Englefield could be denied treatment at hospitals which have benefited from Mr Botnar's generosity. Alternatively, if Mr Englefield would like to send me his cheque for £5 million I would substitute it for Mr Botnar's."[252]

Botnar also made numerous smaller gifts to other medical charities. He gave £200,000 to the Mental Heath Foundation; £200,000 to Walk Again Legs Kinetics; £100,000 to the Sharon Allen Leukaemia Trust; £48,000 to the St Barnabas House hospice in Worthing; £50,000 to the Breathlessness Research Trust; £100,000 to install a lift in the Chaseley home for severely disabled people; and £400,000 to Aspire, the charity which raises money to cure spinal injury. He gave £150,000 to the Make a Wish Foundation which supports children with incurable illnesses and £100,000 to the Romanian Orphanage Trust.

However, Botnar did not support only medical charities. He also engaged in more general philanthropy. He gave over £800,000 between 1981 and 1990 to the Motor and Allied Trades Benevolent Fund, a charity which helps retired car workers, for new buildings and to ensure the fund's revenue. In 1985, he and Marcela created La Fondation Camelia Botnar in Villars-sur-Ollon in Switzerland, where they had built their chalet. This foundation was to be generously funded by them over the years, for instance to the tune of 2 million Swiss francs in 1988 alone.[253] The goal of this Foundation was to help elderly people in the village.

Botnar was also interested in the arts, at both the local and national level, giving nearly £1 million to the Chichester Festival Theatre to enable it to build the Minerva Theatre; £860,000 to the Philharmonia Orchestra in London for its productions at the Royal Festival Hall; £750,000 to the Royal Opera House to support its schools matinee productions; £100,000 to the British Museum to help its Japanese galleries and to endow fellowships in Japanese art; £100,000 to the Jacqueline du Pré Memorial Fund for the construction of the music building at St Hilda's College, Oxford; and other donations to schools offering music classes or which needed a new library. He also made a major donation, £500,000, to the Prince's Youth Business Trust, the charity set up by Prince Charles to help young people set up in business: this corresponded of course very deeply to Botnar's own "can do" ethic and to his profound belief that if only people could be given a helping hand then they would be able to realise their full potential.

Taking all these donations together, and combining them with the enormous charitable commitment to the Camelia Botnar Foundation, meant that, by 1994, Botnar had given some £100 million to charitable causes, and he continued to give further huge sums until he died.

Furthermore, through the various ongoing charitable initiatives which he established during his lifetime, support for charitable causes continues to this day. This record makes him one of the greatest philanthropists in Britain in the second half of the 20th Century. It explains why the Prime Minister at the time, Margaret Thatcher, thought fit to write to Botnar from 10 Downing Street on 19 January 1990, as follows:

> *Dear Mr Botnar,*
>
> *I am writing to thank you so very much for the wonderfully generous gifts which you and your Company have made to various charities in the United Kingdom in recent years.*
>
> *I know that your support for handicapped children, for medical research and for the arts has been very greatly appreciated, and has enriched the lives of so many.*
>
> *I want you to know how specially grateful and appreciative I am.*
>
> *Yours sincerely,*
>
> *Margaret Thatcher*

It was not just UK politicians who had reason to thank Botnar. Towards the end of his life, Botnar became interested in Israel and peace in the Middle East. During the 1980s, through his acquaintance with Alistair (Lord) McAlpine – Margaret Thatcher's legendary and colourful adviser and Tory party treasurer, whom Botnar had met through Tim Bell, the man credited with crafting the Tories' election campaigns and who became his PR consultant – Botnar had made substantial donations to the Conservative Party. Botnar's heart beat on the left but he admired Mrs Thatcher for her drive and courage.

This, plus the business and personal friendships he had formed with senior Conservative ministers as a result of discussions linked to the construction of the Nissan factory, had led to him becoming a major donor to the governing party during the heyday of Thatcherism.

It was another unexpected link, observed during his enforced exile in Switzerland, which was to set Botnar off on an entirely new course of charitable giving and political activity. One of the lawyers Botnar engaged briefly was Lawrence Cartier, a London solicitor. In 1996, Cartier travelled to Villars for a meeting with his new client. As he opened his suitcase, Botnar noticed that he had some dreidels in it, the little four-sided spinning tops which are played with at the Jewish holiday of Hannukah. Botnar must have recognised them from his own childhood. In his thick accent, Botnar said to Cartier, "You are *Jude?*" Cartier had not said that he was Jewish and he did not know that Botnar was either. "England has treated me unfairly," Botnar said, and together they started to talk about Israel, where Cartier kept a flat, and which in any case had caught Botnar's attention because the Israeli-Palestine conflict was in the news.

The Botnars had initially emigrated to Israel when they left Romania in 1965, but they had not stayed long because Botnar did not like it and he had no interest in his Jewish roots. However, like many people around the world, he followed the news coming out of the Middle East closely. He was deeply shocked when Yitzhak Rabin, the Israeli Prime Minister, was assassinated on 4 November 1995 by a Jewish extremist who regarded him as a traitor for having negotiated away "Jewish land" (i.e. the occupied territories) at Oslo. These Oslo agreements had been famously signed on the lawn of the White House in September 1993, when Rabin had reluctantly shaken hands with Yasser Arafat, the Palestinian leader.

Botnar, always a voracious consumer of news, was attracted by situations and causes with which he empathised. He resolved to do what he could to make a difference in what appeared to be an intractable conflict. He expressed the desire to meet Yasser Arafat and to help pay for peace. When this proved impossible, he decided instead to finance a number of charitable causes in Israel proper and to give political support to those forces in that country which were favourable to an agreement with the Palestinians.

Cartier took the Botnars on a tour of Israel in February 1997. Cartier recalls that in discussions with potential recipients of his largesse, Botnar would behave with charming idiosyncrasy, making little upward gestures with the upturned palm of his hand when potential sums were suggested: he meant by this that the potential recipient should be bolder and ask for more. Cartier recalls, "He was very modest. He was doing what he liked to do when he gave away money." He generally shunned recognition and laughed when he saw the names of various donors on a glass plaque in a Jerusalem hospital: "I am giving you money," he said, "you know what to do with it." But Cartier also remarked, like everyone, how full of energy Botnar was: "He was very urgent, he felt he had a shortage of time."[254]

Botnar asked Cartier to put him in touch with the then opposition leader, Shimon Peres, who had succeeded Rabin as Prime Minister in November 1995 but who had later been driven from office by the Likud leader, Benjamin Netanyahu, at the elections in May 1996. The initial contact was made in early 1997 through Isaac Herzog, who was then both a senior partner at Herzog, Fox & Neeman (the law firm founded by his father, Chaim Herzog, a former President of Israel) and also a special advisor to Shimon Peres dealing with international relations. (Herzog would later go on to follow a prolific political career as a member of the Knesset, a minister, and the leader of the opposition who ran a neck-and-neck campaign against the incumbent Prime Minister, Netanyahu, in 2015.)

Herzog agreed to meet Cartier and Botnar in Israel. The meeting occurred the following month, in the Beit Amot Mishpat building where Peres, like other former Prime Ministers, had his

*Examples of the outstanding public
and commercial commissions designed
and produced by the apprentices of the
Camelia Botnar Foundation Forge.*

A portrait of Octav Botnar (left) by photographer Jack Burke, of Worthing.

The Duke of Gloucester (right) is shown an example of metalwork in progress on a visit to the Camelia Botnar Foundation Forge, Cowfold (May 2017).

Mahum Bahti (below), a 20-year-old Camelia Botnar Foundation apprentice, became the Young Craftsman of the Year at the prestigious South of England Show. She is pictured receiving her award from British actor and comedian, Romesh Ranganathan.

Portrait (original in oil) of Botnar by Anthony Stones (Fellow of the Society of Portrait Sculptors). Presented to Botnar as a birthday present.

The building of the Nissan factory in Washington, Tyne & Wear is considered the most important foreign investment in Britain since the war. Botnar was sitting immediately behind Prime Minister Margaret Thatcher when she officially opened the factory on 8 September 1986. In the only photograph which exists (above) Botnar is sadly hidden from the camera by the Prime Minister's elbow.

Below, Nissan President Yutaka Kume (left) and Nissan Chairman Takashi Ishihara (right) sit either side of Prime Minister Margaret Thatcher at the opening ceremony.

Botnar with Lord (Richard) Marsh (right) at a press conference linked to the building of the Nissan factory in the North-East – 30 Marsh 1984. Marsh, a former Labour cabinet minister but sitting as a crossbench peer, was acting as a consultant to NMC. Marsh later chaired the PR company which NMC employed to "destroy Botnar's image".

The Nissan factory in Washington, Tyne & Wear is a memorial both to Botnar's vision and his unstinting endeavours. The inward investment now exceeds £4 billion.

Botnar understood the immense importance of printed information from his time with the French Resistance. He constantly put the in-house printing press at Nissan UK to good effect.

Cool as a cucumber. This photograph of Botnar was taken in Nissan UK's offices on the day of the raid by scores of Inland Revenue officials. Botnar was completely untroubled throughout.

Botnar on a rare day off, pictured in Paris, the city he considered his own.

office. Herzog recalls that, having first met Cartier, he then noticed a small man with a deep voice. It was Botnar, who cut immediately to the quick. "How do we get this man Netanyahu out of power?" Botnar asked.

Botnar was virulent in his hatred for Netanyahu and he told Herzog that he had seen him on television and had concluded that he was a liar.[255] (He had come to the same conclusion, evidently, as that expressed by the French President, Nicolas Sarkozy, to Barack Obama in November 2011.) It was music to Herzog's ears. The Israeli left largely blamed Netanyahu for the Rabin assassination: they accused him of fomenting the atmosphere of revenge which inspired the assassin. For instance, the museum of the Yitzhak Rabin Center in Tel Aviv shows a video of Netanyahu addressing a rally at which images of Rabin in the crosshairs of a gun were prominently displayed.

Herzog arranged for Botnar to meet Shimon Peres and Leah Rabin, the widow of the slain Prime Minister, who by then had started to create the Yitzhak Rabin Center, a vast complex in the centre of Tel Aviv housing a large permanent exhibition about the history of Israel and the life of Rabin.[256] Botnar was to give $4 million to this foundation, which now plays a major educational role in Israel, as tens of thousands of schoolchildren and Israel Defense Forces (IDF) soldiers are taken there on organised visits every year. Botnar would also make a similar donation to the Peres Center for Peace, created in 1996 by the former Prime Minister before he became President of Israel, and where he worked until his death in 2016.

The relationship between Botnar and Herzog quickly blossomed. Herzog and his wife Michal became very fond of both the Botnars, whom they would often visit in Villars. Herzog later wrote of Marcela that she always impressed him "as so strong, wise and friendly, haunted by the pains of the past and the tragic loss of Camelia."[257] The Botnars were especially affectionate towards the Herzogs' children, which naturally touched the Herzogs greatly.

Botnar was determined to support those Israeli political forces working for peace. He wanted to change the attitude of the Israeli public and, to this end, decided to finance a "soft power" operation. This meant giving money to non-governmental organisations, rather as the billionaire George Soros did across Eastern Europe after the fall of Communism. Having started with the Rabin Center and the Peres Center, he then, through Isaac Herzog, gave money to grass-roots organisations which had been created in the immediate aftermath of the Rabin assassination. These included *Dor Shalem Doresh Shalom* ("An Entire Generation Demands Peace"), known as *Dor Shalom*, which had considerable success in the early years of its existence.[258] An offshore Camelia Trust was created, which Herzog helped set up and which channelled money into these NGOs, and then later made a series of very large donations into various other charitable projects in Israel.

Armed with this and other sources of finance – Israeli industrialists and businesspeople who had supported Rabin gave money too – these NGOs in turn created subsidiaries which engaged in political lobbying, speaking to settlers in the occupied territories, challenging those on the Israeli right, and arguing the cause for a peace settlement. In terms of Israeli politics, this soft power operation effectively meant campaigning for Ehud Barak, who was seen as the man who could beat Netanyahu at the ballot box and negotiate peace. Barak would indeed successfully wrest the Prime Ministership from Netanyahu in 1999. Isaac Herzog took Barak to meet Botnar in Villars in early 1998: they flew in by helicopter and were entertained to lunch. (Barak was by no means the only dignitary to go to see the Botnars in Villars; on one occasion, Queen Anne of Romania was also a visitor.) A few months later, Barak called Marcela to offer his condolences after Botnar died. Isaac Herzog opined that Botnar would have been very pleased at his election. Herzog remarked, "Octav Botnar was a fighter. He was from a generation of revolutionaries, of the kind you do not see any more."[259]

Botnar's financing of groups who were effectively campaigning for Barak's election was to get both Barak and Herzog into trouble in later years, after Botnar's death. During the May 1999 Israeli election campaign, which was very heated, Netanyahu's team claimed that their opponents had been receiving foreign money, a claim designed to make them appear unpatriotic. Allegations were made that Barak's campaign had been illegally funded. The state controller called for foreign campaign funding to be regulated, which it later was, but the then Attorney General ruled initially that there was a loophole in the law. When the scandal blew up again after the election, in December 1999, shortly before Barak started negotiations with Syria, the main name which was quoted in the papers was that of Octav Botnar.[260] There was a police investigation which dragged on for years but in due course died down. The case was eventually closed in 2004.

While the issue was still live, the physicist Haim Harari, then president of the Weizmann Institute of Science, one of the leading academic research institutes in the world with thousands of members, wrote to the editor of *Haaretz*, the famous liberal daily, to defend Botnar's name. He told the paper that Botnar had made his first donation to the Institute completely anonymously, through an intermediary, which enabled them to establish a research centre in microelectronics. They then opened centres for reseach into genetics and cancer, also with his help. Botnar gave $12 million in total over the years, making him one of the 10 most generous donors to this institute. Harari wrote:

"Octav Botnar was a latter-day version of the Biblical Job, to whom fate continuously dealt a cruel hand. In his youth, like many other Jews, he fought the fascist regime in Romania and later volunteered to join the anti-fascist forces in Spain, then the Resistance in France. Following the war, he returned to Romania only to be imprisoned by the Communist regime in one of its anti-Jewish purges. He left Romania at the age of 56 with his wife, daughter, a single suitcase and not a penny to his name."

Apart from the small mistake about Botnar's age in 1965, this was right on the nail.

On the occasion of his and Marcela's visit to Israel in 1997, a dinner was held at the Hebrew University of Jerusalem, attended by the rector of the university, Yehoshua Ben-Arieh, and a professor of Jewish studies, Yair Zakovitch, also an expert on Biblical studies. They got on extremely well. Botnar agreed to pay for what is now the Yitzhak Rabin Building housing the Mandel Institute of Jewish Studies at the university. Although there is a sign outside this beautiful stone building, calling the area the Camelia Botnar Plaza, Botnar did not want his own name on the building itself, even though he had given $12.5 million towards its construction, but instead that of the late Prime Minister of Israel he so admired. The building was completed in 2000. Camelia Botnar's name is now prominently visible at the entrance to the domed building on Mount Scopus, the historic original location of the Hebrew University founded in 1925, before the creation of the state of Israel itself. From here you can see for miles across the eternal landscape of the arid lands of Eastern Israel and out towards the Dead Sea.

On a visit by Herzog to Villars in November 1997, Botnar told him he wanted to continue making big donations to Israel. Herzog suggested hospitals, a suggestion Botnar took up with gusto. In a very short space of time, Botnar agreed to pay for three major construction projects in different parts of the country. The first to be completed was the Camelia Botnar Maternity Wing at the Ichilov hospital in Tel Aviv. This hospital, formally known as the Sourasky Medical Center, is the largest in the city and the third largest in the country. The maternity wing is physically in the heart of the hospital complex, and the fact that the bereaved and childless Botnars chose this project is poignant. When Marcela Botnar toured this new building in 2000, shortly after its completion and after Botnar's death, a woman gave birth during her visit. The baby was handed to Marcela and she burst into tears: one can only imagine her emotion.

The next project was even bigger. Through Isaac Herzog's father-in-law, a contact was established with the Soroka Medical Center in the Southern Israeli city of Be'er-Sheva. Herzog told the hospital that a major donation might be in the pipeline. Botnar said that he wanted to meet the hospital's Director first. "I want to look him in the eye. If I like him, I'll give him the money," he told Herzog. Professor Yitzhak Peterburg asked for a large model to be made of the proposed building. The model had to be transported to Switzerland, itself a considerable logistical operation because an engineer had to be sent ahead to receive it. Peterburg, Isaac Herzog, his wife Michal, and the Deputy Director of the hospital, all travelled to Villars to show the model to Botnar. He was very excited by what he saw. Botnar asked Peterburg a few questions and then said, "You've got the money." It was a characteristically quick decision.

Botnar was to give US $20 million to construct a new building, which is now the central and largest part of the whole hospital complex. This Camelia Botnar Surgical Building, which houses the main entrance of the hospital and its principal operating theatres, was inaugurated in 2003. The entire structure is built around a method of sterilising operating material, which is unique in the world: an elaborate set of lifts transports "dirty" material down into the sterilisation unit and clean material back up into the operating theatres. The building is also equipped to function even in conditions of biological and chemical warfare. It was opened in 2003 and now treats 100,000 patients a year. Seven minutes by helicopter from Gaza, the hospital plays a strategic role in Israel's ongoing conflict with that province and is also part of the Israeli Government's plans for the region as a whole, which it intends to develop further, not least because of the growth of military bases in the area. But Botnar was also very pleased to learn that the hospital treats everyone, Arabs and Israelis alike, as one immediately notices on a visit there. Ironically, at the opening ceremony, numerous speakers naturally praised the generosity of Octav Botnar. But, as Isaac Herzog wryly recalls, not a single journalist made the link between the philanthropist who was being so profusely thanked, and the so-called shadowy businessman who had been posthumously accused of illicitly funding the Barak campaign in 1999.

The final major project was the enormous new medical faculty building at the Hadassah hospital in Ein Karem in Jerusalem, part of the Hebrew University. Finished in 2010, in traditional stone like the Rabin Building he also paid for, this building houses lecture halls and laboratories for use by the medical students learning clinical practice at the hospital: it is named the Octav and Marcela Botnar Medical Research Building. Botnar gave US $12 million to this project, which together with his other donations to the Hebrew University made him one of the biggest donors in the university's history.

CHAPTER 13·

TRIAL AND PREJUDICE

Being lied about, don't deal in lies…

Botnar's philanthropy was therefore immense by the time of the Inland Revenue raid in June 1991. It was to continue after it until the end of his life. The Fiat deal having collapsed, and with the acrimonious row with Nissan about to make its way into the courts, the Botnars left England in December 1991 for their annual Christmas break at their Swiss chalet in Villars.

Having failed to secure a prosecution of the company's financial advisers in October 1991, the Inland Revenue instead initiated criminal proceedings, principally against Michael Hunt, the company's then General Manager, and Frank Shannon, a former Finance Director. Shannon had left the company five years earlier, since when he had spent most of his time in the United States.

Although Botnar settled all of his Nissan UK shares in a charitable trust, Hunt and Shannon personally held shares in the company which Botnar had given them years before. The large dividends they had received from their shares had made both men very rich.

Three days before Botnar was due to return to the UK from Switzerland, in late January 1992, an arrest warrant was issued for Hunt, Shannon, Botnar and a Norwegian shipping agent, Tore Thorsen. The warrant meant that Botnar was never to return to England, the country he had adopted 25 years earlier.

Hunt and Shannon were arrested. Thorsen, who was in Newcastle at the time, was also arrested and charged. Botnar, by contrast, who the Revenue knew was in Switzerland, was not pursued.

No attempt was made to extradite him, nor from any other country he subsequently visited. Botnar concluded that the Revenue did not want him to defend himself in court.

Thorsen removed himself from the equation. Expressing disdain for the proceedings, he jumped bail and went back to Norway. The Revenue made no attempt to get him back to Britain to be tried.

Eventually the Revenue abandoned all but one of its various lines of enquiry and concentrated on one only: transport – the very issue which Inland Revenue officer David Hugo had said in September 1991 would not impress anyone. The Revenue were aware that in 1975 the terms on which Nissan UK had bought cars from NMC had changed, from CIF (Cost of car, Insurance and Freight, an all-inclusive price paid to NMC in yen) to C&I plus F – the cost and insurance being paid in yen to NMC and the cost of the freight being paid as a separate item in US dollars (the global currency for freight), to a Dutch shipping agent, Autocontex (during the years 1976-1983), and later on to a Norwegian shipping agent, Scansiris, a company owned and managed by Tore Thorsen (from 1983-1991). The shipping agents were invoiced in turn by NMC's shipping firm, Nissan Motor Car Carrier (NMCC), for the freight costs of the vehicles.

The crux of the Revenue's case was that Nissan UK, specifically Botnar, had initiated this change of trading terms from CIF to C&I plus F, that he had insisted NMC accept the proposed changes to the trading terms, and that the purpose of the change of terms was to facilitate a fraud on the Inland Revenue, by enabling the difference in price between what Nissan UK paid to the agent and what the agent paid to NMCC to be paid into a tax haven for the benefit of Botnar, Hunt and Shannon. The Revenue alleged the shipping agents actually did nothing.

Nissan UK denied that it was involved in any such scam. It argued that NMC was the principal partner in the trading relationship and that it was NMC who had requested the change in terms. Furthermore, it would have been impossible for an independent distributor such as Nissan UK to have any influence over the fundamental trading terms of the global giant which NMC was. Nissan UK had no choice as to what shipper was used to transport the vehicles from Japan – it had to use NMCC or shippers appointed by NMCC.

It took a year for the case against Michael Hunt and Frank Shannon to come to trial. Given the complexity of the case and the enormous volume of documents, the building at Southwark Crown Court was considered unsuitable to try the case. A special courtroom was set up in an overflow building off the Royal Courts of Justice in Chichester Rents, Chancery Lane. This gave the lawyers, the judge and the jury individual access to television monitors to view materials. Shannon and Hunt were thus tried in "Southwark Crown Court sitting at the Royal Courts of Justice".

As the final preparations were being put into place, the prosecution tried at the eleventh hour to play for time. It admitted to the judge that it had no proof that the payment arrangements had been set up by Nissan UK, or that Hunt or Shannon had been the beneficiaries of it. On 13 January 1993, as the trial was due to begin, the Revenue applied for a delay. Prosecuting counsel Peter Rook QC told the judge:

"It is indeed unsatisfactory… that we should be embarking upon a trial which is going to be very costly for the country where there is a dark void in relation to very important evidence."[261]

The "dark void" was the lack of evidence that the defendants controlled, or benefited from, directly or indirectly, the Swiss bank accounts into which monies were paid by the shipping agent. In fact, the prosecution could not find those accounts at all. From its point of view, the money vanished into thin air. In the words of the authoritative account of the Hunt trial and the subsequent appeal in 1994, the Revenue was "unable to prove that the shareholders of Nissan UK benefited from the proceeds of the fraud".[262]

This was very embarrassing. The Revenue argued that the fact that they had failed to find proof did not mean that it did not exist: this is not the sort of argument which should cut much ice with a British judge. The Revenue blamed its failure to find evidence on the length of time required for the legal procedure to lift the secrecy on bank accounts in Switzerland; but when the Swiss did eventually divulge what they could, no information useful to the Revenue was found either. No evidence was found in Botnar's own bank accounts, which he voluntarily opened for the Revenue's inspection in 1992. The judge rejected the Revenue's application and the trial went ahead as planned.

This lack of evidence remained a fundamental weakness in the Revenue's case. The weakness was all the more striking because the Japanese clearly had good motives for wanting to divert cash into secret havens for use when dollars were needed to open doors: the defence narrative that the payment scheme had been set up by the Japanese for their own benefit was plausible, to say the least. A similar case was discovered in the United States around the same time, in which Japanese motor companies were overcharging their own subsidiaries and squirrelling the extra money out of the country to avoid tax.[263]

The Revenue, however, could not afford to lose face. It had billed the Nissan UK affair as the biggest tax fraud in British history. The raid had been launched with spectacular publicity and one of Britain's most successful companies had been put into liquidation. How could the Revenue now admit that there was no evidence for its main charges?

Equally, it was politically impossible for the British state to accuse NMC of fraud. Britain had given substantial subsidies to the company for the construction of the factory in Sunderland, in the form of regional aid, and it depended on the continuing goodwill of NMC for the thousands of jobs the factory provided in the North East. Subsequent events, for instance after the Brexit referendum on 23 June 2016, when Nissan sought and obtained immediate assurances from the British Government that its trade with the EU would not be affected, have confirmed the extent of Nissan's political clout.

At this point an event occurred which helped the Revenue out of the hole into which it had dug itself. Unknown to Nissan UK, Shannon had been engaged in tax evasion in his own personal tax affairs. With the fortune he had earned from Datsun (later Nissan) UK dividends, he had acquired a large network of assets, mostly property abroad, held by various offshore companies he controlled, and a series of industrial properties in the United Kingdom. Shannon also had undeclared bank accounts in Spain.[264]

Having been caught red-handed in his personal tax affairs, Shannon agreed to plead guilty, albeit only very partially, to the criminal charges laid against him in connection with his work at Nissan UK. He agreed to say that he had stumbled upon the freight fraud in 1985 but that he had left the company a year thereafter. A new count was thereupon added to the original indictment, tailor-made for what Shannon was prepared to admit, the original indictment having alleged that Shannon was one of the original conspirators in, and beneficiaries of, a fraud which had operated since 1976.

In return for his guilty plea to this greatly reduced charge, in which he admitted no active conspiracy, and knowledge of the fraud for only one year and not 20, the Revenue agreed not to prosecute him under the other counts.[265] Shannon also argued in his plea that he had not benefited personally from the freight fraud, a version of events which the prosecution accepted and stated in open court.[266] This version of events was quite incompatible with the terms of the original indictment.[267]

Armed with his guilty plea, which it was agreed with Shannon would be entered before Hunt's trial started, the Revenue proceeded with the case against Hunt, who always protested his innocence. The prosecution requested that the guilty plea be revealed to the jury during the trial. Hunt's defence counsel, Michael Sherrard QC, initially appealed against the admission of this guilty plea as evidence but then changed his mind. He persuaded Hunt to abandon the appeal against the admission of the plea and so the prosecution's request was granted on 11 February 1993. This meant that Shannon's plea was accepted as evidence but never tested in court. The decision was to prove fatal to Hunt's Defence, and to his subsequent appeal.

Perhaps even more important than the lack of evidence against Hunt was the fact that the Revenue's narrative did not even prove that the UK had been defrauded. The facts were also compatible with an entirely different theory: that the Japanese had set up the payment arrangements for their own reasons.

Following Shannon's guilty plea, Michael Hunt was tried alone. His trial started on 20 April 1993. Hunt's Defence believed that the Revenue would be unable to prove its case, given the absence of any evidence. No doubt the lawyers assumed that one man's (partial) guilty plea could not be used against their own client, against whom there was no evidence at all. Botnar's solicitors, Herbert Smith, who received and forwarded to him a copy of Shannon's Defence Case Statement containing the guilty plea, similarly advised Botnar that it was "not necessarily damaging to your position or to that of Mr Hunt."[268] This turned out to be an excessively optimistic piece of legal advice.

Behind closed doors, on 4 May 1993, while the trial of Hunt

was taking place, Shannon agreed to pay the Revenue £10 million as settlement of his undeclared liabilities. As part of the deal, the Revenue expressly agreed not to pursue him for any money allegedly siphoned off from Nissan UK or obtained by means of the alleged freight fraud.[269] The agreement reached with the Revenue included an admission from Shannon that the Scansiris invoices were artificially inflated, but an acceptance by the Revenue that Shannon himself had not profited from the scam. In other words, the Revenue's position was that the £10 million settlement represented taxes owing from his own personal affairs and not from any fraud committed by Nissan UK.

As Hunt's trial was about to conclude, on 23 June 1993 – its 33rd day – the judge delivered his summing-up.

"In fact, members of the jury, I am reminded by Mr Sherrard (counsel for Michael Hunt), and he is quite right, that there is no direct evidence of a fraud either way. It is only inference, is it not? If there were a fraud on the United Kingdom Revenue, there is no direct evidence, you may infer from all the surrounding circumstances that we have been through at great length."[270]

This was an astonishing admission by the judge. The trial was about to conclude and the judge had said that the prosecution had not produced any direct evidence of a fraud. The "inference" to which the judge referred was an allusion to the prosecution claim that the freight arrangements had been set up by Nissan UK, that Botnar and his associates controlled the unidentified accounts in Switzerland into which extra money was allegedly paid, and that they had access to that money. These were the points for which the prosecution had, according to the judge, not produced any "direct evidence".

This extraordinary statement by the judge puzzled the jury.

Having withdrawn shortly thereafter, on 24 June, the jury sent a note to the judge asking a very specific and simple question:

"Is there any direct evidence of fraud (tax evasion) upon the UK Revenue?"[271]

The jury clearly felt that it had not been given any such evidence. The jurors believed, therefore, that the defence counter-argument that the payment arrangements had been set up by the Japanese had not been disproved, and that therefore Hunt's guilt had not been established beyond reasonable doubt. After the trial, indeed, a senior Nissan executive, Shiro Ozawa, who had signed the 1975 agreement with Nissan UK converting the shipping arrangements from cost, insurance and freight (CIF) to cost and insurance (C&I plus F) only – an agreement which, the Revenue argued, Nissan UK had initiated – testified in a letter that the slush fund had in fact been set up by the Japanese:[272]

"During the 1970s when I was in charge of Nissan Motor Company's Export Department for Europe and the Middle East, I travelled round some of the Arab countries and distributed cash in US dollars to members of the Arab boycott. The origin of the dollars was a matter to be kept secret because it violated Japanese laws of Foreign Exchange Control and Income Tax. It is my understanding and belief that these US dollars were from Nissan Motor Car Carrier's accounts in Switzerland."[273]

This version of events was also corroborated by Norman Tebbit, who testified on a separate occasion that another Director of NMC had told him exactly the same thing: that NMC used the money paid into the slush fund to bribe Arab countries into buying its cars, which they otherwise did not want to do because Nissan also traded with Israel.[274] Moreover, the Swiss banker, Kurt Vogelsang, sent an affidavit, which was submitted in evidence at the Hunt trial, saying that neither Botnar, Hunt nor Shannon had ever received any money from any account in Switzerland.[275]

The judge did not know quite how to answer the jury's question. His first response was to repeat what he had said the previous day and to say, "There is no direct evidence of a fraud on the UK Revenue."[276] The judge and the defence counsel then agreed that facts were essential before anyone drew any inferences and that:

"The only primary facts that they know on this question is that Datsun UK paid on the Autocontex higher invoices, let us call it that; that the amounts paid were included in the accounts of the company; those accounts were submitted to the Revenue and as a result tax was paid on the diminished profits that resulted."[277]

Michael Sherrard, Hunt's defence counsel, tried to press his advantage by saying, "There is no direct evidence, or any primary evidence, as to what the contractual arrangement was." The judge replied, "No, that is right"[278] before adding, "There is no direct evidence of a fraud either way. It is only inference, is it not, if there was a fraud on the UK Revenue, there is no direct evidence." He said that one might as well infer that the Japanese had been committing a fraud, but reiterated that there was no direct evidence either way.

Seeing his prey about to escape him, counsel for the prosecution intervened. He insisted that Shannon's guilty plea did count as evidence. The judge started to get confused. "It is not in itself direct evidence, I think, or is it?" he said. "I do not know." The lawyers argued back and forth with the judge, who seemed to agree with whichever one of them had spoken last. At one point, the judge repeated that Shannon's confession was "not direct evidence of your client (Hunt) being part of a conspiracy."

Shannon, indeed, had pleaded not guilty to conspiracy under the terms of the other counts for which Hunt was being prosecuted, so his limited guilty plea could not possibly apply to Hunt, who was charged with crimes committed years before Shannon claimed he had stumbled upon the fraud. Time and again the defence counsel urged that the court did not know on what basis Shannon had pleaded guilty, or for what reason. Shannon was not called as a witness and his guilty plea, and the evidence to support it, were never the subject of cross-examination. The Defence also insisted that Shannon had not pleaded guilty to a conspiracy. So what possible relevance could his plea have to Hunt?

However, under pressure from the prosecution, the judge started to shift his ground when he got the Defence to agree that Shannon's guilty plea could be taken as evidence for Shannon's own guilt. This was of course impossible to deny. Defence counsel Michael Sherrard countered that one man's guilty plea could not be used as evidence against another. It was in vain. The judge moved away from his earlier position and the jury came back into the courtroom. The judge addressed them:

"Members of the jury, you have asked a question, 'Is there any direct evidence of fraud (tax evasion) upon the UK Revenue?' The answer that I give you is, yes, there is. Shannon's plea of guilty to Count 5 is direct evidence that Shannon cheated the Revenue in the year alleged, 1st November 1985 to 31st October 1986. That is direct evidence, his plea of guilty...

What you do not know is the basis on which he pleaded. In other words, was he pleading to using false invoices, false agreements or false correspondence? You do not know that. What you do know is that Shannon pleaded guilty to cheating Her Majesty's Commissioners of Inland Revenue of Public Revenue Corporation Tax in that year. The rest of the particulars follow because all this is admitted. The sums were entered in the accounts having been paid by the company, the accounts were submitted to the Inspector of Taxes for the purposes of assessing profits and if there was cheating that means the profits on which tax was charged were made to appear less than they were.

Let me make it plain: that is the only direct evidence. All the rest must be inference. It is an inference you may feel follows from the direct evidence, but it is for you to judge how strong the inference is. In other words, Shannon's plea to guilty of cheating in 1985/1986 does not prove a conspiracy by itself. You need other evidence to decide that. It certainly does not prove Mr Hunt's being concerned in that cheat of the Revenue."[279]

The nuances of his reply were lost on the jury. They had asked him a question and he had replied yes. After two further days deliberation, ignorant of the most important facts about Shannon's plea and faced with the prospect of a weekend together in a hotel, the jury found Hunt guilty by a majority of 10 to 2 of the charge which related to the period covering Shannon's guilty plea. Significantly, the jury found him innocent in relation to the earlier period. Hunt was convicted on the basis of Frank Shannon's guilty plea alone, and not on the basis of evidence that Nissan UK had committed a fraud. Hunt was sentenced to eight years in prison.

Among the thousands of documents the Revenue had seized in several different countries, and which it had taken away with the highest possible publicity, the judge in the trial which resulted from that raid had just admitted that "the only direct evidence" for the alleged fraud was Shannon's plea, which was itself unsubstantiated by any evidence or explanation, and which in any case concerned only one out of an alleged 17 years of fraud.

The judge did not say that the prosecution had proved its case by producing demonstrably false freight invoices, as the men from the Revenue had claimed they had on the day of the raid, or by showing any other direct evidence. He did not say that they had traced a trail of money leading back to Botnar or his associates, which they themselves admitted they had not.

Moreover, the judge had ruled against Hunt's lawyers and admitted Shannon's guilty plea because to do otherwise would "have a marked effect on the most time-consuming aspect of the trial, namely the proof of the trail of false invoices and overpayment."[280] In other words, the limited guilty plea, based on an amendment to the original indictment, was declared admissible as a short cut to save the prosecution the bother of proving its case. At no point was the jury told about Shannon's private tax affairs, or about the agreement which the Revenue had reached with him. On the contrary, the jury were given the impression that the guilty plea was made freely and with contrition. The jury was kept in the dark about the key facts concerning Shannon.

The issue of Shannon's guilty plea, and what evidential status to accord it, was at the heart of the appeal which Michael Hunt lodged immediately after his conviction. The appeal was heard in 1994. Hunt again denied that he was involved in a conspiracy and said that, if there had been a conspiracy to avoid tax, the Japanese were the authors of it. He had denied throughout the trial that there was proof of fraud committed by him and said that the Revenue's version of events was also consistent with a fraud practised by the Japanese.

Hunt's new defence counsel – Hunt had sacked his original lawyers and complained bitterly about how badly they had handled the case – tried to convince the Appeal Court judge that Shannon's guilty plea should not have been admitted in evidence against him. Their argument had solid basis in English law, which has a substantial body of jurisprudence governing what may or may not be admitted as evidence in a criminal trial. It was in vain. The various arguments by his new lawyers alleging that the trial judge had erred in law were rejected and the sentence upheld. Nissan UK, through the conviction of its General Manager, had been criminalised.

Hunt's new barrister, Alun Jones QC, wrote several years later, "In my opinion, the legal history of this matter is flawed, shoddy and mean. The conviction of Mr Hunt was wrongly procured by the presentation to the jury of a confession, which was in reality a deal to the benefit of the Revenue and Shannon. Justice has not been done."[281] Norman Tebbit agreed: "Octav Botnar was wrongly accused."[282]

The guilty plea also made a nonsense of the warrant which had been issued for the arrest of Botnar. That warrant pertained to the allegation that Botnar had committed two successive tax frauds, involving two different shipping agents, the first from 1975-1983 and the second from 1983 onwards. Shannon's guilty plea pertained only to the period 1983-1991 and, as far as he was concerned, only to one year of that period, 1985-1986. It was therefore for this second period alone, 1983-1991, that Hunt was convicted. Hunt was in fact acquitted on the charges relating to the first period, 1975-1983. In the trial, moreover, the Revenue offered no evidence against Hunt for the first period, yet this first period was the legal basis for the arrest warrant issued in January 1992 against Botnar. No doubt aware of this inconsistency, the Revenue eventually issued a second arrest warrant against Botnar on 8 November 1995, this time in relation to allegations about the period 1983-1991, and after Botnar's lawyers had argued that the original warrant was invalid because his associate had been acquitted for the first period.

Many years later, when the original arrest warrant against Botnar was finally withdrawn, albeit – and much to Botnar's annoyance – only on the grounds of his ill health, a leader in *The Daily Telegraph* elegantly summed up the whole saga in a few quick paragraphs, an account it concluded by using the killer word "conspiracy", which it alleged had been hatched between the British Government and Nissan in Japan.

> "It is quite a story. At its heart is the allegation that Botnar was effectively sacrificed by the British authorities to pacify the gods of Nissan. Like the best conspiracies, what sounds at first like fantasy is backed up by a pile of circumstantial evidence, much of it quite convincing.
>
> The Revenue's case was that Nissan UK... inflated its input costs by putting the cars through the books of an offshore company and thus understated its British profits. But Nissan UK's declared profits were already more than the whole of the British motor distribution trade put together. The idea that they were really even higher, enough to generate another £238 million for the Revenue, always seemed patently absurd. Once Botnar scarpered, the taxmen never sought his extradition either from Switzerland or during his frequent visits to France or Spain. He was not on Interpol's wanted list despite the criminal nature of the charges. The taxmen's action discouraged the Swiss authorities from granting him permanent residency and pressured him to cough up a decent sum in settlement. Eventually, this tactic worked.
>
> Then, there is what his advisers describe as the Revenue's complete failure to establish any evidence of fraud, even in its successful prosecutions of other Nissan UK directors. The Revenue never produced a single falsely inflated invoice, despite the size of the deception it claimed to have uncovered...
>
> Nissan of Japan was faced with the prospect of being unable to sell its British-built cars except through this curmudgeon, who had frequently told them how stupid they

were. For the new guard at Nissan, this was more than they could take. The British government desperately needed the first transplant to be successful and so the conspiracy to crush Mr Botnar was born."[283]

CHAPTER 14

THE FIGHT WITH THE REVENUE

And lose, and start again at your beginnings...

Having spent nearly two decades making huge donations to charities in Britain, Botnar found it ironic that he and his company were now being accused of tax fraud. He had always kept a very low profile as a philanthropist. Much of his charitable giving was therefore unknown, maybe even to the Revenue itself. He started to mention his donations only once the Revenue launched its accusations, in order to show that its claims were quite implausible: who would cheat and give away money at the same time? He also felt betrayed by the British establishment and was convinced that it was somehow in cahoots with the Japanese – what *The Daily Telegraph* called "a squalid deal between the British authorities and Nissan".[284]

Having obtained the conviction of Michael Hunt through the guilty plea of Frank Shannon in 1993, the Revenue then pursued Nissan UK for the allegedly unpaid tax. Botnar was determined to fight the Revenue's accusations. He insisted that there was nothing to justify any of them. He repeatedly told anyone who was willing to listen that the Revenue had not produced a single document – not a single false invoice, for instance – demonstrating a fraud at Nissan UK. This was in spite of the fact that the Revenue had taken away lorry loads of documents in June 1991, practically emptying the head office of Nissan UK in the process, and that it claimed to have uncovered a fraud involving hundreds of millions of pounds and spanning 20 years.

Botnar simultaneously continued to fight NMC over the termination of the franchise. He had tried and failed to have the dispute determined by the High Court in London, rather than settled by arbitration. During 1992, he had flown twice to Tokyo, in March and July, first to prepare for the arbitration panel and then for its first hearings.[285] Later in the year, in August[286], he flew to the United States for a further hearing before the arbitrators, which took place at the Massachusetts Institute of Technology. On this occasion, he was detained by US immigration as he arrived in Boston. In 1997, the Inland Revenue admitted that they had tipped off the American authorities about his arrival in Boston in 1992. Again, no attempt was made to extradite him.

The Japanese allegation that he had a dubious war record emerged during his interrogation by the American immigration officials, and no doubt some bogus credence was lent it by Botnar's German passport. Nevertheless, after a few hours of questioning, he was released without further ado.

During this gruelling period, Botnar fought NMC with determination but also with his famous mischievous humour. During the arbitration hearings in Tokyo, evidence was given for NMC by the first Managing Director of the Sunderland plant. Ian (now Sir Ian) Gibson was sitting in a hot, improvised courtroom trying to keep himself cool with a plain bamboo fan as he spoke. During the lunch break, Botnar instructed his team to go out and buy a garish and brightly coloured ladies' fan. They replaced Gibson's fan with this new one and waited for their prank to succeed. When proceedings recommenced, Gibson instinctively picked up the fan in front of him and, raising a wry smile as he realised the joke, carried on regardless. The Nissan UK team struggled to conceal their laughter and Gibson knew perfectly well who was responsible. Nissan UK's solicitor, Richard Fleck of Herbert Smith, gave the naughty boys from Worthing a very stern telling off. Botnar would have appreciated the absurdity of the situation: he was not averse to slapstick himself, for instance donning a wig and a party mask with slitty eyes on his trips to Japan.

In November 1992, the ruling of the Japan Commercial Arbitration Association went against Nissan UK. The Association ruled in NMC's favour for two reasons, first because of the transfer of the AFGH business to UBS, and second because of the abrasive tone which Botnar often adopted in his dealings with the Japanese. This latter point also came up in British court hearings and there seems little doubt that it is true. Botnar was notorious in Nissan UK board meetings and lunches for speaking his mind, with great force if necessary, and for calling his employees all kinds of things to their faces. Some people resented this; others dealt with it.

In late 1992, before he was temporarily too ill to travel, Botnar had tried to negotiate terms for bail with the Revenue so that he could come back to England and take part in the trial. These discussions came to nothing. The Revenue even repeatedly threatened to arrest him if he came back to Britain, and refused to guarantee that they would not seize his passport, which he needed in order to travel in pursuit of his ongoing dispute with Nissan. By early 1993, the Revenue had clinched Shannon's guilty plea, and Botnar was regularly portrayed in the press as "shadowy" and "reclusive", in line with the smear tactics first outlined in the Petition for Arbitration drawn up by NMC in Japan. The media was also happy to portray him as "a fugitive from justice", and this of course further damaged his reputation, as well as causing him problems with the Swiss authorities who refused to grant him full residency. (He continued to live in Switzerland on an annual permit until the day he died.)

His age and health notwithstanding, Botnar continued a punishing work schedule. The Fiat deal having fallen through in 1991, he remained the owner of the large network of AFG car dealerships. These dealerships had been selling Renault, Fiat, Citroën and Peugeot cars since the withdrawal of the Nissan franchise. Botnar wanted to dispose of them and the other parts of the AFGH group, including the finance company.

The eventual sale of AFGH in November 1994 to the business empire of Sir David and Sir Frederick Barclay was a good example of Botnar's own special business style. Concluded to the satisfaction of both parties in a matter of months, Botnar appeared to put the whole deal in jeopardy when, at the meeting in Geneva convened to sign the agreed deal, he asked for an extra £5 million for redundancy costs. He suggested the costs be split 50:50 between buyer and seller. The Barclay brothers were initially taken aback and everyone retired for half an hour's reflection to consider this unexpected 11th-hour proposition. In the end, all was agreed and the deal went ahead.

Botnar later told Otto Bruderer, the banker who had handled the fine detail of the transaction, that he had done this only to show Bruderer that he could have got a better deal. The Barclays remained in contact for several years afterwards, including after Botnar's death.

For the purposes of claiming that Nissan UK owed some £238 million in unpaid tax, the Revenue again relied on Frank Shannon. This time, Shannon told a much more detailed story than the rather minimalist one he had told in his partial guilty plea at the trial. At the trial he had said, and the prosecution and judge had accepted, three things – that he had derived no benefit from the alleged freight fraud, that he had not been a party to a conspiracy, and that he had only stumbled across the fraud in the last year of his employment at Nissan UK.

In the case mounted against Nissan UK for unpaid corporation tax, by contrast, he claimed in writing that he had been a co-conspirator for 17 years and said repeatedly that he had personally benefited from the fraud.[287] Whereas he had said at the time of the trial that Botnar had run a reign of terror at Nissan UK, he now alleged that he had been his willing co-conspirator for nearly two decades. These discrepancies came up in a hearing before the Special Commissioners in income tax held in November 1994 when Botnar's counsel asked Shannon, "Which of the two versions of the facts on this do you want to tell us today was a pack of lies?"[288]

Initially, the Revenue tried to insist that Nissan UK pay the disputed tax as a condition of being allowed to appeal against its claim. Such a sum was beyond the company's ability at that point, the business having been thrown into disarray by the cancellation of the Nissan franchise and by the fact that the Fiat deal had been sabotaged by the raid. The Revenue then applied to have Nissan UK put into liquidation, on the basis that its claims against the company, untested in court, exceeded Nissan UK's net assets (audited at £96.6 million at the end of July 1992).[289] It made this application *ex parte*, meaning that no one at Nissan UK knew it was happening.

The application therefore went unchallenged and so, early one Saturday morning, on 19 November 1993, teams of people from Price Waterhouse, who had been appointed to wind the company up, arrived at the Worthing head office. They took numerous documents including those relating to Nissan UK's defence against the Revenue's tax assessments and said that they would henceforth decide whether the company would contest the Revenue's claims. During this time, salaries and utility bills went unpaid.

A month later, Nissan UK successfully applied for the liquidators to be discharged. This was on the basis of a compromise agreement reached which meant that, for many years, the company had to work under very strict conditions: large payments had to be approved by the Revenue in court, for instance, and no dividends could be paid. Nissan UK's solicitor, Mark Spragg, recalls showing the agreement to Botnar. "Bloody rubbish!" Botnar shouted. "We must fight on." As they went through each provision of the agreement, however, he agreed that each one was "OK". When Spragg asked whether that meant they could agree the draft, Botnar again said it was all bloody rubbish. "What do you think you are doing?" he demanded. They started again and went through the whole text and Botnar agreed that each provision was acceptable.

"Why can't we agree it, then?" Spragg asked. "You can," said Botnar. So it was that the company operated under severe constraints which were not lifted until after the settlement was reached with the Revenue in October 1996.

All this led Botnar to make the comparison between the treatment he received from the Revenue and the way he had been treated by the Securitate in Romania. In 1996 he told *The Times* that the Inland Revenue's tactics "bear a striking resemblance to those of the terror police in former Communist countries of which I have had first-hand experience and which I thought I had left behind when I came to England."[290]

As the date of the hearing on tax claims approached, the Revenue informed Nissan UK that it would not be calling its witnesses from abroad to appear but would instead take their evidence in accordance with the Civil Evidence Act. This meant that Nissan UK's lawyers would not be able to cross-examine them, as they would not be physically present. The Revenue also told Nissan UK that if certain of the company's own witnesses came to the UK, they would be arrested as co-conspirators of Hunt and Shannon.

Faced with unfairness bordering on extortion, and with his health continuing to weaken, Botnar became gradually convinced that he had no choice but to settle. Part of the reason was that Marcela could not bear the stress and did not want the affair to drag on any longer. In September 1996, the Botnars were interviewed together by *The Mail on Sunday*. Botnar confided: "If I do a deal with the British taxman I will do it for Marcela, because I don't think she can take much more..."[291]

Thus it was that, in October 1996, he reluctantly agreed to put an end to a painful and destructive battle against what seemed to be the unchecked and unaccountable powers of the Revenue, agreeing to pay them £59 million. The Revenue had said it would settle for £60 million but Botnar could not resist gaining a last little victory against them. By some calculations, the full amount originally claimed by the Revenue could have been 10 times this figure – £238 million in allegedly unpaid tax plus interest over 17 years, and penalties could have brought it to £600 million.[292]

Nonetheless, Botnar was determined, up to the bitter end, to show that he was innocent as charged. On the contract document setting out the terms of the settlement Botnar added by hand the following statement underneath his signature, a statement which was countersigned by the representative of the Commissioners of the Inland Revenue:

"The sum of £59 million is paid irrevocably but I deny on behalf of myself and Nissan UK Ltd that we do owe this amount to the Inland Revenue and the Inland Revenue have not in five years proved their case…"[293]

Five years after the Inland Revenue had mounted raids of an unprecedented scale against Nissan UK, and had done so in the most publicly damaging way, a conclusion had been reached. Along the way, a highly successful business had been destroyed, along with the jobs of 4,000 people. The Revenue may have walked away with £59 million, but that was to be the only payment it would receive. £59 million is a similar figure to that which Nissan UK and AFGH would together have paid in corporation tax for each and every one of the intervening five years, and into the future as well. The Inland Revenue had destroyed one of the country's biggest corporate taxpayers.

While this whole saga was going on, Botnar was also fighting a separate battle with the Revenue over his personal tax affairs. Botnar had had a heart attack in 1970 when he was in his late fifties. With no heir after 1972, if he had he died at that point, his estate, which he wanted to go to charity, would have been taxed out of existence. In order to realise his intention that, after both his death and that of Marcela, only charity should be entitled to his fortune, Botnar decided to settle his Datsun UK shares in a trust based in Liechtenstein set up by his lifelong lawyer, the Basel-based Dr Peter Lenz.

It should not be forgotten that 1974 was the era of socialism red in tooth and claw. Labour had just been elected to power in February and the new Chancellor, Denis Healey, who had briefly joined the Communist Party in 1937, had reportedly said that his intention was to squeeze the rich until the pips squeaked. In fact, "squeeze the rich until the pips squeak" is one of the greatest quotes never made: rather as with Enoch Powell's "rivers of blood" speech – also a misquoted phrase that was in fact never pronounced – it appears that this famous quotation is false. Healey insisted later that he had said that he would squeeze property speculators until the pips squeaked, not the rich in general. However, the misquote did accurately sum up the Labour Party's punitive taxation policy at the time. It aimed at reducing retained earnings above a certain level to nearly zero. Healey's first budget, passed on 26 March 1974 within weeks of the election, put the top rate of tax up to 83 per cent for incomes over £20,000 per year, with a marginal rate of 98 per cent for the highest earners.[294] In other words, people like Botnar kept a mere two per cent of their income.

The terms of the trust were explicitly framed to exclude Octav and Marcela Botnar from benefiting from the proceeds because its goal was to accumulate money for charity. Clause 23 of the settlement provided that no excluded person (Octav and Marcela Botnar were listed as such) was to be capable of taking any benefit in accordance with the terms of the settlement.[295] Clause 23 provided as follows:

"No Excluded Person shall be capable of taking any benefit in accordance with the terms of this settlement and in particular but without prejudice to the generality of the foregoing provisions of this Clause:

(a)   The trust fund shall henceforth be possessed and enjoyed to the entire exclusion of any such Excluded Person and of any benefit to him by contract or otherwise

(b)   No part of the capital or income of the trust fund shall be paid or lent or applied for the benefit of any such Excluded Person."

Indeed, neither Marcela nor Botnar ever did benefit from it. The statutes of the trust were drawn up to provide for it to last for a maximum of 80 years and for the trustees to be able to use the funds "for charitable purposes" earlier if they so decided (clause 2).[296] The trust therefore had charitable status in the eyes of the British tax authorities, and in Liechtenstein, and, as such, was not subject to tax. Because the bulk of the money Botnar had made – the capital value of the shares and the substantial dividends they paid – was settled into this trust, the Botnars in fact lived modestly, relatively at least to the income which his companies generated. Indeed, people who knew Botnar have testified independently of one another that he was in fact not interested in money at all.[297]

Although the Liechtenstein trust was therefore chosen as a means of avoiding Labour's taxation rates – the goal was laid out in the very first provisions of the memorandum written by Dr Peter Lenz in October 1974 when it was set up – such tax avoidance was perfectly legal, especially as Botnar was not a British national and owned no property in Britain. The advice he followed in creating the trust was similar to that given to countless other people in comparable situations at the time, when it was common for people who had made money to leave the country altogether to avoid tax.

The Revenue, however, had the bit between its teeth. It

was convinced that it had uncovered a fraudster. The case was heard by the Special Commissioners of the Inland Revenue in May 1996, a few months before the agreement to settle the outstanding claims against Nissan UK with a payment of £59 million. The Commissioners found in favour of Botnar's claim that he and his wife were excluded as beneficiaries and that he therefore should not be taxed on the trust's income.[298] So the Revenue lost.

It appealed, insisting that Botnar owed tax on the money in this trust because he would have "the power to enjoy" it in some hypothetical future scenario, as opposed to the actual situation in which he did not. The Revenue invoked a clause in the Income and Corporation Taxes Act of 1970 to argue that Octav and Marcela might "in the event of the exercise or successive exercise of one or more powers... become entitled to the beneficial enjoyment" of the income from the trust.[299] The Revenue argued that the trustees could create another trust, pay money into that new trust, and that the Botnars could therefore benefit from the money that way. In other words, the Revenue argued that Botnar had already committed fraud because he might at some future point commit one, and that he should therefore be taxed now for earnings which he might one day make in some hypothetical scenario. The Revenue's case was nothing other than the presumption of guilt.

On 29 July 1996, so before the final settlement over Nissan UK (in October) but after the Revenue had lost the Trust case (in May), Botnar, accompanied by accountants from Coopers & Lybrand, agreed to meet representatives of the Revenue in France. During the course of the conversation, one of the Revenue officers repeatedly said that the Revenue would continue to make Botnar's life very difficult until he handed over very large sums of money. They asked for £60 million. At this point, the conversation went as follows.

1O DOWNING STREET
LONDON SW1A 2AA

19 January 1990

Dear Mr. Botnar,

I am writing to thank you so very much for the
wonderfully generous gifts which you and your Company
have made to various Charities in the United Kingdom in
recent years.

I know that your support for handicapped children, for
medical research and for the arts has been very greatly
appreciated, and has enriched the lives of so many.

I want you to know how specially grateful and
appreciative I am.

Yours sincerely

Margaret Thatcher

Octav Botnar Esq

A letter from an appreciative Prime Minister. Botnar's heart beat on the left but he admired Margaret Thatcher for her drive and courage. With typical modesty, though, he declined the opportunity to be presented to her.

The Octav Botnar Wing, Great Ormond Street Hospital for Children, London.

Topping out ceremony for the Octav Botnar Wing, Great Ormond Street Hospital (GOSH) – 16 March 2004. Sir Anthony Tippet, former Chief Executive, GOSH (left); Marcela Botnar (centre); and Dr Jane Collins, Chief Executive, GOSH (right).

The Camelia Botnar Laboratories, Great Ormond Street Hospital for Children.

THE BOARD OF THE
GREAT ORMOND STREET HOSPITAL
FOR CHILDREN NHS TRUST
are deeply grateful to

Mr Octav Botnar

for his generous donations which have
made possible the creation of the

CAMELIA BOTNAR LABORATORIES
and the beginning of the redevelopement
of the old parts of the Hospital to
complete the upgrading of all wards to
take the Hospital into the 21st Century

He is the greatest benefactor the
Hospital has ever had in its long history

Sir Brian Hill
Chairman

on behalf of all who work for and in the Hospital

*TRH the Prince of Wales and
the Duchess of Cornwall visit
the newly-opened Octav Botnar
Wing, Great Ormond Street
Hospital for Children –
21 November 2006.*

As Patron of the Nuffield Orthopaedic Centre, HRH the Duchess of Cornwall opens Phase 2 of The Botnar Research Centre at the Institute of Musculoskeletal Sciences, Oxford, accompanied by Lord Tebbit CH PC – 9 May 2014.

The Botnar Research Centre at the Institute of Musculoskeletal Sciences, Nuffield Orthopaedic Centre, Oxford.

Apprentices from the Camelia Botnar Foundation install a life-size metal sculpture of a horse at the Botnar Research Centre, Oxford. The horse was built at the Foundation's Cowfold workshops.

The Camelia Botnar Plaza in front of the Yitzhak Rabin Building at the Hebrew University of Jerusalem, to which Botnar gave $12.5 million for its construction. It houses the Mandel Institute of Jewish Studies.

Botnar made a donation of $20 million towards the construction of a new building at the heart of the Soroka Medical Center in the Southern Israeli city of Be'er-Sheva.

The Octav and Marcela Botnar Medical Research Building, The Hebrew University, Ein Karem Campus, Jerusalem. A unique facility with laboratories designed to conduct leading-edge microbiological research and training. Botnar's combined donations to the Hebrew University made him one of the biggest donors in the university's history.

Ion Rațiu (left) and the Rt Hon Lord Tebbit CH (right) speaking at the Memorial Ceremony to celebrate Botnar's life. The ceremony was held in the grounds of the Camelia Botnar Foundation, Cowfold, West Sussex on 21 October 1998, on what would have been Botnar's 85th birthday.

Ivory's House in Cowfold, West Sussex, the home of the Camelia Botnar Foundation. Designed by Arts & Crafts architect Walter Brierley, the house sits in a 500-acre estate from which the Foundation operates its many workshops, rural estates activities, plants nursery and large garden centre.

Botnar: What for?

Revenue officer: Well, we want to include something for the Trust case.

Botnar: But you lost the Trust case!

Revenue officer: We will appeal it.

Botnar: You have destroyed my company. Now you want
to hang me and you expect me to pay for the rope!

It is clear from the Revenue's various turgid reasonings and rulings
that their officials were not criminal lawyers, and probably not lawyers at
all. At the beginning of one of their documents, which has entered the
official record, they even managed to get Botnar's name wrong, referring
to him as "Otto".[300] They were deaf to the arguments made by Botnar's
lawyers that the wording of the trust precluded the transfer of funds to
him or Marcela, even in the event of the closure of the trust and the
transfer of its funds to a new structure. It was essentially a matter of
discretion whether the Commissioners decided that the relevant clause
in the 1974 Act could be interpreted one way or another to make him
liable, or not, for tax. The Revenue's claim was additionally odd because
by then Botnar clearly did have a very established track record as a major
philanthropist. The Botnars' argument that the trust had been set up to
amass money to give to charity was not, by any means, implausible.

The oddness was only aggravated by the fact that the Revenue
had known since the 1970s that Botnar's Datsun UK shares had been
settled in this trust. They had sent their first enquiries to Botnar's
accountants about it on 10 November 1975.[301] On 23 October 1978,
in response to a letter from the Revenue expressing disbelief that the
trust had been created for any reason other than to benefit Mr and Mrs
Botnar secretly, Botnar's accountants, Thornton Baker, had written
to the Revenue to tell them that by 1974 the Botnars had more than
enough money to live off and that, their only daughter having died,
their motives in setting up the trust were "entirely charitable".[302] By
that stage, the trust had indeed begun to make charitable donations

to the Camelia Botnar Foundation in Cowfold. The Revenue had not taken matters any further and the file was closed in 1979. Botnar had had every reason, therefore, to believe that the matter was settled.

The Special Commissioners, who heard the case, appeared to be unaware of the principle of non-contradiction. On the one hand, when they ruled on the appeal in November 1997, the Commissioners continued to accept that Botnar had never benefited from the money paid into the 1974 trust:

"Subject to only one point of minor detail, we have no hesitation in accepting the conclusions (of a report commissioned by Mr Mainz of Coopers & Lybrand) set out in para 202:

'In summary, I conclude that:

(a)   the 1974 settlement has been the ultimate beneficial owner of the controlling shareholding in NUK since 1974;

(b)   the 1974 settlement's ownership of the shares in NUK has been channelled through various structures;

(c)   Dr Lenz has at all times been the protector of the 1974 settlement and has, in practice, controlled it since 1974;

(d)   apart from two transactions in relation to which I have not been able to reach a final conclusion, there is no evidence that Mr or Mrs Botnar have benefited personally from the dividends and subsequent investment income received by the 1974 settlement or its underlying companies.'"[303]

On the other hand, though, they also insisted that the trust was nothing but a smoke and mirrors operation to enable Botnar to enjoy the proceeds of the fund at some future date:

"In the light of the evidence as a whole, and in particular the Lenz memorandum, we record at the outset that we are clearly satisfied that the establishment of the settlement was part of a series of steps, including the exchange of shares with Octav Botnar Ltd, which were taken to ensure that the Datsun UK shares and the income therefrom could at some time in the future be utilised for the benefit of Mr and Mrs Botnar, while in the meantime minimising taxation and establishing a cloak which concealed that intended future result."[304]

The Revenue also disregarded, and did not challenge, the evidence given by a QC whom it called as an expert in the case, and who is referred to in the ruling as "a leading member of the Revenue bar at the relevant time", who confirmed that the arrangements did indeed mean that Mr and Mrs Botnar could not enjoy the funds and that they should therefore be treated as charitable and exempt from tax.[305]

For all these reasons, Botnar told the press at the time that the claims being made against him in the trust case were designed to complete the Revenue's blackening of his name by adding a personal tax fraud onto the corporate one allegedly practised by Nissan UK. He again rejected the accusations en bloc, accusing the Revenue of sabotaging his charitable giving:

"The accusations about personal tax were put into the package of tax evasion allegations to help to justify the raid on my company in 1991. The Revenue had to do so to make its case. That made me very angry because it perverts the true purpose of the trust money, which is all for charity. I have never taken any for myself. I am 82 going on 83. What exactly do you think I am going to get up to with all that cash? And sadly, I have no one to leave it to. I just want to see it do some good. If I had not been so busy fighting the corporation tax case I would have set about distributing the money by now. I would rather have the pleasure of seeing it used in my lifetime."[306]

As part of his attempt to have the arrest warrant dropped, Botnar enlisted the help of his old friend, Norman Tebbit, whom he authorised to negotiate on his behalf. A meeting was held with the Inland Revenue at Somerset House in London on 22 October 1997. The atmosphere was tense and disagreeable. The most senior of the Revenue men present, Stephen Matheson, the Revenue's Deputy Chairman, held the meeting with his feet on his desk, a deliberate act of disrespect towards the former Cabinet Minister. Another peppered his comments with vague and supercilious accusations, a situation made surreal by the fact – which Tebbit was happy to point out – that Botnar was a foreign national living abroad and that his assets were, in any case, a long way out of the Revenue's reach.

Tebbit asked the officials why they had not applied for Botnar's extradition to Britain when he had been briefly detained by US immigration in Boston in 1992. One of the Revenue officials said, "We informed American immigration that he was arriving from Paris on a plane."[307] Tebbit put it to the Revenue's lawyer that this incident proved that the arrest warrant had been issued "for a collateral purpose", to keep Botnar out of the UK, because otherwise the Revenue could have applied for his extradition from the US, which the American authorities would have doubtless granted.[308] Indeed, no attempt was ever made to extradite him from Switzerland, even though other alleged tax fraudsters have been extradited to Britain from that country. Had Botnar returned to the UK, he might well have been able to argue his case more forcefully. The Revenue never applied for Botnar's extradition from Switzerland, nor from any of the other European countries he travelled to during this period. He was never put on an Interpol list. The Revenue never requested the Swiss authorities to commence any prosecution against him either.

On a personal level, Botnar's enforced absence from the UK meant that it was impossible for him to visit his daughter Camelia's grave in Gunnersbury, or any of the charitable projects he had endowed like the Camelia Botnar Foundation or Great Ormond Street Hospital. He maintained a strong interest in their activities but could never inspect them for himself after 1991.

At one point in the meeting, Matheson suggested that the Revenue might have further claims on Botnar, above and beyond the already enormous ones being made against the trust. When asked what these other claims might be, Matheson asked the Revenue's solicitor, Richard Walters, also present, to reply:

"It is a difficult question. I think Mr Botnar may have other liabilities but at the moment they are essentially inchoate. We take the view that the liability on the trust was so high that we did not want to waste our time with other claims. But we have very fertile imaginations. We could raise an assessment or two."[309]

Undeterred by such threats, and notwithstanding his failing health, after five years of fighting Botnar remained determined to clear his name. A year after he had settled with the Revenue on the Nissan UK case, but with the trust case still under appeal, Botnar's lawyers applied in October 1997 for the arrest warrant from the Nissan UK case to be quashed. This was six years after the original raid. The application was made to the magistrates' court in Worthing, where the original warrant had been obtained. Before the hearing, the Revenue, realising that it could lose, decided to withdraw the warrant on the grounds of Botnar's bad health.

Ever the fighter, undaunted and dogged to the end, Botnar immediately shot back. He did not want the warrant to be withdrawn on a mere pretext, but only on the basis that it had been unfounded in the first place. He demanded full exoneration and issued a statement rubbishing the Revenue's excuses. "The Revenue has known for four and a half years of the perilous state of my health, following surgery for the removal of my entire stomach in 1993. We had asked for the warrants to be cancelled on the grounds that the Revenue had applied for them and maintained them for ulterior motives, and had no intention whatsoever of bringing me to trial."[310]

Having obtained their agreement to withdraw the warrant, Botnar's lawyers tried to get the Revenue to agree to a warmly worded press release which acknowledged his philanthropy, and in which the Revenue would have admitted that Botnar had never been charged with anything, and that it had never proved that he, or any other director of Nissan UK, had siphoned off hundreds of millions of pounds. The Revenue refused.

CHAPTER 15

THE DETERMINATION TO CLEAR
HIS NAME

If neither foes nor loving friends can hurt you...

Since the termination of the distribution agreement by NMC and the raids by the Inland Revenue, Botnar's life had been overwhelmed by the need to fight his corner, often against the odds. Botnar believed that he was the victim of an alliance between NMC and the Inland Revenue. However, "victim" was not an epithet which sat comfortably with a man who consistently and repeatedly stood up to injustice. He was not about to change.

As *The Mail on Sunday* had reported in 1996, the Botnars had "endured five years of lonely isolation under a cloud of suspicion". Marcela had explained what this had meant in everyday life: "Sometimes I feel as though the Inland Revenue simply wants to reduce us to nothing. To humiliate us even in Switzerland. We can't go anywhere without being reminded of it. Octav was in a hospital waiting room and he flicked through a magazine and found an article about us. We took it home so no one else there would see it and recognise us."[311]

It hurt Botnar every time he read the frequent press reports, many of which appeared to been generated by the Inland Revenue or by NMC, which referred to him as a "fugitive" or the "prime mover" in the alleged fraud. Although neither statement was true, both were repeated endlessly.

For a man with few material wants, and for whom money was surprisingly unimportant, something had been stolen which to him was invaluable: his good name. When the Revenue refused to allow the settlement to be presented as he saw it, he considered that he was left with only one option. In order to clear his name he chose to sue personally, bringing a claim of malicious prosecution against the Inland Revenue, and naming openly as co-defendants Revenue officers Robert Brown and Tom Cawdron, the architects of the raid.[312]

A writ of summons was issued on 18 February 1998, alleging that the defendants had "maliciously", and "without reasonable or probable cause", applied for arrest warrants against Botnar in January 1992 and November 1995, and that the original raid, executed in June 1991, was "malicious and designed to destroy Nissan UK".[313] His lawyers wrote, "We will argue that the issue of the arrest warrants was and continues to be for a collateral purpose, namely the extraction of money from Mr Botnar by the Inland Revenue."[314] Botnar was claiming that the Revenue was guilty of extortion.

In drafting the writ, the lawyers pointed out to the High Court that, in December 1990, NMC had purported unilaterally to terminate the 1971 agreement, and had established a wholly- owned subsidiary in the United Kingdom as the sole importer of its cars. NMC's intention was to take over the distribution business and network of dealerships and garages established by Nissan UK and thereby secure the profits then being made by Nissan UK without paying for them. The writ stated that it had been the intention of NMC "to destroy the public standing and reputation of the plaintiff".

The writ went on to point the finger at the Inland Revenue, saying that it "had ensured the publication of the invasions [the raids] would be as widespread and dramatic as possible in order that serious damage would be caused thereby to the plaintiff [Botnar] and Nissan UK over and above the highly damaging effects of the invasions themselves". And although the business of Nissan UK "had been brought to a standstill by the invasions, no attempt was made to recover allegedly unpaid tax, and no particulars of tax fraud were provided". Furthermore, it had been "improperly concealed from the

Court that the only evidence of a tax fraud committed by Nissan UK came from the tainted and self-serving admission of Shannon".

The writ continued: "There has never been any proof, notwithstanding the passage of eight years, that Nissan UK nor anyone connected with the company had participated in the alleged fraud." It then referred to Shiro Ozawa, the senior NMC executive, who had testified in a letter that the slush fund in Switzerland had in fact been set up by the Japanese.[315]

The writ then made clear what Botnar's objectives were in bringing this claim: "The Plaintiff wishes to clear his name and will donate all damages found owing to the Nuffield Orthopaedic Centre Appeal."

The Revenue stalled for time. The original defence was due to be given on 19 March 1998. Extra time was accorded until 3 April. On the last day, the Revenue said it needed more time to prepare its defence and asked for three months. The judge allowed them six more weeks, until 15 May. Again on the last available day, the Revenue applied for the writ to be struck out rather than filing a defence. Unsurprisingly, that tactic failed.

Eventually, the case was heard at the High Court in London on 7 July 1998. The judge seemed particularly interested in the fact that the Revenue defended the arrest warrant only on the basis of the Hunt and Shannon convictions. These had been obtained over a year after the warrant had been issued against Botnar. The judge repeatedly asked the Revenue's lawyers how a conviction obtained in June 1993 could be used to justify an arrest warrant issued in January 1992, and whether the Revenue really had had evidence in January 1992 to justify applying for it. He said, "I have nothing before me to suggest what the evidence was in January 1992."

The Revenue argued its corner but the judge persisted. "There may be ample evidence but I am worried. I am very troubled, I tell you. I think there is a strong chance the Plaintiff's case may fail, for a number of reasons, but to strike it out without knowing what information there was would be wrong."[316] This means that he had not been provided with evidence showing what the Revenue had known when it applied for the warrant.

The judge became very irritated. He even started to go over some of the old material of the Hunt trial, for instance asking the Revenue what proof it had for claiming that the initiative to change the shipping arrangements from cost, insurance and freight (CIF in the jargon) to only cost and insurance (C&I) had been Nissan UK's. Botnar had always tried to explain that a distributor like himself was never in a position to change the fundamental purchasing terms in this way, but that such a change could be made only by the principal partner, Nissan in Japan.

"I think it is wholly incredible," the judge said, starting to lose his temper and adding that the Revenue had not demonstrated its case properly at all. He ordered the Revenue to pay the costs of the hearing and ordered it to produce its material by Thursday 9 July, with the plaintiff given until Friday 10 July to respond to the defendants' affidavit. A hearing was scheduled for 13 July 1998. However, fate intervened and prevented this hearing from ever taking place. The judge's statements on 7 July, rubbishing the Revenue's case, were therefore to be the last words in the futile seven-year tax case mounted against Botnar.

CHAPTER 16

DEATH IN VILLARS

If you can force your heart and nerve and sinew
To serve your turn long after they are gone
And so hold on when there is nothing in you...

The arrest warrant in 1992 had been issued during the Botnars' annual Christmas holiday in Switzerland, where they usually stayed until the end of January. Historically, business was usually very quiet in December, January and early February. This was because the annual quota of cars had to be sold by November, and there were therefore usually no cars left to sell in December. The following year's cars would not begin to arrive until the end of January, given the time it took to ship cars from Japan.

The Botnars had built Chalet Marcela in the 1970s. It was situated in the mountains in Villars-sur-Ollon in the canton of Vaud, and the Botnars tended to go there two or three times a year. The plot of land was bigger than the planners usually allowed, but they had come to an agreement with the village authorities which meant that it was bequeathed to the commune on their deaths.

Once the implications of the arrest warrant had sunk in, it became clear to the Botnars that they would have to turn their holiday home into a permanent base. They found themselves faced with the unexpected challenge of transporting their lives to Switzerland from England, where they had lived for nearly 30 years, having made no prior arrangements to do so. Colleagues who made the trip to Switzerland from Britain to see the Botnars were occasionally asked to bring items over from their homes in Worthing and London.

The Botnars had had housekeepers in Switzerland for many years, the couple they employed having an easy life, only really on duty for a few weeks a year. Once Villars became the Botnars' main home, the Swiss couple were replaced by their full-time UK housekeepers, a Portuguese couple and their small son. This couple and their child ended up becoming part of the Botnars' closest circle, effectively part of their family.

Luisa Calheno had started working for the Botnars in 1986, at first for a few hours a day and then full-time. She had come to them through Claude Bunford, Max's second wife. Luisa worked for the Botnars first at Eaton Place, later at Eaton Square. She hardly spoke a word of English. Within only a few days, Botnar offered to pay for her to have English lessons. This was a typical gesture, which flowed from his profound belief in the necessity and possibility of self-improvement. Luisa gladly accepted.

Shortly after her son, Sergio, was born, Luisa and her husband Costa moved into a lodge at the Botnars' company house in High Salvington, a house Botnar had designed and which overlooked Worthing and the sea. (Costa's first name was in fact Porfirio, a bit of a mouthful for non-Portuguese speakers, so the Botnars called him by his surname from his mother's side.) Here, Luisa worked as housekeeper and cook while Costa managed the house and grounds. This was no small task: the house had a large engine room which served the gymnasium and the swimming pool, and these had to be kept in running order. There was an acre of land including a large koi pond, a dramatic water feature and a large aviary, all of which Costa looked after. (Amongst other things, Botnar kept an extensive collection of ornamental pheasants and softbills.) In the main reception room of the house, there was a large tank of marine fish, the composition of whose water had to be kept just right or else the fish died. This, too, was Costa's job. The Calhenos were in the property when the Revenue arrived early in the morning for the June 1991 raid, so they had been through that experience together. (Marcela was in the flat in Eaton Square and had to deal with the men from the Revenue on her own.)

In Switzerland, Costa was given other tasks too. In April 1992, *The Mail on Sunday*, which appeared to have become somewhat obsessed with Botnar, sent a junior reporter from the UK to Villars to ask questions locally, and then to knock on the door of Chalet Marcela. When the journalist announced who he was, Botnar instructed Costa to drench him with the hosepipe – a refreshing experience, no doubt, given that this was halfway up a mountain in April and snow was still on the ground.

The resulting newspaper article nevertheless made no mention of the dousing shower, but was instead peppered with the sort of tabloid hyperbole that is often the product of journalistic indolence rather than serious investigation. Amongst other inaccuracies, the report suggested that the Botnars were living in a six-bedroomed luxury chalet overlooking Lake Geneva. The truth was rather different. The chalet, although comfortable, reflected the Botnars' comparatively simple needs and had only two bedrooms. As for the view of the lake, it was non-existent as the chalet was separated from it by ten kilometres of mountain ridges.

The Calhenos were to remain in Villars for well over 20 years, until after Marcela's death in 2014, occupying a housekeepers' apartment on the ground floor with their own piece of garden and a vegetable patch. They worked all year round except for a four- week holiday in Portugal each summer. Luisa took care of all the housework, including cooking and laundry, while Costa did the driving and looked after the upkeep of the grounds and the house maintenance, just as he had in Worthing. The chalet at Villars also had a koi pond: although it was smaller than the one in Sussex, it had to be heated during the long mountain winter to prevent the fish from dying. There was also a small trout lake, an indoor pool, a gym and a sauna.

With no children of their own, the Botnars practically

adopted the Calhenos' little boy, Sergio. They treated him with immense affection, as if he were their own flesh and blood: in fact, they told the boy to address them as "uncle" and "aunt". The Calheno family repaid this with intense loyalty and affection of their own, which was remarked on by all those who visited the Botnars in Villars. Sergio was sent to the local international school, paid for by the Botnars, and was encouraged to study medicine, which he did, also thanks to support from them, before switching to law. As a boy, the Botnars would take him with them whenever they went out to a restaurant. Botnar would always be pushing Sergio, just as he pushed everyone, testing his times tables and encouraging him to learn.

"They were very kind and good people," recalled Costa Calheno in 2016. "He was a brilliant man," agreed his wife, Luisa, tearfully.[317] The housekeepers recalled that the Botnars always wanted things done in a very precise way, but that they were always good-hearted. Some people might have found them demanding, but not the Calhenos. Costa testified that Botnar might, for instance, ask him to fix an electrical unit like a plug. If Calheno protested that he was not an electrician, Botnar would say firmly but friendlily, "Try. Just try. You can do it." On other occasions, he would say more abruptly, " 'I don't know' does not exist."[318]

Costa Calheno remembers that Botnar was always working: "He never relaxed." He could not bear to waste time. So, for instance, when he had a flight to catch, he would always leave the house much later than Costa would have liked. If Costa protested that they were going to be late and miss the plane, Botnar would simply tell him to drive faster.

Botnar was always smartly dressed in a suit or jacket and tie. When guests arrived at Villars, Luisa would ask them to wait in the sitting room: when she came in to tell him they had arrived, he would ask her if he was properly dressed. While living in Britain,

Botnar had used a Savile Row tailor, a German wartime refugee from Nazism. Many years before, Botnar had bought his clothes in Paris, and on one such outing acquired a nickname which Marcela used for the rest of his days as a term of endearment. As a result of his mishearing at a Paris tailor's of the French word "taille" (meaning "size"), he was to be known by her thenceforth as "Taila". He and Marcela had a flat in Paris, in rue Albéric Magnard, in the 16th arrondissement of the city he had always loved and where he would eventually be buried. When in Paris he and Marcela would go to the opera, the theatre or the cinema, and of course out to dinner.

Botnar kept fit and tried to look after his health. He had a cycling machine in the chalet and would exercise on it, just as he had had gyms in his other properties in Britain and Spain. As a result, he was a strong man, even in his old age. The Botnars were also voracious readers, Botnar poring over the papers in the morning. The house had a big library, just as he had had wonderful libraries in High Salvington, Eaton Square and Javea in Spain. He was an avid reader, especially of books about the Second World War – there were always plenty of works on Stalin, Hitler and Churchill – but also of other subjects including philosophy and biography in English, French, German and Romanian. He retained a lifelong interest in world history, philosophy and politics and would eagerly keep up with world affairs.

Throughout her life with him, Marcela had always taken great care over Botnar's diet. It was the one aspect of him that she could control. During the days at Worthing, she would ensure that the directors' cook provided him with a square meal at lunchtime, often buying fresh fish herself for the purpose. However, the Botnars' health consciousness was not enough to prevent the worst of all diseases. The year 1992 had another blow in store for the couple, in addition to the fall-out with the Revenue and the effective destruction of Nissan UK. At the end of their first year in enforced exile in Switzerland, Botnar learned that he had stomach cancer. Stomach cancer generally manifests itself as an extremely malignant tumour with few long-term survivors.

Many people in such circumstances might have accepted their fate. Not Botnar. His attitude to this extremely bad news was characteristically combative. A doctor in Lausanne had told him to enjoy life to the full for the coming six months because he was certainly going to die after that. Botnar's reaction was reminiscent of the words attributed to Lord Palmerston: "Die, my dear doctor? That is the last thing I shall do!" Botnar was simply not prepared to accept that death was near. He decided to take action for himself. He contacted Professor MacGregor, his blood pressure specialist from London, and asked him to put together a team of experts to come to Switzerland to see him.

The doctors were largely pessimistic but Botnar was determined to survive. After all, his inner strength had enabled him to rebound from numerous other health scares throughout his life: he had nearly died of malnutrition in the Romanian labour camp, where he had also been diagnosed with asthenia. He had had a heart attack in Britain in 1970. In 1986, he had been treated in London for very high blood pressure, severe vascular disease and the narrowing of several critical arteries; these were no doubt the consequence of his having smoked heavily until 1970, when he gave up completely.

So, faced with the news that he had cancer, he resolved to solve the problem himself, through a combination of sheer willpower and radical action. He announced abruptly to the doctors who came to Switzerland that he had concluded that he needed to have his stomach removed. He managed to overcome their initial scepticism about taking such a step: as Professor MacGregor commented later, "This turned out to be an entirely correct decision that he had taken himself."[319] The operation was conducted in February 1993, and for the next five years of his life Botnar survived by eating normally but only small amounts at a time. In the last 18 months of his life, he was fed through a feeding tube inserted into part of his intestine, and using nutritional advice given him by an Israeli nutritionist, Elliot Berry. Oddly, the removal of his stomach cured his vascular disease; but of course it ruined his ability to indulge his love of good food. He was to survive after the surgery – albeit increasingly weakened – for another five years, again defying all the odds: the magnitude of the surgery involved in removing a stomach means that it is an operation which carries a high mortality rate even in younger and healthier patients than Botnar.

Botnar retained his huge energy in spite of his illness. Even in Switzerland, when he worked from home, he would be on the phone all day. "He never stopped talking," recalled the Calhenos. When he was not on the phone, he would be in the garden giving instructions to the gardener, forever changing things around. Marcela had never liked the fact that he worked all the time, but she could do nothing to stop him, as work was what drove him and what he liked to do.

Elliot Berry, originally from England and who had been at Cambridge with Lawrence Cartier who introduced him to Botnar, devoted himself to working out how to give Botnar the nutrition he required. Having had his stomach removed, Botnar never felt hungry because the body produced no enzymes: the danger therefore existed that he might starve to death without noticing. Berry, in turn, introduced Botnar to US nutritionist Dr Moshe Shike, who was pioneering a procedure whereby a hole is created in the stomach through which high protein fluids can be injected, which act as food and hydration. As in London, where Botnar typically made donations to the institutes in which the doctors worked who were treating him, he gave generously to Berry's Department of Human Nutrition and Metabolism at the Hebrew University of Jerusalem. He also gave regularly to the Centre Hospitalier Universitaire Vaudois where he was looked after by Professeur Pascal Nicod, and where Moshe Shike supervised the operation to create the means by which to keep Botnar fed.

Like many, Elliot Berry became very fond of the Botnars, whom he and his wife used to visit in Villars. Berry recalled of Marcela, "She was a tough woman but always very gracious and polite." But although he did his best to help Botnar after the removal of his stomach, Berry felt that Botnar had been deeply wounded by the treatment he had received at the hands of NMC and the Inland Revenue. "He was deeply stricken by it, to the soul," he recalls. Although Botnar retained until the end the fighting spirit which had been his hallmark, eventually the drastic measures taken to cure his cancer meant that, in Berry's words, he was "like a motor running down".[320]

Botnar tried to force his body to obey his will and continued to fight in spite of the fact that his strength was slowly ebbing away. He would insist on taking a daily walk, pushing himself to an active pace, but the distances he could manage inevitably shortened. On one occasion, walking with Dawn Lawson on a mountain road below Villars, he reflected on his life. "What a stupid life I have had," he said, "always fighting, fighting, fighting," while admitting that he knew no other way.

Lawson remembers a telephone conversation with Botnar during the last weeks of his life. She was in the middle of a field in Norfolk, the only place she could get a decent mobile signal at the time for the daily business call. As they ended the discussion Botnar said to her, "You are a good soldier, Dawn." "And you are an excellent general, Mr Botnar," she replied. She felt at the time, and has done ever since, that this was the best accolade he could ever have given her.

Even in his final days, Botnar continued to make plans for the future. On Wednesday 8 July 1998 he was with Otto Bruderer in Villars when he called Lawson to tell her to prepare for a trip to Romania, where he had been talking about setting up a charitable project for some time. He talked endlessly about the court action against the Revenue for malicious prosecution.

On Thursday 9 July, perhaps sensing that things were getting worse, Botnar telephoned Dr Shike. "Come tomorrow," he told him peremptorily. This was quite a demand since Shike lived in New York. Nonetheless, the doctor dropped everything, got on a plane and arrived at Villars at midnight on Friday 10 July 1998, where Botnar had spent the day in bed, no doubt for the first time in his life.

The next day Botnar seemed fine but he still decided to stay in bed. Lunch was brought up to him, including, as always, soup. Young Sergio, the housekeepers' son and the apple of the Botnars' eye, came up and read children's stories to him. In the garden outside, Sergio's father, Costa, was mowing the lawn. After a while, thinking that perhaps the noise was disturbing Mr Botnar, he put the lawnmower away and went up into the bedroom where Dr Shike was with him, to see if he could help.

Marcela came up and asked Botnar if he wanted some tea, which he gladly accepted. She brought tea and apple pie. Teasingly, Marcela asked whether she should feed him. She then left the room to go back downstairs. He ate some of the pie but started to choke on it and so Costa patted his back and started to massage it. Without warning, Botnar fell forwards. Costa caught his lifeless body before it hit the floor. Dr Shike tried to revive him but to no avail. When Luisa was told he had died, she did not believe it. "We will never forget him," Luisa recalled years later. "When he died, I lost something from my own heart."

The funeral took place in Paris, at the Passy cemetery behind the Trocadéro. Max, Maurice, their mother and other family members were already buried there. A small group of his closest friends and colleagues attended the ceremony. Brian Groves was asked by Marcela to say a few words and he remarked, "Most people go through their lives without ever meeting a man with the stature and ability of Octav Botnar."[321] Although Botnar was an atheist with little or no interest in his roots, and although no religious ceremony had been arranged, Moshe Shike unexpectedly recited the Jewish burial prayer, the kaddish, as his body was lowered into the grave.

Botnar's death meant that the Revenue's claims against him became null and void. His lawyers continued some desultory negotiations with the Revenue officials, who continued to nourish hopes of getting money out of his estate. After a few months they went away and nothing more was heard from them. The last legal words on the gigantic tax claims made against him were therefore those of the judge at the High Court in London, who said that the Revenue had not proved its case on the allegations of criminal fraud, nor produced evidence to justify the original arrest warrant issued against Botnar in 1992.

A Memorial Ceremony to celebrate Botnar's life was held on 21 October 1998, the day which would have been his 85th birthday. It took place in a group of marquees in the grounds of the Camelia Botnar Foundation in Cowfold – the scene could hardly have been more English, even though the guests were celebrating the life of someone who was from faraway Eastern Europe and who first set foot in Britain at the age of 52. Few people there that day knew much about what Octav Botnar had done before he arrived in Britain.

Those close to him, and many who perhaps would not have considered themselves so close, but who had worked with him or had known him, were deeply affected by his death. He had been a powerful and mesmerising character and had successfully dealt with so many vicissitudes: it took time to come to terms with the fact that, finally, he was no more. Many of them felt that he somehow belonged to them; they all agreed that he had been an exceptional man.

Attendance at the Memorial Ceremony had to be restricted and yet more than 250 people gathered together to pay their respects on that wet and windy October day. The ceremony was non-religious, in keeping with Botnar's own outlook on life. Music was played, tributes were given, and there was a reading of Rudyard Kipling's poem *"If –"*.

From the speeches given, by a former Cabinet Minister (Norman Tebbit), by his old friend Ion Raţiu, by Professor Graham MacGregor, by his old colleagues Brian Groves, Dawn Lawson and Jim North, by his niece Amalie, and others, a picture emerged of a hard-working, energetic, courageous and driven man; kind and generous; a firm idealist with a strong sense of fairness and justice; and, above all, a fighter.

Despite the wind whistling outside and the flapping of canvas, the audience hung on every word.

EPILOGUE

BRIAN GROVES
FORMER MARKETING DIRECTOR, NISSAN UK

And – which is more – you'll be a Man, my son!

Octav Botnar may no longer be around but his legacy remains, and is as tangible as it is significant. Nissan UK, the business which he created from scratch and which became such a powerhouse, may no longer employ thousands of people, but the company still exists, albeit in a different form, and continues to give millions to charities. One of Botnar's final wishes was to extend his philanthropic work into Romania and, respecting that vision, today the company gives substantial financial support to community projects in the magnificent central region of Transylvania.

In Britain, Botnar's profound and lasting impact upon the multi-million pound motor industry is to be found everywhere in the marketing and distribution of cars. Many of the concepts which he pioneered – single-tier distribution, parallel car finance and highly sophisticated stock control – are now universally practised.

Botnar built one of Britain's most successful private companies, created thousands of jobs and paid millions in taxes. He was also instrumental in persuading Nissan to build its European factory in one of Britain's most disadvantaged regions at Washington, in Sunderland, Tyne & Wear. The inward investment, now exceeding £4 billion, would never have been made without Botnar, and the factory is thus a memorial to his vision and unstinting endeavours.

Today, there are approximately 7,000 employees working at the factory in Sunderland, with components being supplied by more than 200 European companies, of which 150 are British. It is the most productive car plant in the UK, building one in five of all British-made cars. It is one of Britain's greatest ever success stories.

Botnar also exercised philanthropy on an enormous scale; philanthropy which will continue for many years to come. After his death, Marcela, in order to fulfil Botnar's will, established Fondation Botnar, a Swiss foundation whose role is to support children's good health, balanced nutrition and quality education, enabling young people across the world to live dignified and rewarding lives. Marcela named Fondation Botnar as the sole beneficiary of her will. The trustees of the Liechtenstein Trust amended the trust deed accordingly and added Fondation Botnar to the Appointed Class of the Trust.

After Marcela's death on 3 November 2014, all the personal assets of the Botnars and of the Liechtenstein Trust were transferred to Fondation Botnar, which thus became one of the biggest charitable foundations in Switzerland. It is a member of Swiss Foundations, the association of grant-making foundations in Switzerland. It is committed to best practice governance in line with the principles and recommendations of the Swiss Foundation Code, and its accounting follows the guidelines of Swiss GAAP FER 21 for charitable social non-profit organisations. The Fondation's activities are supervised by the Supervisory Authority for Foundations at the Swiss Federal Department of Home Affairs.

In 2017, the Board of Fondation Botnar, which had hitherto been itself managing the Fondation's charitable activities, established a management team which was charged by the Board with remaining true to Botnar's approach to philanthropy and of extending his legacy. Fondation Botnar has much to live up to.

The Botnar name is today displayed proudly by hospitals, institutions and charitable projects in Britain, Switzerland, Israel and other countries around the world. The contributions that Botnar made to those establishments have already enhanced the lives of countless thousands of people – and will continue to do so for long into the future.

It is hoped that this biography will contribute to a better understanding of the life of Octav Botnar, and of his enduring legacy.

References

CHAPTER 1 – A CHILD OF CZERNOWITZ

1   Israel Chalfen, *Paul Celan, Eine Biographie seiner Jugend* (Frankfurt: Suhrkamp, 1983), p. 7.

2   Prive Friedjung, *"Wir wollten nur das Paradies auf Erden", Die Erinnerungen einer jüdischen Kommunistin aus der Bukowina* (Vienna: Böhlau, 1991) p. 34.

3   Theodor Herzl, *Der Judenstaat. Versuch einer modernen Lösung der Judenfrage*, Leipzig, 1896, p. 75.

4   The source for these figures is a census carried out in the Austrian province in 1910. *Die Ergebnisse der Volks- und Viehzählung vom 31. Dezember 1910 im Herzogtume Bukowina nach den Angaben der k. und k. statistischen Zentral-Kommission in Wien* (Mitteilungen des statistischen Landesamtes des Herzogtums Bukowina, 17. Heft), Czernowitz 1913, pp. 54 f., 80f; quoted in Prive Friedjung, *"Wir wollten nur das Paradies auf Erden", Die Erinnerungen einer jüdischen Kommunistin aus der Bukowina* (Vienna: Böhlau, 1991), pp. 29 & 32.

5   "Die dritte Invasion von Czernowitz", *Czernowitzer Allgemeine Zeitung*, 28 August 1917.

6   "Die dritte Invasion von Czernowitz", *Czernowitzer Allgemeine Zeitung*, 28 August 1917.

7   These photographs can be seen on Edgar Hauster's web page under the title "The Revolution Comes to Czernowitz, May Day 1917", here: http://hauster. blogspot.fr/2012/11/october-revolution-in-czernowitz.html

8   Interview with Irma Mico (née Rosenberg) concerning Czernowitz in 1914, conducted in Paris in February 2016. Irma Mico's own brother was officially called Siegfried but his "temple" name was Shlomo.

9   Ion Rațiu: address at Octav Botnar's memorial ceremony, held at the Camelia Botnar Foundation in Cowfold, West Sussex, on 21 October 1998.

10 This account is taken more or less verbatim from the report in the local German-language newspaper, *Der Tag*, dated 22 March 1932, p. 2, entitled "Die Kommunisten demonstrieren". Copies of the newspaper are available online at http://dertag.forenworld.com/index.php

11 "Aufruhr im Gerichtssaal, Urteilsverkündung gegen die Kommunisten, Kerkerstrafen bis zu 16 Monaten verhängt", by Helios Hecht, *Der Tag* (Czernowitz), 16 July 1932.

12 Ion Rațiu recounted the story in his funeral address at Octav Botnar's memorial ceremony held at The Camelia Botnar Foundation in Cowfold on 21 October 1998. The episode is also referred to in his Securitate files from the 1950s and 1960s. But the practice of young Communists singing the *Internationale* on conviction by a court seems to have been widespread: Bundorf's fellow

Romanian Jewish Communist, Boris Holban (né Baruch Bruhman) tells exactly the same tale in his memoir, *Testament* (Paris: Calmann-Lévy,1989), p. 35 – and his trial took place six years before Bundorf's, and in a different city.

13 Helios Hecht, "Jugend im Gefängnis," *Der Tag*, Czernowitz, 16 July 1932.

14 Quoted by Mircea Chiritoiu, "Radiografiei unui Stalinist" in *Dosarele Istoriei*, No. 3 (8), 1997, pp. 4-5; see Denis Deletant, *Communist Terror in Romania, Gheorghiu-Dej and the Police State 1948-1965* (London: Hurst and Co., 1999), p. 15.

15 Boris Holban, *Testament* (Paris: Calmann-Lévy, 1989), p. 37.

16 On the Bund and Jewish socialism, see Claudie Weill, *Les Cosmopolites, Socialisme et Judéité en Russie 1897-1917* (Paris: Editions Syllepse, 2004), passim.

17 Michael Shafir, *Romania: Politics, Economics and Society* (London: Pinter, 1985), p. 26.

18 His co-defendants were Stefan Somko, Alexander Lanowski, Saveta Andreiczuk, Abraham Wolf, Adolf Ölberger, Julius Bendit, Dawid Beutel, Hermann Schuster, B. Burg, Max Teicher, Victor Mandrici, N. Müller, Mendel Wolf, Leib Scheidmann, Anton Nuricz (acquitted), Alexander Schloimovici (acquitted), Berl Schajowicz (acquitted), Teofil Majewski (acquitted) and Frieda Halm (acquitted).

19 Ben Halpern and Jehuda Reinharz, *Zionism and the Creation of a New Society* (Hanover, New Hampshire: Brandeis University Press, 2002): "Zionism... must be compared to social revolutionary and radical reform movements." (p. 6).

20 Ervin Bodnar, *L'Odyssée d'un Juif roumain aux Temps de la Résistance française et de la Guerre froide*, (Lyon: Editions BGA Permezel, 2014, p. 24). Author's telephone conversation with Erwin Bodnar, June 2016.

21 Prive Friedjung, *op.cit.* p. 52.

22 "Das eigentlich bedeutende von Czernowitz ist für mich die Symbiose der jiddischistischem und revolutionärem Denken." Prive Friedjung, *op.cit.* p. 131.

23 Prive Friedjung, *op.cit.* p. 135.

24 See her chapter in Claude Collin's misleadingly entitled book, *Le "Travail allemand", une organisation de résistance au sein de la Wehrmacht* (Paris: Les Indes Savantes, 2013), p. 58. The title is misleading because the *Travail allemand* was an activity within the French Resistance.

25 Allegations of police torture (beating with a rubber truncheon) were heard in the same court on 2 December 1932, at another trial of Communists. See "Die Rottenberg – 'Mühle' vor Gericht", *Der Tag*, Czernowitz, 3 December 1932.

26 Irma Mico's first husband was a Communist activist called Grischa Rothstein. Perhaps it was the same Grischa.

27 "Prozess Vascauteanu, Die Zeugen sagen aus...", *Der Tag*, 28 January 1933.

28 Interview with Max's daughter, Amalie Molhant Proost, Rougemont, Switzerland, 9 March 2016.

29 Interview with Max's son, Dominic Bunford, Monaco, 5 September 2016.

30 Securitate document 15 September 1950, No. 42/42691, Dossier 29186 Vol. 1, also referred to as 211278 Vol. 1 with a bar code.

31   Boris Holban, *op.cit.* pp. 38-39.

32   According to the memorandum which readmitted him to the Communist Party in 1955, the date of his release was September 1935. However, as he elsewhere refers to a six-month period of detention starting in May, and as OB himself says November in other documents, November seems to be the correct date.

33   Bundorf was to be interrogated about all these events 20 years later by the Securitate, the internal security police of the new Communist regime of which he had been a member but from which he was expelled in 1950. This account comes from the Securitate files from the early 1950s.

34   Securitate document 15 September 1950, No. 42/42691, Dossier 29186 Vol. 1, also referred to as 211278 Vol. 1 with a bar code.

35   OB's written reply to the Party Collegium in 1952.

36   This sum, and the reference to Zina Craciunescu, come from OB's interrogation by the Securitate on 15 August 1960. Dossier P7893 Vol. 1.

CHAPTER 2 – PARIS AND THE WAR

37   According to a statement given by Octav Botnar to the Securitate on 27 May 1960, following his arrest for plotting to overthrow the social order. Dossier 29186 Vol. 2, also referred to as 211278 Vol. 2.

38   Barbu Ollanescu-Orendi relates this in his memoir, *Aşa a fost să fie, amintri din anii mei buni su rai* (Bucharest: Humanitas, 2014), p. 132, but it is not clear when Maurice Bundorf and Maurice Thorez met.

39   Boris Holban, *op.cit.* p. 56.

40   Boris Holban, *op.cit.* p. 57.

41   Stéphane Courtois, Denis Peschanski, Adam Rayski, *Le Sang de l'Etranger, Les Immigrés de la MOI dans la Résistance* (Paris: Fayard, 1989), quote the Soviet Jewish poet Itsik Fefer boasting of the destruction of the spirit of Torquemada, p.40.

42   Georges-Roux, *La Guerre Civile d'Espagne* (Paris: Fayard, 1963), pp. 140-141.

43   William E. Watters, *An International Affair. Non Intervention in the Spanish Civil War, 1936-1939* (New York: Exposition Press, 1971).

44   Stéphane Courtois, Denis Peschanski, Adam Rayski, *op.cit.* p. 15.

45   Karl Marx and Friedrich Engels, *Manifesto of the Communist Party,* Chapter 2. See also Engels, *The Prussian Military Question and the German Workers' Party,* 1865, Part III: "Particularism will hamper the free movement of the proletariat but its existence will never be justified."

46   "National differences and antagonism between peoples are daily more and more vanishing, owing to the development of the bourgeoisie, to freedom of commerce, to the world market, to uniformity in the mode of production and in the conditions of life corresponding thereto. The supremacy of the proletariat will cause them to vanish still faster." *Communist Manifesto,* Chapter 2.

47   Stéphane Courtois, Denis Peschanski, Adam Rayski, *op.cit.* p. 23.

48   Stéphane Courtois, Denis Peschanski, Adam Rayski, *ibid.* p. 41.

49   Stéphane Courtois, Denis Peschanski, Adam Rayski, *ibid.* p. 41 ff.; also Boris Holban, *op.cit.*

50   Bundorf's role in the "Aide populaire" is mentioned in the memorandum of 1955 readmitting him into the Romanian Communist Party. See also Boris Holban, *op.cit.* p. 55, for Holban's own involvement.

51   Much of the information in the passages which follow comes from the marvellous documentary about the RMVE regiments, *Les régiments ficelles, Des héros dans la tourmente de 1940* by Robert Mugnerot, available on DVD.

52   Maurice Sisterman, *A Barcarès il y a 30 ans,* in *Le Combattant Volontaire Juif 1939-1945,* Supplément au No. 130 de "Notre Volonté", bulletin de l'Union des Engagés Volontaires et Anciens Combattants Juifs 1939-1945, Paris, 1971, p. 22 ff. Sisterman produced an affidavit dated 28 November 1945 confirming that he had seen Bundorf in the Stalag at Cambrai and that he had later escaped.

53   Joseph Okonowski, a comrade of Bundorf's in the 22nd RMVE, speaking at 10.26 of *Les régiments ficelles.*

54   The "Journal de Marche" (war diary) of the regiment, which details every stage of these operations and which was written by the regiment's commander while in German captivity, as well as other archives concerning the regiment, are conserved at the Service Historique de la Défense in the Château de Vincennes outside Paris.

55   Albert Valny at 23.33 of *Les régiments ficelles.*

56   At 31.00 of *Les régiments ficelles.*

57   *Citation* published in the *Journal officiel* on 5 December 1941.

58   Testimony of Joseph Okonowski in *Les régiments ficelles.*

59   Interview with Octav Botnar's niece, Amalie Molhant Proost, Rougemont, Switzerland, 9 March 2016.

60   Maurice Sisterman testified to the date of Bundorf's escape in an affidavit signed on 28 November 1945. The details about the civilian clothes come from what Octav Botnar told the Securitate during his interrogations in the 1950s.

CHAPTER 3 – THE FRENCH RESISTANCE

61   Boris Holban, *op.cit.* p. 180.

62   Bundorf mentions Aliona Flom several times in his 1952 reply to the memorandum demanding his expulsion from the Romanian Communist Party. Boris Holban mentions Flom in his acknowledgements, *op.cit.* p. 279.

63   In 2016, Irma Mico recalled this as her address.

64   The story is told by Dora Schaul in Gilles Perrault, *Taupes rouges contre SS* (Paris: Editions Messidor 1986), p. 94.

65   For instance in the preparations for the attack on the USSR in 1941. See Otto Niebergall in Gilles Perrault, *op.cit.* p. 41.

66   *Das Kind* by Yonathan Levy, February 2013.

67   Claude Collin, Le *"Travail allemand", une organisation de résistance au sein de la Wehrmacht* (Paris: Les Indes Savantes, 2013), especially the chapter by Irma Mico, p. 55 ff. See also Boris Holban's brief reference to the *Travail allemand* in *Les Roumains dans la Résistance française*, by G. Vassilichi *et al.* (Bucharest, 1971), pp. 54-55.

68   Heisel tells his story in Gilles Perrault, *op.cit.* p. 77.

69   See Claude Collin, Le *"Travail allemand", origines et filiation* in "Guerres Mondiales et Conflits Contemporains" 2008/2 (No. 230). Available online.

70   Botnar mentions this detail in his 1952 reply to the memorandum expelling him from the Romanian Communist Party.

71   Otto Niebergall in Gilles Perrault, *op.cit.* p. 40.

72   Octav Botnar told the story of the duplicating machines in a long memorandum he wrote arguing against his expulsion from the Romanian Communist Party in 1952. The story about the pram comes from Dawn Lawson, who was his secretary for 17 years at Nissan UK.

73   Stéphane Courtois *et al., Le Sang de l'Etranger,* p. 138.

74   This passage is taken from Octav Botnar's long memorandum to the Party College protesting against his expulsion from the Romanian Communist Party in 1952. The typewritten document is dated 4 June 1952 and this passage is on page 10 of the manuscript. Author's translation from Romanian.

75   Gilles Perrault, *op.cit.* p. 45.

76   Jacob Semel is mentioned as one of Bundorf's comrades in 1935 in the 1955 typewritten memorandum readmitting Octav Botnar to the Romanian Communist Party.

77   Irma Mico is the source of the recollection about Bundorf's love affair with "Coca" Semel, although she recalls the name being spelled with two 'm's, Semmel. She remembers how she was deported to Auschwitz with her daughter, Nadine, who was not yet two years old, in 1942. Regina and toddler Nadine Seinel, both with the same address, and Regina being identified as a Romanian, are listed by the Mémorial de la Shoah as having been deported on that date, Nadine "Seinel" being the only Nadine of that age in the entire list. Mother and daughter are also listed as Seinel on the wall of names in the Paris Memorial of the Shoah in the typewritten list published on their website. However, this "Seinel" is clearly a mis-transcription by the typist of Semel: the correct name, Semel, has been entered into the database of Memorial GenWeb. (www.memorialgenweb.org). Following correspondence with this author, the Memorial of the Shoah has agreed to change the spelling of the name on the wall.

78   Gavin Bowd, *Romanians of the French Resistance,* in "French History" (2014), p. 4.

79   Denis Peschanski claims there were only 65 FTP-MOI agents in total in the whole of the Ile de France between June and September 1943 (at 27.48 in the 2014 documentary film *Ils étaient juifs et résistants* by Alain Jomy, available on YouTube).

80 The story of the Manouchian group is told in the 2009 film by Robert Guédiguian, *The Army of Crime*. It is also the subject of several books, many of which have in their title a reference to *L'Affiche rouge*, the red poster put up by Vichy and the Germans to advertise the fact that the condemned men were foreigners and Jews, and to slander them, and the Resistance in general, as *"l'armée du crime"*.

81 This chilling story is recounted by one of those who executed him, Boris Holban, in *Testament*, pp. 195-206.

82 Handwritten affidavit by Irma Mico, 12 February 1992.

83 Irma Mico, *De la MOI au TA* in Claude Collin, *Le "Travail allemand"*, pp. 72-73.

84 Irma Mico describes and disapproves of the execution in Claude Collin, *op.cit.* p. 73. In correspondence with this author, she expressed her doubts that Botnar had been responsible for Avramescu's death.

85 Henri Amouroux, *La grande histoire des Français après l'occupation*, tome 9: *Les règlements de comptes (septembre 1944-janvier 1945)* (Paris: Robert Laffont, 1991) pp. 83-89.

86 See Ministerul Afacerilor Interne, Dossier 29186 Vol. 3, 8 April 1963, also referred to as 211278 Vol. 3 with a bar code, Report 29 dated 27 August 1960 (handwritten); and Report Number 24 (typewritten) dated 9 August 1960 (p. 2 of that document). This document is a report written by Octav Botnar's "cellmate" (in reality an informer). It reads as follows:
"During the last session, the interrogator asked him: why does his brother not send his correspondence directly to him, to which he gave an inadequate answer: "Because nobody might be at home." To this the interrogator retorted: "Your brother gives another reason." Botnar tells me that the real reason his brother does not send letters to his address is that he was wanted by the French police in connection with the murder of a former agent in the Resistance, AVRAMESCU (of Romanian origin), who having been caught by the Gestapo, became an informer and a traitor, causing the arrest and death of dozens of fighters. Botnar tells me the murder 'occurred' (*'s-a produs'* is in inverted commas in the original, presumably to emphasise that it is a euphemism) after the installation of the provisional government, and as such it is considered an abusive act, which – although (the punishment is) prescribed after the elapse of ten years, would cast his brother in a bad light..."
There are, however, no references to Oswald Bundorf, Octav Botnar or Avramescu in the archives of the Prefecture of Police of Paris.

87 *Proces-Verbal de Interogator*, 15 August 1960, Dossier on Eugen Perian in CNSAS Archives (Consiliul National Pentru Studierea Arhivelor Securitatii), P007893, Vol. 8. I am grateful to Christian Mititelu for finding this passage. Capital letters in the original text.

88 Handwritten letter by Irma Mico to Oswald Bundorf, 12 February 1992.

89 Monique Houssin, *Résistantes et résistants en Seine-Saint-Denis: Un nom, une rue, une histoire* (Paris: Les éditions de l'Atelier, 2004).

90 Written affidavit by Boris Holban, 9 January 1992.

91 Handwritten letter by Irma Mico to Oswald Bundorf, 12 February 1992.

92 In his 1952 statement refuting the charges used against him to expel him from the Romanian Communist Party.

93 *Témoignage* by Georges Filip-Lefort, 3 January 1992, typewritten letter.

CHAPTER 4 – BUILDING SOCIALISM

94 Denis Deletant, *Communist Terror in Romania, Gheorghiu-Dej and the Police State 1948-1965* (London: Hurst and Company, 1999), p. 9.

95 Ervin Bodnar, *L'Odyssée d'un Juif roumain aux Temps de la Résistance française et de la guerre froide* (Lyon: Editions PGA Permezel, 2014), pp. 164-165.

96 Barbu Ollanescu-Orendi, *Aşa a fost să fie* (Bucharest: Humanitas, 2014), p. 131.

97 Barbu Ollanescu-Orendi, *ibid.* p. 131, says Botnar "wept".

98 Dennis Deletant, *op. cit.* p. 52.

99 John Laughland, *A History of Political Trials* (Oxford: Peter Lang, 2007 and 2016), chapter 14.

100 Ervin Bodnar, *op.cit.* p. 181; Boris Holban, *op.cit.* p. 232.

101 Undated *Referat* in Securitate archives, Dossier 211278 Vol. 6, in the name of Octav Botnar.

102 References to a child or a baby (*copil*) of Raymonde Anonge's are in Securitate documents dated 20 and 21 March 1959; Dossier 211278 Vol. 1. As no child is ever mentioned anywhere else, these references might be mistaken, possibly a confusion with Camelia, Octav and Marcela Botnar's daughter born in 1952.

103 Handwritten report, No. 29, dated 27 August 1960, in Securitate Dossier 211278 Vol. 3, p. 9.

104 *Proces-Verbal de Interogator,* 27 May 1960, Octav Botnar questioned, Securitate file 7893 Vol. 8, on Eugen Perian.

105 In an undated memorandum written around this time to the Romanian head of state and Communist Party leader, Gheorghe Gheorghiu-Dej. See Dossier 211278 Vol. 6, document entitled "Memoriu" and described as a letter to Dej in the previous document in the same file.

106 Dennis Deletant, *op.cit.* p. 130.

107 Dennis Deletant, *op.cit.* pp. 127-128.

108 Sarah Oliver, 'We've been destroyed, now we just want to come back', *Mail on Sunday,* 29 September 1996, p. 41.

109 See the Securitate dossiers on Eugen Perian, e.g. 243916 Vol. 1, also listed as 555439 Vol. 1 with a bar code.

110 Note ref. 42/42691 dated 15 September 1950, entitled "232", signed Lt. Col. Gheorghe Petrescu, in Dossier 211278 Vol. 1, in the name of Octav Botnar,

pp. 2-3 of the document, pp. 26-27 of that dossier.

111 Long handwritten memo (*Referat*) dated 19 February 1957, held by the Personnel Service of the Ministry of Foreign Trade. See Dossier 211278 Vol. 1, p. 30 of that dossier.

112 Artur London, *L'Aveu. Dans l'engrenage du procès de Prague* (Paris: Gallimard, 1968).

113 The affair is mentioned, *inter alia*, in Securitate Dossier 540236 Vol. 1 about Marcela Camelia Botnar in a handwritten document dated 7 October 1976, first page of the first document in that dossier. It says: "In 1957 he (Botnar) caught her (Marcela) cheating on him with a friend of his, a police officer." The affair is mentioned in numerous other documents from OB's time in prison, for instance in a note by an informer, Ferdinand Schaffer, dated 22 May 1960, in which Schaffer writes: "The leader of the gang (Ioanid) had formerly been a good friend of OB; they quarrelled because his wife cheated on him with this bandit and, furthermore, she was seeing him even after this quarrel." See Dossier 211278 Vol. 2, p. 1 of the note, p. 56 of that dossier.

114 OB confided to his "cellmate", in reality a Securitate informer, about Marcela's infidelities. See Dossier 211278 Vol. 2, Report No. 3 dated 5 May 1960, pp. 1-2 of the document, pp. 78-79 of that dossier.

115 Report No. 29 dated 27 August 1960, handwritten report, Dossier 211278 Vol. 3.

116 Report dated 20 May 1960.

117 See his Securitate Dossier, 7893 Vol. 1

118 Report No. 3 dated 6 May 1960, MAI Dossier 211278 Vol. 2, pp. 1-2 of the report (pp. 78-79 of that dossier). The report is written by a "cellmate" of OB's, in reality an informer. See his Securitate Dossier, 7893 Vol. 1.

119 Report No. 3 dated 6 May 1960, MAI Dossier 211278 Vol. 2.

120 Note dated 23 May 1960 in Dossier 211278 Vol. 2, p. 54 of that dossier (document marked p. 240 in red pencil), first page of this two-page document.

121 Informer's note by Ferdinand Schaffer, dated 22 May 1960, Dossier 211278 Vol. 2, p. 1 of the Note, page 56 of that dossier. This document is marked 241 in red pencil.

122 Milad Doroudian, 'The not so known Communist bank heist', *Jerusalem Post*, 26 January 2015. See also Jonathan Levin, 'The Jewish gang that pulled off the most famous bank robbery in Communist history', *Tablet Magazine*, 20 February 2014, a review of the film *Closer to the Moon*. The *Guardian's* film critic trashed the film: see John Patterson review, 9 November 2015.

123 *Referat* dated 20 October 1960 and approved on 22 October 1960 in a handwritten addition, Dossier 211278 Vol. 1.

124 Memorandum (*Referat*) dated 1 October 1959 and signed by General Evghenie Tanase. Dossier 211278 Vol. 1, p. 21 of the document and p. 72 of that dossier.

125 Memorandum (*Referat*) dated 1 October 1959 and signed by General Evghenie Tanase. Dossier 211278 Vol. 1, p. 21 of the document and p. 72 of that dossier.

126 Handwritten memo (*Referat*) dated 19 February 1957, held by the Personnel Service

of the Ministry of Foreign Trade. See Dossier 211278 Vol. 1, p. 34 of that dossier.

127 For the alleged remarks about the USSR, see the Securitate report by Lt Gheorghe Antonescu dated 26 March 1959. The remarks were allegedly made in December 1957. See Dossier 211278 Vol. 4, p. 7 of that dossier. See also the Decision (Hotarire) dated 20 March 1959, Dossier 211278 Vol. 1, p. 3 of that dossier, for the story about the plum brandy (*tuica*). The various allegations were all laid out together in a long memorandum (*Referat*) dated 1 October 1959 and signed by General Evghenie Tanase. Dossier 211278 Vol. 1, starting at p. 52 of that dossier (last document).

128 General Evghenie Tanase: (*Referat*) dated 1 October 1959 and signed by General Tanase. Dossier 211278 Vol. 1, p. 20 of the document and p. 71 of that dossier (last document).

CHAPTER 5 – THE ROMANIAN GULAG

129 *Proces Verbal, Interogator de inculpat*, Eugen Perian, 23 May 1961, MAI Dossier 43502 Vol. 4 on Octav Botnar, also referred to as 007893 Vol. 4 with a bar code, p. 3 of that dossier. See also *Sentinta No. 129*, 25 May 1961, MAI Dossier 43502 Vol. 4 on Octav Botnar, also referred to as 007893 Vol. 4 with a bar code, p. 16 of that dossier. See pp. 5-6 of this Sentence for Perian's evidence against Botnar; see p. 12 for the Court's reasoning about the attenuating circumstances (that he had informed on Botnar). See also the interrogation, *Proces Verbal de Interogator*, of Eugen Perian dated 1 July 1960, in *Ministerul Afacerilor Interne*, Dossier 43502 Vol. 1 on Octav Botnar, also catalogued as P 007893 Vol. 1 with a bar code; p. 29 ff. of that dossier.

130 *Concluzii de învinuire* (Concluding act of accusation), 21 January 1961, signed by Stefan Nedelcu, p. 6 in Ministerul Afacerilor Interne Dossier 43502 Vol. 1 on Octav Botnar, also catalogued as P 007893 Vol. 1.

131 *Referat* (Report) on Dumitru Arsenie, 15 January 1960, signed by Emil Macri and Ioan Schiopu, in *Ministerul Afacerilor Interne*, Dossier 29186 Vol. 1 on Octav Botnar, also catalogued as 211278 Vol. 1, p. 35 of that dossier.

132 The letter dated 10 June 1960 is in the MAI (Ministry of the Interior) Dossier 211278 Vol. 1, p. 48 of that dossier. The four pages of the document are marked 307-310 in red pen. The falsehood of Merchea's accusations about Botnar's corruption, and the fact that he was later forced to withdraw them, are noted in *Motive de recurs* (Grounds for appeal) 27 June 1961, p. 2, in *Ministerul Afacerilor Interne*, Dossier 43502 Vol. 4 on Octav Botnar, also catalogued as P 007893 Vol. 4, p. 33 of that dossier.

133 *Nota informativa* dated 10 December 1958 reported to Lt. Gheorghe Antonescu by "Laura"; in Dossier 29186 Vol. 4, also referred to as 211278 Vol. 4 with a bar code.

134 Report No. 2 dated 5 May 1960 in MAI (Ministry of Internal Affairs) Dossier 211278 Vol. 2, p. 66 of that dossier (marked 263 ff in red pen).

135 Ion Raţiu told this story at the address he delivered at Octav Botnar's memorial ceremony, held at the Camelia Botnar Foundation in Cowfold, West Sussex, on 21 October 1998.

136 Report No. 3 dated 6 May 1960, Securitate Dossier 211278 Vol. 2. The report is written by a "cellmate" of OB's, in reality an informer.

137 Report No. 24, Dossier 211278 Vol. 3, p. 7 of that dossier. The actual expression in Romanian means "What a bandit!"

138 Report No. 29, handwritten note dated 27 August 1960. This is the document in which the Avramescu murder is again referred to, and where the cellmate speculates that this was the reason why Botnar had not been able to return to France to join his first wife, Raymonde Anonge.

139 *Concluzii de invinuire* (Investigation Conclusions), by Captain Stefan Nedelcu, Bucharest, 21 January 1960, in MAI Dossier P 7893 Vol. 1, p. 102 of that dossier, see p. 7 of the document for this quotation.

140 Article 209 is widely discussed in the literature on Communist repression, for instance in Radu Stancu, *Ideologie, represiune şi pedeapsa cu moartea in deceniul dinaintea adoptarii Codului penal din 1969* (Ideology, Repression, and the Death Penalty in the Decade before the Adoption of the Penal Code in 1969), *Revista Arhivelor* 2002, pp. 181-203, www.archivelenationale.ro

141 *Ordonanta* (ordinance), 21 January 1960, by Stefan Nedelcu, MAI Dossier P 7893 Vol. 1, one-page document, p. 86 of that dossier.

142 *Proces Verbal, Interogator de Inculpat*, Octav Botnar, Tribunal Militar Bucureşti, public session, 23 May 1961, in MAI Dossier 7893 Vol. 4, pp. 1-2 of that dossier.

143 *Proces Verbal, Interogator de Inculpat*, Eugen Perian, Tribunal Militar Bucureşti, public session 23 May 1961, in MAI Dossier 7893 Vol. 4, pp. 3-4 of that dossier.

144 *Incheiere* (Conclusion) Tribunal Militar Bucureşti, 23 May 1961, p. 5, see MAI Dossier 7893 Vol. 4, pp. 3-4 (p. 13 of that dossier).

145 *Sentinta No. 129* (sentence), Tribunal Militar Bucureşti, 25 May 1961, p. 10, in MAI Dossier 7893 Vol. 4, p. 25 of that dossier.

146 *ibid.*, p. 14 (p. 29 of that dossier).

147 MAI Dossier 7893 Vol. 4, pp. 30-32 of that dossier.

148 Undated letter from Alexa Augustin, General Prosecutor, to the President of the Supreme Court, MAI Dossier 7893 Vol. 4, p. 39 of that dossier.

149 *Decizia No. 108* (Decision), Tribunalul Suprem al RPR, Colegiul Militar, 3 June 1963, MAI Dossier 7893 Vol. 4, pp. 42-45 of that dossier.

150 *Decizia No. 108* (Decision), Tribunalul Suprem al RPR, Colegiul Militar, 3 June 1963, p. 4 (p. 45 of that dossier).

151 Barbu Ollanescu-Orendi, *Aşa a fost să fie* (Bucharest: Humanitas, 2014), p. 132.

152 Author's interview with Barbu Ollanescu-Orendi, Botnar's fellow prisoner, in Bordesholm, Germany, 10 February 2016.

153 Interview with Barbu Ollanescu-Orendi in Bordesholm, Germany, 10 February 2016; see also *Aşa a fost să fie*, p. 132.

154 Dossier P007893 Vol. 5.

155 This story was recounted to the author by Barbu Ollanescu-Orendi who also tells it in his memoir, *Aşa a fost să fie* (Bucharest: Humanitas, 2014), pp. 147-148.

156 Dossier R194491, memo dated 27 May 1962. R dossiers are for Securitate agents.

157 Dossier P7893 Vol. 5, Eugen Perian, letter signed by Marcela Botnar, p. 5 of that dossier.

158 *Proces-Verbal de Interogator,* 28 May 1950, Octav Botnar questioned, Securitate file 7893 Vol. 8 on Eugen Perian.

159 MAI (Interior Ministry, i.e. Securitate) file 7893 Vol. 8 on Eugen Perian, pp. 39-46 of that dossier.

160 Transcript of telephone call, 26 January 1965, in Dossier 211278 Vol. 6, p. 6 of that dossier.

161 *Nota* by Lt. Col. Fleanu, 23 April 1965, in Dossier 537437, Eugen Perian, p. 9 of that dossier.

162 The exact date of his departure is given in document D/304659 dated 13 October 1965, a note from the Passport Office of the Romanian Foreign Ministry, held in Dossier No. 29186 of the Romanian Ministry of the Interior, Vol. 6, dated 13 December 1965.

CHAPTER 6 – A FRESH START

163 Max Bundorf's story is told in Isaac Berman's memoir, *Stormy Days*, published in Hebrew, and in Tuvia Friling, *Istanbul 1942–1945: The Kollek-Avriel and Berman-Ofner Networks* in D Bankier, ed. *Secret Intelligence and the Holocaust* (New York: Enigma books and Yad Vashem, 2006), pp. 105-156. (2006). Article also available on line at www.academia.edu.

164 Report of the Emergency Committee to Save the Jewish People of Europe, by E Jabotinsky, Ankara, 14 June 1944, document transmitted to this Committee via the US Department of State.

165 Speech by Barry Clarke at the Octav Botnar Memorial Ceremony, Cowfold, 21 October 1998.

166 Datsun is an automobile brand which is owned by Nissan, and which was first used in 1931. From 1958 to 1984 vehicles exported by Nissan were branded Datsun. By 1984 Nissan had phased out the Datsun name, instead using the Nissan brand worldwide. Datsun was re-launched in 2013 as a low-cost brand for emerging markets.

167 Witness Statement of Octav Botnar, 6 September 1996, pp 40 and 82 ff.

168 In 1990, Botnar's head office in Worthing employed 246 people, mostly in the parts warehouse, at a cost of £5 million. By comparison, Volkswagen Audi UK, selling roughly the same number of cars, employed 1,000 people in its head office, at a cost of £22.4 million.

169 Ion Rațiu, speech to the Octav Botnar memorial ceremony, Cowfold, 21 October 1998.

CHAPTER 7 – CAMELIA

170 Sarah Oliver, "We've been destroyed, now we just want to come back", *Mail on Sunday*, 29 September 1996, p. 41.

171 Interview with Lady Meyer, née Catherine Laylle, London 9 November 2016. Telephone interview with Charles Buchet, 28 November 2016. Interview with Dawn Rose, née Dawn Lawson, London, 8 December 2016.

172 Family anecdote recounted by Charles Buchet, telephone interview 28 November 2016.

173 This information is gleaned from the short police file on Maurice Bundorf in the archives of the Prefecture of Police of Paris.

174 Catherine Laylle mentions Camelia Botnar in her memoir, *Two Children Behind a Wall* (London: Arrow Books, 1997), p. 20.

175 From the papers of Catherine Laylle (Lady Meyer).

176 Interview with Lady (Catherine) Meyer, London, 9 November 2016.

177 Telephone interview with Charles Buchet, 25 November 2016.

178 "German girl killed", *Swindon Evening Advertiser*, Wednesday 27 December 1972; "Black Weekend on Wilts Roads as Four Die", *Wiltshire Gazette and Herald*, undated news clipping from around the same date.

179 Testimony of Dawn Rose, née Dawn Lawson, March 2017.

180 Interview with Porfirio Costa Calheno, Braga, Portugal, 30 May 2016.

CHAPTER 8 – THE RISE AND RISE OF DATSUN UK

181 By 1974, Datsun UK was outselling Toyota, its closest Japanese competitor, by more than three to one. The UK became the only market in the world in which Datsun outsold Toyota.

182 Interview with Otto Bruderer, Zurich, 6 October 2016.

183 Interview with Paul Yallop, now General Manager of the Camelia Botnar Foundation, Cowfold, West Sussex, 20 July 2016.

184 Interview with Tony Stone, London, 2 March 2017.

185 Interview with Richard Smith, London, 9 December 2016.

186 Interview with Brian Groves, London, 22 March 2016.

187 Interview with Tony Stone, London, 2 March 2017.

188 Interview with Richard Smith, London, 9 December 2016, email from Smith 15 December 2016.

189 Ion Rațiu, speech at Octav Botnar's memorial ceremony, Cowfold, 21 October 1998.

190 Interview with Otto Bruderer, Zurich, 6 October 2016.

191 Interview with Brian Groves, London, 22 March 2016.

192 Interview with Otto Bruderer, Zurich, 6 October 2016.

193 Speech by Barry Clarke at the Octav Botnar Memorial Ceremony, Cowfold, 21 October 1998.

194 Interview with Otto Bruderer, Zurich, 6 October 2016.

195 Amalie Bunford, address at the Octav Botnar Memorial Ceremony, Cowfold, 21 October 1998.

196 Ion Raţiu, speech to the Octav Botnar memorial ceremony, Cowfold, 21 October 1998.

197 'Wo ich herkomme, haben Berge keine Gipfel,' Botnar said. Interview with Otto Bruderer, Zurich, 6 October 2016.

198 Interview with Tony Stone, London, 2 March 2017.

199 Interview with Richard Smith, London, 9 December 2016.

200 Interview with Tony Stone, London, 2 March 2017.

201 Interview with Dawn Rose née Lawson, Camelia Botnar Foundation, Cowfold, West Sussex, 20 July 2016.

202 Anecdote told by Otto Bruderer, Zurich, 6 October 2016.

203 Industry and Companies House statistics.

CHAPTER 9 – THATCHER'S FLAGSHIP

204 Letter from Octav Botnar to Masataka Okuma, 14 February 1980.

205 Record of meeting between Nissan Motors Ltd and UK Department of Industry, 31 July 1980, London, drawn up by Department of Industry and dated 8 August 1980.

206 Letter from Octav Botnar to Norman Tebbit, Minister of State at the Department of Industry, 23 January 1981.

207 Signed statement on House of Lords letterhead from Lord Tebbit, 27 February 1997. See also Norman Tebbit, Upwardly Mobile (London: Futura, 1991), pp. 173-4.

208 Interview with Lord Tebbit, House of Lords, 11 May 2016.

209 Norman Tebbit, op.cit. pp. 174-175.

210 Norman Tebbit, Minister of State for Industry, Statement about the Motor Industry, House of Commons, 29 January 1981, Hansard HC Deb 29 January 1981 Vol. 997 cc 1081-8.

211 Hansard HC Deb 29 January 1981 Vol. 997 cc 1085.

212 Paul Ingrassia and Kathryn Groven, Wall Street Journal, 1 November 1989, quoted by John E Walsh, Jr., Nissan United Kingdom Ltd., in International Business Case Studies for the Multicultural Marketplace eds. Robert T. Moran, David O. Braaten and John E. Walsh (Oxford and New York: Taylor & Francis, 1994), p. 47.

213 Carl Aaron, The Political Economy of Japanese Investment in the UK and the US (Basingstoke: Macmillan, 1999), p. 89.

214 Notes of a meeting held in London on 1 October 1983 between Octav Botnar and Teiichi Hara.

215 Norman Tebbit, Secretary of State for Trade and Industry, Nissan Project,

House of Commons, 1 February 1984, *Hansard* HC Vol 53 cc 265-75.

216 Interview with Lord Tebbit, House of Lords, London, 11 May 2016.

217 Giles Edwards, "Was this Thatcher's greatest legacy?", BBC Radio 4, 14 September 2009.

218 This article can be read online here: http://news.bbc.co.uk/2/hi/business/8253169.stm

219 Numerous news reports including Peter Campbell and George Parker, "May assures Nissan of shield against Brexit tariffs", *Financial Times*, 14 October 2016.

220 Alex Morales, "Nissan Only Automaker to Receive Brexit Letter, Minister Says", *Bloomberg*, 20 January 2017.

221 Philip Garrahan and Paul Stewart, *The Nissan Enigma: Flexibility at Work in a Local Economy* (London: Mansell Publishing, 1992).

CHAPTER 10 – THE BREAKDOWN OF THE RELATIONSHIP WITH THE JAPANESE

222 *Nissan United Kingdom Ltd.*, in *International Business Case Studies for the Multicultural Marketplace* eds. Robert T. Moran, David O. Braaten and John E. Walsh (Oxford and New York: Taylor & Francis, 1994), p. 48.

223 From 1983 to 2001, new car registration numbers in Britain contained a prefix indicating the year of registration: A for 1983, B for 1984, and so on. The change in prefix occurred each year on August 1st, resulting in a disproportionate level of registrations in August each year.

224 According to the *Financial Times*. See "Controversy dogs the secretive man behind Nissan UK" by Kevin Done, *Financial Times*, 27 June 1991, p. 8.

225 Article in *Automotive Magazine*, 15 November 1990.

226 English translation of Petition for Arbitration, 10 May 1991, Nissan Motor Company et. al. v Nissan UK, p. 4.

227 English translation of Petition for Arbitration by Nissan Motor Company, p. 4.

228 Nissan UK Press Information, 4 January 1991.

229 Philip Garrahan and Paul Stewart, *The Nissan Enigma: Flexibility at Work in a Local Economy* (London: Mansell Publishing, 1992), p. 70.

230 Judgment in the High Court of Justice Chancery Division before the Vice Chancellor, between Nissan (UK) Ltd and Nissan Motor Manufacturing (UK) Ltd., heard on Tuesday 2 March 1993, transcription of the computerised stenograph notes of Smith Bernal Reporting Ltd.

231 Letter from Octav Botnar to C. Signoroni, 5 June 1991.

CHAPTER 11 – A KNOCK ON THE DOOR

232 Minutes of a meeting between Inland Revenue officials and Nissan UK's advisers, Grant Thornton and Coole & Haddock, held at Somerset House, 4 July 1991.

233 Paul Ham, "Exposed: the bullying tactics of the taxman", *Sunday Times, Money*, 5 October 1997.

234 Letter from Robert (Bob) Brown of Ernst & Young to Mark Spragg of Jeffrey Green Russell, 22 October 1996.

235 Michael Kemp, "Taxmen raid car giant", *Daily Mail*, 27 June 1991.

236 "Tax Raid on Nissan UK" by Roland Gribben and Michael Fleet, *The Daily Telegraph*, 27 June 1991.

237 "The Revenue drives head-on into Nissan UK", City Comment, *Daily Telegraph*, 27 June 1991, p. 21.

238 Minutes of a meeting between Inland Revenue officials and Nissan UK's advisers, Grant Thornton and Coole & Haddock, held at Somerset House, 4 July 1991.

239 "Controversy dogs the secretive man behind Nissan UK" by Kevin Done, *Financial Times*, 27 June 1991, p. 8, quoting an interview from late 1990.

CHAPTER 12 – THE CHARITIES

240 Interview at Camelia Botnar Foundation, 20 July 2016.

241 Email to author from Professor Roger Greenhalgh, 27 November 2016.

242 Testimony of Professor Roger Greenhalgh, sent by email to the author, 28 November 2016.

243 See Lives of the Fellows of the Royal Society of Physicians, http://munksroll. rcplondon.ac.uk/Biography/Details/7006

244 Professor Graham MacGregor, address to the Octav Botnar Memorial Ceremony, Cowfold, 21 October 1998.

245 Professor Graham MacGregor, interview in London, 9 November 2016.

246 Telephone interview with Marion Allford, former director of the Wishing Well Appeal, 23 November 2016.

247 Letter from Cecil Parkinson to Octav Botnar, 4 January 1989.

248 *Lifeline*, the in-house magazine of Great Ormond Street Children's Hospital, summer 1996, p. 6.

249 Robert Creighton, address to the Octav Botnar Memorial Ceremony, Cowfold, 21 October 1998.

250 Email from Jeanette Franklin MBE, 20 January 2017.

251 Interview with Professor Andrew Carr, Oxford, 4 October 2016.

252 Lord Tebbit, Letter to the Editor, The Daily Telegraph, 11 July 1997. Tebbit recalled this exchange with relish in his speech to the Octav Botnar Memorial Ceremony held at Cowfold, West Sussex, on 21 October 1998.

253 Inland Revenue Commissioners v Botnar, Chancery Division, 1998, Simon's Tax Cases 38, hearings dated 23, 24 October, 19 November 1997.

254 Interview with Lawrence Cartier, Tel Aviv, 19 August 2016.

255 Interview with Isaac Herzog, Tel Aviv, 18 August 2016.

256 www.rabincenter.org.il

257 Email from Isaac Herzog, 22 February 2017.

258 Tamar S Hermann, The Israeli Peace Movement: A Shattered Dream (Cambridge University Press, 2009), p. 146 f.

259 Interview with Isaac Herzog, Tel Aviv, 18 August 2016.

260 Alan Philips, "Israeli police to investigate illegal funds for Labour," *The Daily Telegraph*, 28 January 2000; Phil Reeves, "Mr Barak and the millionaire car dealer who funded his victory", *The Independent*, 28 January 2000.

CHAPTER 13 – TRIAL AND PREJUDICE

261 Court transcript, 13 January 1993, p. 4, quoted in Witness Statement by Octav Botnar, 6 September 1996, par 99 (p. 43).

262 Simon's Tax Cases 1994, R v Hunt, Appeal Court ruling, 5 May 1994, by Lord Justice Stuart-Smith, p. 823.

263 "The corporate transfer trick that could wreck Clinton's tax plans", *The Times* Business Comment, 6 January 1993.

264 These were all disclosed in a letter to the Revenue signed by Shannon on 4 May 1993 and forwarded to the Revenue by Ernst & Young, his accountants. Frank Shannon's personal tax liabilities were settled in a similar letter from the same accountant dated 22 April 1993.

265 Southwark Crown Court sitting at the Royal Courts of Justice, transcript of pre-trial hearing before the Honorable Mr Justice Gatehouse, 1 February 1993, p. 3.

266 See the account of the trial in the Appeal Court ruling of 5 May 1994, Simon's Tax Cases, 1994, p. 825.

267 Prosecution case statement, quoted in hearing before Mr Justice Gatehouse, 10 February 1993, transcripts pp. 14-15, pp. 9, 12 and 22 of the statement.

268 Letter to Octav Botnar from J. D. Sissons of Herbert Smith, 31 December 1992.

269 Letter from Ken Duxbury, Head of Revenue Investigations, Ernst & Young, 4 May 1993.

270 Quoted in the Appeal Court ruling of 5 May 1994, Simon's Tax Cases 1994, p. 835.

271 Mr Justice Gatehouse, Southwark Crown Court, trial transcript, Day 34, 24 June 1993, p. 56, lines 11-14. Emphasis original: "direct evidence" was underlined in the jury's note, as the judge said in court.

272 Roland Gribben, "Botnar's Final Assault on the Inland Revenue", *Daily Telegraph*, Business News, 19 February 1998.

273 Octav Botnar v The Commissioners of the Inland Revenue, Revised Applicant's

Submissions, prepared for hearing on 19 & 20 November 1997, submitted by Alun Jones QC and James Lewis, par. 17.

274 Interview with Lord Tebbit, House of Lords, 11 May 2016.

275 Roland Gribben, "Botnar's Final Assault on the Inland Revenue". *The Daily Telegraph*, Business News, 19 February 1998.

276 Mr Justice Gatehouse, Southwark Crown Court, trial transcript, Day 34, 24 June 1993, p. 56, lines 19-20.

277 Mr Justice Gatehouse, Southwark Crown Court, trial transcript, Day 34, 24 June 1993, p. 57, lines 18-23.

278 Mr Justice Gatehouse, Southwark Crown Court, trial transcript, Day 34, 24 June 1993, p. 58, line 5.

279 Mr Justice Gatehouse, Southwark Crown Court, Day 34, 24 June 1993, trial transcript, pp. 71-72.

280 See Appeal Court ruling, 5 May 1994, Simon's Tax Cases 1994, p. 826.

281 Alun Jones QC, "English Law, Nissan UK and Mr Octav Botnar", Opinion dated 5 January 1997 (typed note).

282 Lord Tebbit, interview at the House of Lords, London, 11 May 2016.

283 "Maddening Nissan link that will merely keep us guessing", leader, *Daily Telegraph*, 5 November 1997.

CHAPTER 14 – THE FIGHT WITH THE REVENUE

284 "How Botnar weathered the storms in a life and a half", City Comment, *Daily Telegraph*, 14 July 1998.

285 The dates in his passport are 19-27 March 1992 for the first trip and 5-18 July 1992 for the first set of hearings.

286 He arrived on 21 August 1992.

287 Statement by Frank Shannon, typewritten document dated 18 October 1993, paragraphs 11, 20, 37, 81 and elsewhere. See also par 123 for Shannon's claim that he benefited from another fraud. Contrast this with pars 1 and 2 of Defence Case Statement on Behalf of Frank Shannon, submitted in the Central Criminal Court in R. v Michael Hunt & Frank Shannon, undated document from December 1992.

288 Special Commissioners in Income Tax, before Mr Theodore Wallace and Mr Malcolm Palmer, Mr Octav Oswald Botnar and the Inland Revenue, 21 November 1994.

289 Kevin Done, "Inland Revenue seeks order for the winding up of Nissan UK", *Financial Times*, 27 November 1993. "Revenue request over Nissan UK", *Daily Telegraph*, 29 November 1993.

290 Jon Ashworth, "Botnar strikes deal with 'draconian' Revenue," *The Times*, 15 October 1996.

291 Sarah Oliver, "We've been destroyed, now we just want to come back", *The Mail on*

Sunday, 29 September 1996.

292 Jon Ashworth, "Botnar strikes deal with 'draconian' Revenue", *The Times,* 15 October 1996, calculated that the total amount allegedly owing could have been £600 million.

293 Agreement between Nissan UK Ltd, Octav Botnar and the Commissioners of the Inland Revenue, 5 October 1996.

294 Tom Clark and Andrew Dilnot, *Long Term Trends in British Taxation and Spending,* Institute for Fiscal Studies, Briefing Note No. 25, 2002.

295 Inland Revenue Commissioners v Botnar, *Simon's Tax Cases 1999,* p. 711.

296 Quoted in Inland Revenue Commissioners v Botnar, Chancery Division [1998], Simon's Tax Cases 38, paragraph 60, available online. Hearing dates 23, 24 October, 19 November 1997.

297 This statement has been made on two quite independent occasions by people who do not know each other, Lord Tebbit in the House of Lords, 11 May 2016, and Effi Cartier, Lawrence Cartier's wife, in Tel Aviv on 19 August 2016.

298 Sarah Oliver, "Botnar Victory", *Financial Mail,* 22 September 1996.

299 IRC v Botnar, *Simon's Tax Cases 1999,* p. 712.

300 Appeal dated 17 December 1997, see IRC v Botnar, *Simon's Tax Cases 1999,* p. 715 and elsewhere. "Otto" is used several times in this official report.

301 Inland Revenue Commissioners v Botnar, Chancery Division, 1998, *Simon's Tax Cases 38,* hearing dates 23, 24 October, 19 November 1997.

302 The letter is quoted in Inland Revenue Commissioners v Botnar, Chancery Division, 1998, *Simon's Tax Cases 38,* hearing dates 23, 24 October, 19 November 1997, par 293.

303 Inland Revenue Commissioners v Botnar, Chancery Division, 1998, *Simon's Tax Cases 38,* hearing dates 23, 24 October, 19 November 1997, paragraph 142.

304 Inland Revenue Commissioners v Botnar, Chancery Division, 1998, *Simon's Tax Cases 38,* hearing dates 23, 24 October, 19 November 1997, par 151.

305 Inland Revenue Commissioners v Botnar, Chancery Division, 1998, *Simon's Tax Cases 38,* hearing dates 23, 24 October, 19 November 1997, par 299.

306 Quoted by Sarah Oliver in "Botnar victory", *Financial Mail,* 22 September 1996.

307 Notes of a meeting with the Inland Revenue at Somerset House, 22 October 1997. Richard Walters, then of the Revenue, made this claim in the meeting with Norman Tebbit, Alan Kilkenny and Dawn Lawson.

308 Interview with Lord Tebbit, House of Lords, 11 May 2016.

309 Richard Walters, meeting at Somerset House, 22 October 1997.

310 Quoted by Jason Nisse in "Revenue drops charges against ex-Nissan chief", *The Times,* 5 November 1997.

CHAPTER 15 – THE DETERMINATION TO CLEAR HIS NAME

311 Sarah Oliver, "We've been destroyed, now we just want to come back", *The Mail on Sunday*, 29 September 1996, p. 41.

312 This was widely reported in the press. See "Botnar sues Revenue to get day in court", "Botnar's final assault against the Revenue" and "Ex-Nissan UK chief takes action against Revenue" all by Roland Gribben, *Daily Telegraph* 19 February 1998; "Botnar sues Revenue for 'malicious prosecution'", Chris Godsmark, *The Independent*, 19 February 1998; "Botnar issues writ against Revenue", by Jason Nisse, *The Times*, 19 February 1998.

313 Writ 1998 B No. 321, delivered to the High Court on 18 February 1998.

314 Revised applicant's submissions by Alun Jones QC and James Lewis, undated document.

315 Roland Gribben, "Botnar's Final Assault on the Inland Revenue," *The Daily Telegraph*, Business News, 19 February 1998.

316 Notes taken by Dawn Lawson at the hearing at the High Court, 7 July 1998.

CHAPTER 16 – DEATH IN VILLARS

317 Interview with the Calheno family, Braga, Portugal, 30 May 2016.

318 Interview with the Calheno family, Braga, Portugal, 30 May 2016.

319 Address by Professor Graham MacGregor to the Octav Botnar Memorial Ceremony, Cowfold, West Sussex, 21 October 1998.

320 Interview with Elliot Berry, Jerusalem, 19 August 2016.

321 Brian Groves' speech to the Octav Botnar memorial ceremony, Cowfold, Sussex, 21 October 1998.

Index

Acknowledgements

The author would like to thank the following people for their help during the writing of this book.

Marion Allford

Elliot Berry

Erwin Bodnar

Gavin Bowd

Charles Buchet

Dominic Bunford

Dr Otto Bruderer

Professor Andrew Carr

Lawrence Cartier

François Delpla

Cristina Diac

Jeanette Franklin MBE

Charles Goldlazgier

Professor Roger Greenhalgh

Brian Groves

Edgar Hauster

Isaac Herzog

Michal Herzog

Bruno Leroux

Dr Peter Lenz

Professor Graham MacGregor

Lady Meyer

Irma Mico

Christian Mititelu

Amalie Molhant Proost

Ivan Mulcahy

Barbu Ollanescu-Orendi

Sue Parmenter

Claude Pennetier

Dalia Rabin

Dawn Rose

Richard Smith

Mark Spragg

Tony Stone

François Szulman

Lord Tebbit CH PC

Paul Yallop

Henri Zytnicki

Photographic credits

xviii	Bottom:	The South of England Agricultural Society
xx	Top:	Charles Knight/REX/Shutterstock
	Centre:	Trinity Mirror/Mirrorpix/Alamy Stock Photo
	Bottom:	Sunderland Echo
xxi	Top:	PA/PA Archive/PA Images
	Bottom:	Commission Air/Alamy Stock Photo
xxiii		Clive Limpkin/REX/Shutterstock
xxvii	Bottom:	Tim Graham/Corbis Historical/Getty
xxviii	Top & bottom:	Paul Grover
xxix	Bottom:	Oxford Mail
xxx	Top:	Hanan Isachar/Alamy Stock Photo
	Bottom:	Shay Levy/Alamy Stock Photo
xxxi		G Shifman-Nathan, Ilia Kruvorechko
xxxii	Top left & right:	Richard Dawkins

With special thanks to Jason Keffert and Les Wilson